TEACH YOURSELF BOOKS

TEACH YOURSELF BOOKS

HAUSA

Charles H. Kraft, Ph.D.

Department of Linguistics, University of California

in association with

A. H. M. Kirk-Greene, M.A.(Cantab.)

*Senior Research Fellow in African Studies, St. Antony's College,
Oxford University*

*Formerly Head of the Department of Languages,
Ahmadu Bello University, Zaria, Nigeria
Sometime Member of the Hausa Language Board and
Chairman of the Higher Standard Hausa Board of Examiners*

NTC *Publishing Group*

Hodder & Stoughton

A MEMBER OF THE HODDER HEADLINE GROUP

Library of Congress Catalog Card Number: 94–65385

First published in UK 1973 by Hodder Headline Plc, 338 Euston Road, London NW1 3BH

First published in US 1994 by NTC Publishing Group, 4255 West Touhy Avenue, Lincolnwood (Chicago), Illinois 60646 – 1975 U.S.A.

Printed and bound in Great Britain by Cox & Wyman Ltd, Reading, Berkshire

First published 1973
Reissued 1990
10 9 8 7 6 5 4 3 2
1999 1998 1997 1996 1995 1994

Contents

Preface

Were it not for the fact that we have three matters to record, no prefatory note would be necessary in a volume in the well-established Teach Yourself series.

First, a note on the history of the materials in this Hausa grammar. The original lessons were used from 1962–1968 by Mr. Kirk-Greene in regular African language courses in the Summer Schools at the University of California, Los Angeles, and for faculty and post-graduate classes at Ahmadu Bello University. A parallel and advanced version was used by Dr. Kraft in his credit-earning courses at Michigan State University between 1964 and 1968, and at UCLA from 1968 to the present. On the experience gained from this considerable testing period we have combined and revised our course materials. Since 1966, Dr. Kraft has worked on the task of incorporating them into the eventual text of *Teach Yourself Hausa*. If the foundations of this volume lie in the original work of one of us, the credit for the final version is essentially that of the other.

Secondly, a reference to some of the distinctive features of this Hausa grammar. In most existent grammars, insufficient attention has been paid to the questions of marking tone and vowel length; we have given special attention to these essential aids to acquiring fluency. The supplementary sections of the book, such as the bibliographical guide to further reading, referential lessons, quick-look tables of grammatical synopsis and a two-way vocabulary of some 2000 words will place the student who completes this course in a promising position to sit formal examinations in Hausa and then, hopefully, move to the field to put into practice what he has learned at home. Again, we have sought to support the morphological and syntactical analysis by a series of lively dialogues and typical situational conversations, and, later on, of traditional fables, proverbs and stories. Where the student has the advantage of working with a Hausa informant, he may conveniently have these conversation-pieces read or recorded. But since we are aware that, in the nature of the Teach Yourself series, many students will initially be faced with the problem of literally teaching themselves, we have here and there eschewed an approach that holds that grammars should be purely descriptive and never prescriptive, and have taken advantage of our class experience where we have found that a didactic ' laying down of the basic rules ' is very often a helpful and appreciated framework for those beginning to learn an African language.

Thirdly, and most importantly, the acknowledgement of our debts of gratitude. To name all those—scholars, informants, research assistants, students—who have so readily co-operated in our work on this new Hausa course would be impossible. But we hope that if we specify those to whom our greatest thanks for information, explanation and clarification goes, and happily dedicate our book to all students of Hausa, be they Nigerian or otherwise, past or future, we shall have achieved our aim of due acknowledgement. Those to whom our special thanks are due include Mr. F. W. Parsons, Reader in Hausa at the School of Oriental and African Studies, University of London, whose exhaustive comments on the text were so helpful and upon whose scholarly analyses of Hausa verbs and noun plurals we have leaned so heavily ; Dr. D. W. Arnott, Professor of West African Languages at the University of London, for his suggested improvements ; Messrs. G. P. Bargery and R. C. Abraham, whose monumental dictionaries we rarely turned to in vain ; the numerous and enthusiastic students registered for our respective courses over the years; our various research assistants, Yahaya Aliyu, Benjamin Ishaku, Salisu Abubakar, Ibrahim Wada, Sani Abdullahi, Katherine (Powers) de Blij and Marguerite G. Kraft; and our typists, Jean Gorman and Dorothy Pelton, who have dealt so nobly with a language quite strange to them. In hoping that this book may be a helpful contribution to the learning of one of the two most important languages of Africa, we conclude by reminding our readers of the Hausa proverb **Kàràtū, farkonkà madàcī, ƙarshenkà zumà**: *it may be bitter to begin study but the end is sweet.*

CHARLES H. KRAFT, Ph.D.

Department of Linguistics,
University of California at Los Angeles

in association with

A. H. M. KIRK-GREENE, M.A.

St. Antony's College, Oxford

1973

Part One

Introduction

Lesson 1

The Hausa Language

1. Hausa historically is primarily the name of a language rather than of a people. By extension, it has come to be used to describe the majority group of northern Nigerians, linked by a sense of unity based on a common language, history and customs. Ethnically, however, there exists some heterogeneity within this group, and religion-wise there are a few Christian and animist Hausa as well as Muslim Hausa.

2. The present-day Hausa people originate from the **Hausā Bakwài,** the seven historical states of Kano, Katsina, Daura, Zazzau (Zaria), Biram, Gobir and Rano, which form the nucleus of the Kano, North Central and North-western states of Nigeria and of the contiguous portion of Niger Republic. These states flourished some 400 years ago ; Kano city is reputed to be a thousand years old. At the beginning of the nineteenth century, the Fulani of Sokoto incorporated the governments of the **Hausā Bakwài** into the Sokoto empire, the foundation of the political entity recognized up to 1966 as the Northern Region of Nigeria. The kingdom of Bornu, along with the remainder of present-day North-eastern, Benue-Plateau and Kwara states, remained outside the mainstream of Hausa and later Fulani influence.

Those ancient states where Hausa was spoken, but not as a mother tongue, were known as the **Banzā Bakwài,** the seven ' illegitimate ' ones. They included such areas as Ilorin (Yoruba), Nupe, Yauri, Kebbi, Kwararafa (Jukun), Gwari and Zamfara. **Gwārī** is a term still used to refer contemptuously to one who haltingly stammers out pidgin-Hausa : **Bàgwārī nè**. Its opposite, the flattery given to a foreigner who speaks fluent Hausa, is **yā iyà Hausā kàmar jàkin Kanò**, literally *he speaks Hausa like a Kano donkey*. The Kano dialect is that normally accepted as ' standard ' Hausa for teaching purposes, and is the one preferred in this book.

3. The Hausa language is generally recognized to be the largest West African language. Fifteen to twenty million people can claim Hausa as their mother-tongue with some ten million non-native speakers demonstrating varying degrees of competence in the language. It is the predominant language of the northern states of Nigeria and of neighbouring Niger Republic. Sizable Hausa-speaking communities (often itinerant and trading) are also found in many of the major cities of West, North and Equatorial Africa.

In the former Northern Region of Nigeria up to 1966, Hausa shared with English the status of ' official ' language and both were written into the constitution. In 1964 the Northern House of Assembly considered the adoption of Hausa as the only language of business throughout the Government and in the legislature. Regulations towards implementing this were introduced but were rescinded in early 1966. Without a knowledge of Hausa, however, it is awkward to move very far from northern Nigeria's urban circles and difficult to communicate effectively with any but the English-speaking elite.

4. Hausa is classified by Greenberg as a member of the Chadic group of the Afroasiatic family of languages.[1] It is, therefore, more closely related genetically to Arabic, Hebrew, Berber and other members of the Afroasiatic

[1] See Greenberg, J. H., *The Languages of Africa*. Bloomington, Indiana : Indiana University, 1963.

family than are most of the rest of the languages of sub-Saharan Africa. To this extent Hausa is not a ' typical ' African language.

The conceptual framework of the Hausa-speaking peoples expressed through the language is, however, definitely African and bears a close relationship to that expressed through more ' typically ' African Niger-Kordofanian languages to the south of Hausa.

The cultural influence of the Near East upon the Hausa people is, however, quite prominent and is reflected in the language. The influence of Muslim thought and culture may be said to permeate many aspects of Hausa life and language. Borrowings of concepts (especially religious and philosophical) and vocabulary are recognizable at every turn.

As one result of early Muslim influence, Hausa has a literary tradition extending back several centuries before contact with Western culture. Hausa was first written in an Arabic script known as **àjàmī**. Today this representation of the language is largely restricted to Muslim scholars, divines (**màlàmai**) and their Koranic schools, having been superseded for most purposes by the Roman script (minus the diacritics) which is used in this book.

A large amount of printed literature is available in Hausa, and a variety of periodicals have appeared over the years, at least two of which are still produced regularly. Foremost among the secular producers of Hausa literature has been the Gaskiya Corporation, Zaria. In recent years, however, the Northern Nigeria Publishing Corporation at Zaria has emerged as the principal publisher of Hausa texts. The weekly newspaper *Gaskiya Ta Fi Kwabo* is the most prominent of the Hausa periodicals, and is supported by a relatively large number—when compared to the number of publications in other vernaculars—of books printed in Roman script and published by various commercial and mission groups

in Northern Nigeria. Since its removal to Kaduna in
1966, however, it has failed to retain the standard
orthography (especially with respect to the ' hooked '
letters), and should not, therefore, be imitated by those
sitting for formal Hausa language examinations.

Lesson 2

Hausa Pronunciation I : Consonants and Vowels

1. Twenty-one written symbols will be employed to represent the twenty-four Hausa consonants (three of the consonants, **sh**, **ts** and **'y**, are represented by double letters).[1] The following chart provides a fairly accurate indication of the sounds of sixteen of these consonants :

b as in *big* : bābù, bàbba, bàkī [2]
c as the *ch* in *church* : can, cikà, màcè
d as in *dog* : don, bàdūkù, darē
g as in *good* (never as in *gist*) : gudù, gērō, dōgō
h as in *hat* : hūtà, habà, rahà
j as in *jot* : jāwō, kujèrā, jìkī
k as in *king* : kàrē, kūkā, kōwā
l as in *like* : lādā, lallē, lāfiyà
m as in *man* : mōtà, makòyī, dāmā
n as in *not* : nāmà, hannū, nīsa
s as in *son* : sanyī, sanì, Hausā
sh as in *shut* : shìga, shā, tāshì
t as in *tin* : tàfi, tēbùr, fìtō
w as in *win* : watà, wurì, rawā
y as in *yet* : yārò, hanyōyì, yunwà
z as in *zero* : zuwà, zāfī, kàzā

---

[1] The letters *q*, *v* and *x* are not used in Hausa except sometimes in the spelling of foreign names. The letter *p* is sometimes seen as a non-standard representation of the sound regularly written as *f*, which, however, often sounds more like English *p* than English *f*. The sound represented in English by *qu* occurs regularly in Hausa words, but is written **kw**.

[2] See pages 9–11 and 14 for explanations of the diacritical marks.

2. The remainder of the consonants require special treatment.

ẛ sounds very much like the English *f*, but is produced between the lips rather than between the lower lip and upper teeth as in the English *f*. Often, too, Hausa ẛ is pronounced nearer the English *p*, e.g. **fĩlĩ, lāfiyằ, fĩta, fātằ, farĩ.** In some words it is interchangeable with **h**, e.g. **fuɗu/huɗu, tsōfō/tsōhō.**

' is a glottal catch like that which precedes each vowel in English exclamations such as *oh-oh* or *uh-uh*. In Hausa ' is written when it occurs in the middle of a word, e.g. **ā'ằ, nằ'am.** Every word beginning with a vowel in Hausa actually starts with a glottal catch, but this, since it is predictable, is not written either in the official orthography or in this book, e.g. **aikì, ằddā, ĩ.**

'**y** is a very rare Hausa sound which consists of *y* preceded by a glottal catch, e.g. '**yā'yā, 'yarsằ.**

The consonants **ɓ, ɗ, ƙ** and **ts** are known technically as *glottalized consonants*. That is, each is produced with a simultaneous glottal catch and released with a rather explosive quality to it. The **ɓ** and **ɗ,** in addition, are often produced implosively, i.e. with the air stream pulled into the mouth rather than expelled from the mouth as with **ƙ** and **ts.** In the schools of Hausaland the letters representing these sounds are referred to as *hooked* letters.

ɓ is like **b,** but with a simultaneous glottal catch and an explosive quality to the release, e.g. **ɓērā, lēɓề, haɓằ.**

ɗ is like **d** (though the tongue position is a bit farther back), but with a simultaneous glottal catch and an explosive quality to the release, e.g. **ɗākì, ɗaya, kuɗĩ.**

ƙ is like **k,** but with a simultaneous glottal catch and an explosive, click-like quality to the release, e.g. **ƙōfằ, zāƙĩ.**

ts is like **s,** but with a simultaneous glottal catch, an explosive quality to the release and, for many speakers, an initial *t* sound, e.g. **tsāfĩ, yātsằ, tsūtsằ.**

r is either a short trill or a flap which often sounds

much like an l. Though many Hausa speakers will maintain a distinction between the two **r** sounds, consistently employing one in certain words and the other in other words, the processes of linguistic change have so affected the use of these sounds that it is often impossible to predict accurately which **r** will be employed in a given word. The majority of Hausa speakers employ a trilled **r** before most consonants (except labial and velar), e.g. **murnà** ; in final position, e.g. **har** ; regularly in words borrowed from other languages, e.g. **barkà, karàntā** ; and in a relatively small number of other words. The flap **r** occurs in most other contexts. The student is encouraged to discover what the pattern followed by his informant is, and to learn to employ that pattern in his own speech. He may find it convenient to add a tilde (r̃) throughout these lessons to indicate when the trill occurs in his informant's speech. The present authors have weighed the relative merits of consistently indicating the difference between the two **r** sounds throughout these lessons and felt that it would be less confusing to omit such indication here.

3. Hausa makes use of five short and five long vowels. However, only five written symbols are used in Hausa literature to represent these ten sounds. It is, therefore, necessary to supplement the accepted writing system in order to enable the student to know which sound is to be employed in a given word. *Long vowels* will thus be indicated in these lessons by the presence of a macron (ā) above the letter. Vowels with no macron are therefore short.

Due to the wide dialectal differences in the pronunciation of English vowels, it is very difficult to illustrate Hausa vowels unambiguously by employing English words. The following attempt to do so is only a general guide and must not therefore be depended upon too

heavily. The student must do his best to imitate his
informant's production of the vowel sound carefully,
whether or not the English illustration of the Hausa
sound given below is accurate for his dialect. He may
later find it profitable to substitute other English (or
non-English) key-words for those given below. In any
event, the long vowels (ā, ē, ī, ō, ū) are always ' pure '
vowels in Hausa, unlike English where they are usually
phonetic diphthongs (technically known as glides).[3] The
student should keep this basic difference between Hausa
and English vowels in mind as he refers to the English
' key-words ' below.

   a most frequently [4] similar to the *u* in *butter, cuff* :
      habà, àllō, tàfi
   ā similar to *a* in *far, car, psalm* : **rānā, fātà, tàfī**
   e similar to *e* in *bet, check* : **fensìr, màcè, gòbe**

---

[3] The student unaware of this characteristic of English pronunciation might profitably watch his lips in a mirror as he pronounces
slowly a word such as *hope* or *loaf*. He will note that as he completes
the vowel segment of the word his lips become more tightly pursed
into a *w*-like position in anticipation of the final labial consonant.
This process is technically known as a *vowel glide*, and these words
are spelled phonetically *howp* and *lowf* to indicate the fact that the
vowel segment in them is a complex of *o* plus *w*. Less easily observ-
able but nonetheless real vowel glides occur on most other ' long '
vowels in English as well. The vowel in *feet*, for example, involves a
sliding (gliding) forward of the tongue into a *y* position (phonetically
spelled *fiyt*) as does that in *rate* (phonetically *reyt*). Likewise the
vowel in *far* involves a tongue glide which may be phonetically
represented by an *H* (e.g. *faH* or *faHr*). The point is that Hausa
vowels are not characterized by this type of ' diphthongizing '.
Hausa long vowels are, therefore, phonetically representable as *oo*
rather than *ow*, *ii* rather than *iy*, *aa* rather than *aH*, *uu* rather than
uw, *ee* rather than *ey*. The English learner of Hausa must, therefore,
give some attention to keeping his lips still as he produces a
Hausa ō or ū, and his tongue in its starting position when he
produces Hausa ī, ē and ā, regardless of the consonant that follows.
[4] In proximity to **y** or **i**, **a** is often pronounced as short **e**, e.g.
yànzu, sai. Other slight variations also occur in the pronunciation
of **a.** The student should be on the lookout for them and seek to
imitate the native speaker's production at all times.

ē similar to *a* in *rate, mate, date* : lēɓè, gēmū̀, tēbùr
i similar to *i* in *pin, bit* : cikì, gidā, idò
ī similar to *e* in *she, feet* : kīfī, shī, rìgā
o similar to *o* in *obey* (very short) : Bellò
ō similar to *o* in *open, goal* : dōkì, tuwō, mōtà
u similar to the vowel in *foot, put* : ukù, mùtûm, dubū
ū similar to *oo* in *boot, root, toot* : sūnā, tùlū, hùlā

4. Short vowels are *quantitatively shorter* in duration than long vowels and very often differ in *quality* as well. That is, if a given short vowel requires a certain length of time to be produced, its long counterpart may require twice as much time. The fact that a given vowel is short rather than long may also be signalled (especially in closed syllables) by the fact that the short vowel *sounds* different from its long counterpart. Thus, the difference between **tàfi,** *go away,* and **tàfī,** *palm of the hand,* is signalled both by the differences in the actual length of the two **a**'s and by the fact that they ' sound ' different (i.e. have a different phonetic quality).

5. In addition to the ten vowels, there are in Hausa two diphthongs. These are combinations of a short *a* plus *y* or *w* which occur in a single syllable. They are, however, written as **ai** and **au**:

ai usually approximates the *u* in *cuff* + *y* : **kâi, nai ;** or the *e* in *bet* + *y* : **sai, zâi**
au usually approximates the *u* in *cup* + *w* : **ƙauyè, launì.**

6. The student should always keep in mind the fact that a language is made up primarily of *sounds* rather than written symbols. Written symbols are used in this book only as guides to the spoken sounds of the Hausa language, not as an end in themselves.

The system of written symbols here employed is designed to be as true a guide as possible to the spoken language. Therefore, *each written symbol represents one, and only one, meaningful unit of sound in Hausa.*

Lesson 3

Hausa Pronunciation II : Tone and Intonation

1. No language is known to be spoken without the systematic use of pitch distinctions in addition to the distinctions between the various vowels and consonants. English, for example, is characterized by a very intricate intonational system (the specifics of the system vary from dialect to dialect) in which pitch distinctions play a major part.

A large proportion of the world's languages—including all but a very few African languages—employ pitch *tonally* rather than intonationally. This is a usage quite distinct from that of English. Such languages are known as *tone languages*. Hausa is a tone language.

Each Hausa syllable consists of a given set of consonants and vowels plus an assigned tone. Each word must, therefore, be learned and pronounced with its proper tone pattern as well as its proper vowels and consonants.[1] In order to facilitate proper learning, and to avoid ambiguity, we have considered it helpful to employ accent marks in this book to indicate the proper tone of each syllable. In the traditional orthography (which does not indicate either tone or vowel length), for

---

[1] It is important to observe that *tone* and *tone pattern* are terms employed to designate a system which employs pitch distinctions in a relative manner—not in an absolute manner like notes in music. Different speakers, e.g. men and women, have different voice pitches and these may be varied for emotional reasons. It is the *relative interval* between successive syllables of speech that determines the tonal (and intonational) patterns being employed in language, *not* the absolute pitch on which these speech segments fall.

example, the spelling **jibi** represent two distinct words
and the spelling **fito** represents three distinct words,
differing in tone (see below).

2. In Hausa there are two tone levels (termed *high* and
low), and a less frequent combination of high and low
resulting in a *falling* tone. These tones are not necessarily
assignable to absolute pitch levels such as those of a
musical scale, but rather are important because they
contrast with each other in a systematic way within the
language. That is, Hausa high tone is of importance
because it contrasts with low tone to account for the
difference in meaning between words like **jībi**, *day after
tomorrow*, and **jībì**, *a meal*, or between **fitō**, *come out*,
fitò, *ferrying*, and **fitō**, *guinea corn beer*.

3. In this book the grave accent (**`**) is employed over the
vowel of the relevant syllable to indicate *low tone*. A
high-tone syllable is signalled by the *absence of any tone
mark* over the vowel. The circumflex (**^**) accent over a
vowel indicates a *falling-tone* syllable (i.e. one which
starts high and falls to low). A few examples of words
differing only in tone are :

a cry	**kūkā**	**kūkà**	baobab tree
inside	**cikī**	**cikì**	stomach
he went	**yā tàfi**	**yâ tàfi**	he will go
(particle of assent)	**na'àm**	**nà'am**	(reply to a call)

4. Hausa also has an *intonational system*. This system
involves the specifying and modification of the pitch
levels in the tonal system. Hausa intonation applies to
whole utterances, not to each syllable as is the case with
tone.
  While every syllable has its own tone, the specific
pitch level of each syllable in an utterance is determined

by the intonational system in accordance with the position of the given syllable in the utterance. The tonal pattern of a word determines whether the pitch of the syllable is the same, higher or lower than the pitch of the immediately preceding and following syllables in the utterance. The intonational system specifies how much difference there will be between contiguous syllables with different tones.

The total pitch component (tone plus intonation) of a Hausa utterance can be conveniently described in terms of five pitch levels.[2] These can be numbered from 1 to 5, with 1 referring to the lowest and 5 to the highest pitch level.

5. The most characteristic type of Hausa intonation may be termed *declarative intonation*. This type of intonation has a generally descending pitch pattern and may be represented on a chart as follows :

Bàbansà yā shīga dākìn Audù. Father-his he entered
room-of Audu.

The first high tone in a declarative pattern is on pitch level 5. The next low is on pitch 3, the next high on 4,

---

[2] See also Hodge, Carleton T., *Hausa Basic Course*, pp. 3 ff., and Kraft, Charles H., and Marguerite G., *Spoken Hausa: Introductory Course*. An annotated bibliography will be found on pages 289 ff. (Lesson 43).

etc. The pattern, therefore, is to drop two steps from a high to a low, and to climb one step from a low to a high, but with two qualifications :

(i) An initial low tone will be on level 3 and the following high on level 5.

(ii) A final low will drop to level 1, even if the utterance is not long enough to force it there, but will go no lower than level 1.

6. *Interrogative intonation* is of two types :

(*a*) When the utterance includes no interrogative word, the last high tone will jump to a pitch level at least one step higher than the pitch level of the previous high-tone syllable. Often, in fact, the whole utterance is pitched on a higher level than in the corresponding statement. If the final syllable is high, it will slur from the very high level to a level at least one step lower. A following low tone (if present) will drop only one step rather than all the way down to level 1 as in the declarative pattern :

5	ka		fi		su			ne
4		lā	yā			ai		e
3	nā				nā			
2							kī	
1								

Kanà   lāfiyà ?   Sunà aikì nē ?
Are you well ?   Are they working ?

These utterances as statements (declarative intonation) would be as follows, in contrast with the interrogative patterns above :

Kanà làfìyà.   **Sunà aikì nè.**
You are well.   They are working.

(*b*) When the utterance includes an interrogative word it employs the declarative pattern with two modifications :

   (i) The whole utterance may be on a slightly higher pitch.

   (ii) A final high-tone syllable becomes a falling slur to a level at least one step lower. If the final syllable is a low tone, the second modification does not apply.

5 nā gida	zā	nā ai
4 a	zo	
3 i	yaushe ka o	i
2		
1		kĭ

Ìnā gidā ?   **Yàushè zā kà zō ?**   **Ìnā aikì ?**
How's (your)   When will you   How's (your)
   family ?   come ?   work ?

7. *Vocative intonation,* employed when using a person's name or title in addressing him, is the same as that described under 6 (*b*) above :

5	nu Mūsa	Nā gaishē			nu Au	
4	a	dā				
3	san	ka	bi	san		
2			li	i		
1					du	

Sànnu, Mūsā. **Nā gaishē kà, dālìbì.** **Sànnu, Audù.**
Greetings, I greet you, Greetings,
  Musa. student. Audu.

8. *Stress* is also present in Hausa, but is not nearly as important in Hausa as in English. The student must, however, learn to recognize and imitate the stress as well as the pitch pattern of each utterance. The following generalizations concerning Hausa stress may be helpful:

(i) Differences in stress alone do not account for differences in meaning between words.

(ii) Stress generally, though by no means always, falls on syllables possessing high tone (as exceptions note the following—the underlined syllable takes the stress: màcè cē, *it is a woman*; <u>kà</u>wō àkw<u>à</u>tì, *bring the box*).

(iii) When a series of high-tone syllables is followed by a low tone, the high-tone syllable immediately preceding the low syllable carries greater stress than the preceding high syllables unless such a syllable is both word-final and possesses a short vowel (e.g. <u>i</u>ta cè, *it is she*).

9. The importance of mastering the tone and intonation patterns of Hausa cannot be overemphasized. To 'learn' Hausa words and longer utterances without taking the trouble to acquire the proper pitch pattern suggests an indifference by the speaker that indicates disrespect or

even ignorance. Foreigners have insulted Hausa-speakers too long by simply carrying their own intonational patterns over into Hausa. It is an everlasting tribute to the patience and kindness of the Hausa people that they have not only put up with such carelessness but even learned to understand some of the things we have attempted to say in our bastardized form of their language !

The tone pattern of each word is fully as integral to it as are the vowels and consonants, and it must be as completely mastered. It is for this reason that the effort has been made to indicate the tone and vowel length of each Hausa syllable in this book.

Part Two

Grammar

Lesson 4

Greetings I

1. In Hausa society, greetings are usually more than a casual ' hello ' or nodded ' morning '. They are the hallmark of courtesy and good manners. Different greetings exist for different times of the day and for different activities. The more common of these greetings are given below. Other important greetings are given in Lesson 31.

2. The following greetings can be used with anyone, at any time.

Greeting		*Reply*	
hello	sànnu	yâuwā, sànnu (kàdai)	hello
are you well ?	lāfìyà ?	lāfìyà lau	I'm fine
how's (your) tiredness ?	ìnā gàjiyà ?	bâ gàjiyà	there is no tiredness
how's (your) work ?	ìnā aikì ?	aikì da gòdiyā	I'm thankful for it
how's (your) family ?	ìnā gidā ?	lāfìyà	fine
what's the news ?	ìnā làbārì ?	(làbārì)sai àlhērì	all is well
fine	tò mādàllā		
see you later	sai an jimà	yâuwā, sai an jimà	okay, see you later

3. A typical greeting situation will include some such sequence as that listed in section 2 above. The following more specialized greetings are substitutable for the first (lines 3 and 4) or the last (line 5) greeting in the above list when appropriate :

(a) Morning greetings

Greeting		Reply	
how did you sleep ?	ìnā kwānā ?	lāfiyà	fine
did you sleep well ?	kwal lāfiyà ?	lāfiyà	fine

(b) Midday and afternoon greetings :

Greeting		Reply	
how's (your) day ?	ìnā wunì ?	lāfiyà	fine

4. Greetings for special situations :

Greeting		Reply
greetings at (your) work	sànnu dà aikì	yâuwā, sànnu
greetings at (your) coming	sànnu dà zuwà	yâuwā, sànnu
greetings (on entering a home)	sàlāmù àlaikùn	yâuwā, àlaikà sàlāmù

5. Parting greetings :

Greeting		Reply
see you later	sai an jimà	yâuwā, mù jimà dà yawà
see you tomorrow	sai gòbe	yâuwā, sai gòbe
see you sometime (soon)	sai wani lōkàcī	yâuwā, sai wani lōkàcī
until morning	sai dà sāfē	yâuwā, sai dà sāfē
until evening	sai dà yâmmā	yâuwā, sai dà yâmmā
see you some day	sai wata rānā	yâuwā, sai wata rānā

A common alternative reply to any of these greetings is :

> tò Allà yà kai mù   may God bring it about (lit. okay, may God take us [to that time])

to which one responds in turn :

> àmin   may it be so

VOCABULARY

Nominals

aikì	work
Allà	God
an jimà	after a while (this is actually a verbal construction but often functions as a nominal)
gàjiyà	tiredness
gidā	home, household
gòbe	tomorrow
inā	where ?, how ?
kwānā	period of night
làbārì	news
lāfiyà	health, well-being
lōkàcī	time
sāfē	morning
yâmmā	early evening ; west
wani (*m*.),	
wata (*f*.)	a certain, a
wunì	period of daylight

Verbals		*Particles*	
bâ, bābù	there is no/none	**àmin**	amen, may it be so
jimà	wait a while		
kai	carry, take, convey	**dà**	with, and
		mādàllā	splendid, thank you (*lit.* thanks be to God)
		sai	until, except
		sànnu	greetings
		tò [1]/**tô**	well, okay
		yâuwā/	
		yâuwa [1]	fine, okay

[1] The low-tone form **tò** and the form **yâuwa** (with the short final vowel) only occur if no pause (indicated in these lessons by a comma) occurs between these particles and a following word.

Dialogue

Bellò : Sànnu dà zuwà, Ìsā.

Ìsā :   Yâuwā, sànnu.

Bellò : Ìnā gàjiyà ?

Ìsā :   Bâ gàjiyà.

Bellò : Ìnā aikì ?

Ìsā :   Aikì dà gòdiyā.

Bellò : Ìnā làbārì ?

Ìsā :   Làbārì sai àlhērì.

Bellò : Tò mādàllā.

Ìsā :   Kwal lāfiyà ?

Bellò : Lāfiyà.

Ìsā :   Ìnā gidā ?

Bellò : Lāfiyà lau [2]

Ìsā :   Tò mādàllā. Sai gòbe.

Bellò : Tò Allà yà kai mù.

Ìsā :   Àmin

---

[2] **Lau** is an emphasizing particle equivalent to ' very well '.

Lesson 5

Gender of Nouns

1. All singular nouns are either masculine or feminine.
There is no neuter in Hausa.

2. Most nouns ending in **-a** are feminine. Many, however,
are masculine. Following are some of the more common
nouns which have a final **-a** but are masculine:

gidā	home, compound	**sūnā**	name
ruwā	water	**gùgā**	bucket
wàsā [1]	game	**ɓērā**	mouse
watà	moon, month	**nāmà**	meat

3. Words for acceptedly male and female things, regardless of their final vowels, express the expected gender.
(See Lesson 6 for use of **nē** with masculine nominals, **cē**
with feminine.)

Mùtûm nē.	It is a man.
Màcè cē.	It is a woman.
Sâ nē.	It is a bull.
Zàkarà nē.	It is a rooster.

4. No gender distinction is made in the plural. **Nē** is used
with all plural nominals, even if they refer to females.

Mātā nè.	They are women.
Ɓēràyē nè.	They are mice.
Jākunà nē.	They are donkeys.

[1] But this is feminine in some areas.

5. The common names of most animals, though grammatically either masculine or feminine, refer to either sex.

Bērā nè.	It is a rat (either sex).
Giwā cè.	It is an elephant (either sex).
Àkwiyà cē.	It is a goat (either sex).[2]
Tunkìyā cè.	It is a sheep (either sex).[2]

6. The names of towns, countries and rivers are feminine.

Nìjériyà	Nigeria	**Bīnuwài**	River Benue
Fàransà	France	**Ìkko**	Lagos
Ingìlà	England	**Kanò**	Kano
Amirkà	America	**Sakkwato**	Sokoto
Kwârà	River Niger	**Baucī**	Bauchi

7. A feminine of many nouns referring to persons or animals and of many adjectival nominals may be formed by changing the masculine ending as follows :

(a) A final -ō or -ū to -uwā :

tsōfō (*m.*)	old person	**tsōfuwā** (*f.*)
dōgō (*m.*)	tall person	**dōguwā** (*f.*)
tsuntsū (*m.*)	bird	**tsuntsuwā** (*f.*)

(b) A final -ē to -ìyā :

Bàhaushè (*m.*)	Hausa person	**Bàhaushìyā** (*f.*)
Bàlārabè (*m*)	Arab	**Bàlārabìyā** (*f.*)
Bàtūrè (*m.*)	white man	**Bàtūrìyā** (*f.*)
shēgè (*m.*)	bastard	**shēgìyā** (*f.*)

(c) A final -ī to -ìyā :

majèmī (*m.*)	tanner	**majēmìyā** (*f.*)
ɗālibī (*m.*)	student	**ɗālibìyā** (*f.*)
mahàifī (*m.*)	parent	**mahaifìyā** (*f.*)

---

[2] Unless the animal referred to is known to be male, in which case the words **ràgō**, *ram*, and **bùnsurū**, *he goat*, are used.

or to a high tone -**ā** :

jàkī (m.)	donkey	jàkā (f.)
jārùmī (m.)	brave person	jārùmā (f.)
gwànī (m.)	expert	gwànā (f.)
mālàm(ī) (m.)	teacher	mālàmā (f.)
ɗālìbī (m.)	student	ɗālìbā (f.)

8. Some nouns, especially kinship terms, may be either masculine or feminine :

kàkā	grandfather *or* grandmother
jikà	grandson *or* granddaughter
àutā	youngest brother *or* sister

VOCABULARY

Nominals

àkwiyà (f.)	goat
Amirkà (f.)	America
Bàtūrè	white man
ɓērā	mouse, rat
ɗālìbī (pl. ɗàlìbai)	student
gīwā (f.)	elephant
gùgā	bucket
Ingìlà (f.)	England
jàkī	donkey
kàkā	grandparent
Kanò (f.)	Kano
màcè (f.) (pl. mātā) màcè + -r = màtar ...	woman, wife wife of ...
mālàm	teacher, Mr.
mè/mènē/ mènēnè	what ?
mùtûm (pl. mutànē	man, person (pl. people)

Nìjēriyà (*f.*)	Nigeria
ruwā	water
sâ	bull
sūnā	name
tsuntsū	bird
tunkìyā (*f.*)	sheep
wannàn	this
wàsā	game, play
watà	moon, month
zàkarà	rooster, cock

Particles

nē (*f.* cē)	is, are, were

EXERCISES

Translate into English :

1. Ruwā nè.
2. Jākunà nē.
3. Giwā cè.
4. Tsōfuwā cè.
5. Bàtūrè nē.

6. Tsuntsū nè.
7. Kàkā nè.
8. Bērā nè.
9. Dālìbì nè.
10. Mùtûm nē.

Translate into Hausa with either nē (*m.*) or cē (*f.*) :

1. It's a name.
2. It's a bull.
3. They are mice.
4. He's a Hausa person (*m.*).
5. They are women.

6. She's a woman
7. It's a game.
8. It's a rooster.
9. It's a home.
10. It's the moon.

Dialogue

Mūsā : Sànnu dālìbì.
Audù : Yâuwā, sànnu mālàm.
Mūsā : Mènēnè wannàn ?
Audù : Wannàn jàkī nè.
Mūsā : Tò, mènēnè wannàn ?

Audù : Tsuntsū nề.
Mūsā : Mềcēcề wannàn ?
Audù : Àkwiyà cē.
Mūsā : Tò, mềcēcề wannàn ?
Audù : Wannàn tunkìyā cề.
Mūsā : Tò mādàllā, sai gồbe.
Audù : Yâuwā, Allà yà kai mù.

Lesson 6

' To be ' : Nē, Cē and Kè nan [1]

1. The sense of *am/is/are/was/were* is, regardless of aspect (or ' tense '), expressed by **nē** if the subject is masculine or **cē** if it is feminine. As no gender distinction is made in noun plurals, **nē** is always used with plural forms. (See Lesson 5, section 4.)

2. **Nē/cē** typically occurs at the end of a phrase or clause and its tone is always opposite to the tone of the preceding syllable.

Sarkī nè.	It is a chief.
Yārò nē.	It is a boy.
Makarantā cè.	It is a school.
Yārinyà cē.	It is a girl.
Yârā nè.	They are children.
Yā tàfi gidā nè.	He went home (emphatic).

3. The construction **kè nan** can often be used to express the same meaning as **nē/cē**. The use of **kè nan**, however, typically implies greater emphasis than would the use of **nē/cē**.

Kuɗī kè nan.	It is money.
Sarkī kè nan.	It is the king !
Yā sàmi kuɗī kè nan.	He's become really wealthy !
Tô, mun dāwō gidā kè nan.	Well, we're back home.

---

[1] These forms are not, however, the only ways to render the English verb ' to be '. For other renderings, see Lessons 18 and 19.

4. The phrase **shī kè̀ nan,** literally meaning *it is this*, is common in the Hausa language, and is used to express finality and, often, to signal transition to a new topic similar to the notion of *that's all, that's that, that's all there is to it, that's the end of the matter.*

> **Yā mutù. Shī kè̀ nan. Bāyan wannàn...** He died. That was that. After this...

5. In the negative, **bà̀ ... ba nè̀/cè̀** or **kè̀ nan** is used.

Bà idò̀ ba nè̀.	It is not an eye.
Bà kudī ba kè̀ nan.	It is not money !
Bà giwā ba cè̀.	It is not an elephant.
Bà yârā ba nè̀.	They are not children.

6. The independent pronouns commonly occur with **nḕ/cḕ** and **kè̀ nan.**

nī nè̀	it is I (*m.*)	**ita cè̀**	it is she
nī cè̀	it is I (*f.*)	**mū nè̀**	it is we
kai nè̀	it is you (*m.*)	**kū nè̀**	it is you (*pl.*)
kē cè̀	it is you (*f.*)	**sū nè̀**	it is they
shī nè̀	it is he (*m.*)		

Wà̀nē nè̀ ? Nī nè̀.	Who is it ? It's I.
Shī nè̀ zâi tàfi.	It is he who will go.
Wà̀ ya [2] zō ? Nī kè̀ nan.	Who has come ? I.

VOCABULARY

Nominals

gà̀rī	town
idò̀	eye
kâi	head
kà̀suwā (*f.*)	market

---

[2] The reason for a short vowel on this (and other) person-aspect pronouns when following an interrogative is explained in Lesson 20, section 7 (*b*) (ii).

kuɗī	money
kyâu	goodness
lâifī	fault, sin
makarantā (*f.*)	school
sānìyā (*f.*)	
(*pl.* **shānū**)	cow (*pl.* cattle)
sarkī	chief
yārinyà (*f.*)	girl
yārò (*pl.* **yârā**)	boy (*pl.* children)
wà, wànē,	
wànēnè ?	who ?

Verbals

dāwō	return (here), come back
shìga	enter, go in
tàfi	go (away), go (to)

Particles

ā'à	no
ī	yes
ƙalau	very

Important Phrases

bâ lâifī	that's okay (*lit.* there's nothing wrong), never mind
dà kyâu	good !
shī kè nan	that's that

EXERCISES

Translate into English :

1. **Wànē nè ?**
2. **Gàrī kè nan.**
3. **Bà sarkī ba nè.**
4. **Makarantā cè.**
5. **Gùgā nè.**
6. **Bà gidā ba nè.**
7. **Bà yârā ba nè.**
8. **Nī nè.**
9. **Ita cè.**
10. **Mū nè.**

Translate into Hausa :

1. It is a school
2. He is a man.
3. They are boys.
4. He is a chief.

5. That's all.	8. It is money.
6. It is not a bull, it is a cow.	9. It is not an eye.
7. They are not children.	10. It is not a market.

Dialogue

Yūsufù : **Sànnu dà zuwà, Daudà.**
Daudà : **Yâuwa sànnu.**
Yūsufù : **Kwal lāfiyà ?**
Daudà : **Lāfiyà ƙalau.**
Yūsufù : **Wànē ya tàfi gàrī ?**
Daudà : **Audù nḕ.**
Yūsufù : **Yā dāwō nḕ ?**
Daudà : **Ā'à, sai gòbe.**
Yūsufù : **Tò dà kyâu**

Lesson 7

Completed Action

1. In Hausa, the *aspect* (termed aspect rather than tense since it denotes kind of action rather than time of action) of verbs is shown by changes in the *person-aspect pronoun*, not in the verb itself. This precedes the verb.

2. The *completive aspect* indicates action regarded as completed or as occurring at a specific point (rather than as a process) in time. This point in time may be past, present or future as indicated by the context. In the absence of contextual evidence to the contrary, however, it is usually possible to assume that the reference is to a point in time in the past.

3. There are two forms of the completive aspect. The first set of *person-aspect pronouns* here listed with the verb **zō**, *come*, is the most commonly used.[1] Note the feature in Hausa of distinct masculine and feminine forms in the second person singular as well as the third person singular.

nā zō	I have come	**mun zō**	we have come
kā zō	you (*m.*) have come	**kun zō**	you (*pl.*) have come
kin zō	you (*f.*) have come		
yā zō	he has come	**sun zō**	they have come
tā zō	she has come		
an zō	one has come		

[1] See Lesson 20, section 2, for the other set.

4. In every aspect in Hausa, except the imperative, the verb must, unlike English, be preceded by a *person-aspect pronoun* (henceforth abbreviated *p-a* or *p-a pronoun*), regardless of whether there is already a noun subject or not.

Examples :

Audù yā zō.	Audu (he) has come.
Yârā sun tàfi.	The boys (they) have gone.

5. The impersonal p-a pronoun **an** is used in translating the English passive :

An kāwō àbinci.	Food has been brought.	(*Lit.* one has brought food.)
An kashè fìtilà.	The lamp has been extinguished.	(*Lit.* one has killed the lamp.)

This difference from English may be easier to remember if one adapts the English passive into Hausa thought patterns—substituting *someone brought the food* for *the food was brought*.

6. The *negative of the completed aspect* is formed by placing **bà** (low tone, short vowel) immediately before the p-a pronoun, and **ba** (high tone, short vowel) at the end of the utterance. The construction thus becomes :

> **bà** + p-a pronoun + verb + **ba**
> **bà**   **tà**   **zō**   **ba**
> not   she   has come   not
> She has/did not come.

7. The negative form of the completed aspect used with the verb **zō** :

Singular	Plural
bàn zō ba	bà mù zō ba
bà kà zō ba	bà kù zō ba
bà kì zō ba	
bài zō ba	bà sù zō ba
bà tà zō ba	
bà à zō ba	

8. Note three differences between the p-a pronouns employed in the affirmative completive and those employed in the negative completive :

(a) The negative p-a pronouns have a low (rather than high) tone and a short (rather than long) vowel.

(b) In all plural forms, in the second person singular feminine, and in the impersonal **an,** the negative forms have no final **-n.**

(c) In the first and third persons singular, the p-a pronoun elides with the first **bà,** so that **bà nà** becomes **bàn** and **bà yà** becomes **bài.** This is virtually always so in spoken and usually so in written Hausa.

Examples :

Bà kà kāwō àbinci ba.   You did not bring food/You have not brought food.

Bài shā ruwā ba.   He did not drink water/He has not drunk water.

9. When the verb is followed by an object or other sentence material, the final **ba** usually (but by no means invariably) occurs at the end of the sentence. An important exception to this rule is the word **tùkùna** (*not*) *as yet*, which regularly comes after the final **ba.** The first negative word **bà** must never be separated from its p-a pronoun.

bà + p-a pronoun + verb + ... + **ba**

bà	**kà**	**zō**	**gidā**	**ba**
not	you	came	home	not

You did not come home.

bà	**sù**	**zō**	**ba**	**tùkùna**
not	they	came	not	(not) as yet

They have not come yet.

VOCABULARY

Nominals

àbinci	food
àbōkī	friend
darē	night
fìtilà (*f.*)	lantern, lamp
gōnā (*f.*)	farm, garden
kōmē	anything
kujèrā (*f.*)	stool, chair
littāfì	book
nōmā (*f.*)	farming
ùbā	father
uwā (*f.*)	mother
yâu	today

Verbals

bi [2]	follow
ci [2]	eat
ji [2]	hear, understand, feel
kāwō	bring
shā	drink
yi [2]	do, make
zō	come

Particles

dàzu	just now
tùkùna,	
tùkùn	(not) yet

[2] Monosyllabic verbs ending in -i (**bi, ci, fi, ji ki, yi**) have a *long* -i before a pronoun direct or indirect object, and a *short* -i before a noun object or when they stand without an object following. The verbal noun has a long -i with falling tone.

Important Phrases

bâ kōmē   there is nothing (wrong), it does not matter,
              never mind

EXERCISES

Translate into English :

1. **Bà sù tàfi ba.**
2. **Bàn ci àbinci ba tùkùna.**
3. **Bà sù kāwō littāfì ba.**
4. **Yārinyà bà tà dāwō ba.**
5. **Audù bài zō makarantā ba.**

Translate into Hausa :

1. The man did not make a farm.
2. He did not come this morning.
3. The girl did not go to [3] the farm.
4. I have not yet done the work.
5. The chair was not brought.

Dialogue

Bàƙo :   Ìnā wunì ?
Garbà : Lāfiyà.
Bàƙo :   Ìnā gàjiyà ?
Garbà : Bābù gàjiyà.
Bàƙo :   Tò mādàllā.
Garbà : Kā zō lāfiyà ?
Bàƙo :   Lāfiyà, bâ kōmē.
Garbà : Gidā lāfiyà ?
Bàƙo :   Lāfiyà ƙalau.
Garbà : Ìnā Bellò ?
Bàƙo :   Ya tàfi Kanò.
Garbà : Tò dà kyâu. Yā tàfi kàsuwā ?
Bàƙo :   Ā'à, bài tàfi kàsuwā ba.
Garbà : Tò bâ lâifī. Sai an jimà.
Bàƙo :   Yâuwa sai an jimà.

                    [3] **tàfi** = *go* (*to*).

Lesson 8

Genitival Link

1. In understanding the possessive construction in Hausa, it is helpful to rephrase the English *the chief's house* as *the house of the chief*. *Of* is expressed by **na** if the noun possessed is masculine, or **ta** if it is feminine. The gender of the possessing noun is immaterial.

2. Usually this genitival link is shortened and suffixed to the noun. **Na** contracts to **-n** and **ta** becomes **-r** (except after the few feminine nouns which do not end in **-a,** when the **ta** becomes **-n**). Note that the final vowel of the possessed noun is always short before the **-n/-r** suffix.[1]

Masculine noun possessed	**gidā na sarkī = gidan sarkī**	the chief's house
	kàrē na Daudà = kàren Daudà	David's dog
	àbinci na kyânwā = àbincin kyânwā	cat's food
Feminine noun possessed	**sāniyā ta Audù = sāniyar Audù**	Audu's cow
	rìgā ta Garbà = rìgar Garbà	Garba's gown

3. The shorter, suffixed forms (**-n/-r**) are far more frequent than the longer forms. **Na/ta,** however, is preferred (or required) :

---

[1] This is because Hausa does not admit a long vowel (or a diphthong) in a closed syllable.

(a) With any noun to indicate possession of something
previously referred to but not re-specified (see
Lesson 9, section 5, for the use of related forms
before pronouns) :

na Audù nē	it (masculine thing) is Audu's
ta Bellò cē	it (feminine thing) is Bello's
bà sù kāwō na	
Daudà ba	they did not bring David's
na Kànde yā yi kyâu	Kande's is nice

(b) When the **na/ta** phrase is the complement of **nē/cē** :

gidā na Audù nē	the house belongs to Audu/is Audu's
rìgā ta Audù cē	the gown belongs to Audu/is Audu's

(c) As a substitute for a possessed word already mentioned to avoid the necessity of repeating it :

Ìnā gidan Bellò dà na Audù ?	Where is Bello's home and that of Audu ?
An kāwō rìgar Garbà dà ta Daudà.	Garba's and Dauda's gowns were brought

(d) When one or more words intervene between the word
modified and the modifying noun or noun phrase
introduced by **na** :

dōkìn nân na Bellò	this horse of Bello's
kèkē biyu na Garbà	Garba's two bicycles

(e) With numbers to form ordinal numbers :

na biyu nè	it is the second (one)
makarantā ta huɗu cè	it is the fourth school

4. There is no gender distinction in Hausa plurals. The
form of the referential used in the plural is always **-n (na)**:

mātan Audù	Audu's wives
mutànen Sarkin Kanò	the Emir of Kano's people

5. Nouns ending in diphthongs **-ai** and **-au** usually drop the second vowel before the referential, and affix the **-n** to the **-a** : [2]

mâi	oil
mân shānū	butter (*lit.* oil of the cow)
kyâu	(visual) goodness
kyânsà	its goodness

6. Many nouns (chiefly Arabic and English loans) ending in a consonant add **-i** before the referential.

mālàm	teacher
mālàmin makarantā	schoolteacher
mùtûm	man
mùtumin sarkī	the chief's man

VOCABULARY

Nominals

cikī, cikin	inside, in . . .
dōkì	horse
dā	son
dākì	hut, room
ìyālì	one's family (wife and children)
iyàyē	parents
kàrē	dog
kèkē	bicycle
kyânwā (*f.*)	cat
mâi	oil
mālàmin makarantā	schoolteacher
mân shānū	butter, cream
nân/nan/nàn	here, this
rìgā (*f.*)	gown, coat
tàimakō	help, aid
Tūrancī	English language

[2] See footnote on section 2 above.

Verbals

gà	here is/are, there is/are (pointing to object)
gōdè [3]	thank
karàntā	read
rubùtā	write
tàmbayà [4]	ask, ask for

EXERCISES

Translate into English :

1. Ìnā gidan sarkī ?
2. Yāròn sarkī nè.
3. Nā kāwō fìtilàr Garbà.
4. Àbincin kyânwā nè.
5. Yārinyà tā tàfi gōnar mālàmin makarantā.

---

[3] Only now are scholars paying the close attention to the correct length of final vowels in Hausa that the phenomenon deserves. There is still some way to go before a definitive set of rules governing final vowel length can be formulated, but we are grateful to Professor Arnott and his colleagues at S.O.A.S. for allowing us to quote this provisional summary of the rules for polysyllabic verbs. In brief it may be said that :

A. Transitive and intransitive verbs with high-low and high-low-high tone pattern :

    1. Those ending in -a and -e

        (*a*) have the final vowel long when

            (i) they are not followed by an object

            (ii) they are followed by a direct object pronoun or by an indirect object

        (*b*) have the final vowel short when they are followed by a noun object.

    2. Those ending in -i and -u (high-low pattern)

        (*a*) have the final vowel short when the verb is intransitive

        (*b*) have the final vowel long when the verb is transitive.

B. Intransitive verbs with low-high and low-high-low tone pattern always have the final vowel short, except when they are followed by an indirect object. The verbal noun has a long final vowel.

C. The vowel length of monosyllabic verbs ending in -i has been dealt with at page 39, note 2.

[4] The student should not attempt to use this word with an object until he has covered the material in Lesson 15.

Translate into Hausa :

1. Is this the chief's house ?
2. The boy's father has gone to Kano.
3. The schoolteacher did not eat food.
4. Where is the horse's food ?
5. There is Audu's cow.

Dialogue

Ùmarù : Mènē nè̀ sūnan wannàn ?
Àlī : Kèkē nè̀.
Ùmarù : Na wànē nè̀ ?
Àlī : Wannàn kèken ɗan sarkī nè̀.
Ùmarù : Tô, ìnā kèken Audù ?
Àlī : Gà shi cân cikin ɗākì.
Ùmarù : Tò dà kyâu, nā gōdè̀.
Àlī : Tò bâ lâifī.

Lesson 9

Possessive Pronouns

1. There are two forms of the possessive pronoun :
inseparable and separable.

2. The *inseparable*, which corresponds to the English
my, *his*, etc., is formed in all persons, except the first
person singular, by adding the genitival link **-n** or **-r** plus
a pronominal suffix to the object possessed. The final
vowel of the noun is shortened as in Lesson 8.

$$\text{yār\`{o}} + \text{-n} + \text{sà} = \text{yàrònsà} \quad \text{his boy}$$
$$\text{yār\`{o}} + \text{-n} + \text{tà} = \text{yàròntà} \quad \text{her boy}$$
$$\text{gōnā} + \text{-r} + \text{sà} = \text{gōnarsà} \quad \text{his farm}$$
$$\text{gōnā} + \text{-r} + \text{tà} = \text{gōnartà} \quad \text{her farm}$$

3. The formation of the inseparable possessive pronoun
differs in the *first person singular*. Here the suffix **-na** or
-ta is suffixed directly to the thing possessed (**-na** to a
masculine noun, **-ta** to a feminine—the gender (sex) of
the speaker is irrelevant). The final vowel of the noun
remains or becomes long.

yārò + **na** = **yāròna**	my boy (said by male or female)
gōnā + **ta** = **gōnāta**	my farm (said by male or female)
àbinci + **na** = **àbincīna**	my food (said by male or female)

4. The complete table of inseparable possessive pronouns is :

Masculine noun		*Feminine noun*	
my boy	yāròna [1]	gōnāta [1]	my farm
your (*m.*) boy	yārònkà	gōnarkà	your (*m.*) farm
your (*f.*) boy	yārònkì	gōnarkì	your (*f.*) farm
his boy	yārònsà	gōnarsà	his farm
her boy	yāròntà	gōnartà	her farm
our boy	yāròmmù	gōnarmù	our farm
your (*pl.*) boy	yārònkù	gōnarkù	your (*pl.*) farm
their boy	yārònsù	gōnarsù	their farm

Note that, except for the first person singular, all the inseparable possessive pronouns have a low tone and a short vowel. Note also that where the genitival link -n precedes -m (first person plural) it becomes -m for euphony. Especially in the western dialects of Sokoto and Katsina, the feminine -r may also assimilate in this way to any following consonant (e.g. **gōnakkà, gōnassà, gōnammù**). This assimilation is not always represented in written Hausa (thus the spelling **gōnarmù** is ordinarily pronounced **gōnammù**). (See footnote to section 7 below.)

5. To form the *separable* possessive pronouns, either **nā-** or **tā-**, depending on the gender of the thing possessed, is prefixed to the inseparable pronouns.

Nāsà nē.	It is his.
Gidā nākà nē.	The house is yours (*m.*).
Kyânwā tākà cē.	The cat is yours (*m.*).
Kyânwā tākì cē.	The cat is yours (*f.*).

6. As with the inseparable forms, an exception to the general pattern is found in the first person singular.

---

[1] The length of the vowel of the first person singular suffix (-na/-ta) is short only when utterance final (e.g. **bà ni àbincìna**, *give me my food*). When another word follows, the vowel of the -na/-ta becomes long (e.g. **àbincìnā nè**, *it is my food*).

Here **nà-** or **tà-** is prefixed to **-wa**. This **-wa** suffix is invariable and disregards the gender of the possessor.

Gidā nàwa nè.   The house is mine (said by male or female).

Gōnā tàwa cè.   The farm is mine (said by male or female).

Note that the tones of these forms are low-high, just the opposite of the rest of the separable forms (and of the similar sounding word **nawà,** *how many* ?, see Lesson 11).

7. The complete table of the separable possessive pronouns is :

Singular	*Plural*
nàwa, tàwa	**nāmù, tāmù**
nākà, tākà	**nākù, tākù**
nākì, tākì	
nāsà, tāsà	**nāsù, tāsù**
nātà, tātà	

A short-vowel form of the feminines is usual when the separable possessives are used to modify other nouns, e.g. **gōnā tasà,** *his farm* ; **uwā takà,** *your mother.*[2]

8. The plural possessive pronoun is generally used in referring to a town or household. Only the chief of the town or head of the house would use the personal ' my ' : **gàrīna** or **gidāna.** Others would say **gàrimmù** or **gidammù.**

VOCABULARY

Nominals
àbù (+ **-n**
   = **àbin**)   thing

---

[2] Some Hausa scholars explain the use of the short-vowel forms, mostly in the third person singular, as a substitute for the inseparable possessive form in order to avoid the non-favoured combinations like **-rs, -rt.**

cân/can/càn	there ; that
farkō	first
gōrò	kolanut
hanyà (*f.*)	path, road, way
jiyà	yesterday
sàbulù	soap
shūkà	planting, sowing
tàre	together
yànzu	now
yàushè, yàushe	when ?

Verbals [3]

fārà	begin
fita	go out (of)
fitō	come out
gamà	finish
jē	go
sâ	put, place
shigō	come in
shūkà	sow (seed)

Particles

à	at, in
dòmin, don	because, in order to

Important Phrases

à kân	on (top of)
dà sāfē	in the morning
dom mè	why ?
nā tàfi	I'm going (now)
tàre dà	together with

EXERCISES

Translate into English :

1. Yārò yā tàfi Kanò tàre dà uwarsà.
2. Mālàminkù yā jē gōnarsà yâu dà sāfē.

[3] See footnote 3, page 44, concerning the final vowel length of verbs before objects.

3. Dom mè ka sâ littāfìnkà à kân kujèrāta ?
4. Dōkìnā yā shìga gàrin àbōkinkù.
5. Yā kāwō kèkēna. Bài kāwō nākà ba.

Translate into Hausa :

1. My mother and my father went to your house yesterday.
2. Where is my soap ? I put it in my room. Here is yours.
3. Our home is in Kano. Where is yours ?
4. Her father went out of town on the Kano road.
5. When did my friend eat his food ? In the morning.

Dialogue

Àdàmū :   Wannàn gidā nākà nē ?
Àbūbakàr :   Ī, nàwa nè.
Àdàmū: Ìnā gōnarkà ?
Àbūbakàr :   Gà gōnātā cân.
Àdàmū :   Tò dà kyâu.
Àbūbakàr :   Nā gamà shūkà jiyà.
Àdàmū :   Tô, yàushè ka fārà ?
Àbūbakàr: À farkon watàn nân.
Àdàmū :   Nī, bàn gamà tàwa ba tùkùna.
Àbūbakàr :   Tò bâ lâifī. Nā tàfi yànzu.
Àdàmū :   Tò sai wani lōkàcī.
Àbūbakàr :   Yâuwā, Allà yà kai mù.
Àdàmū :   Àmin.

Lesson 10

Specifiers—'This', 'That', 'These', 'Those'

1. *Specifiers* are a group of nouns which modify other nouns to make them more specific or less specific. This class of words includes the words often termed *demonstratives*.

Singular	*Plural*	
wannàn (*m.* and *f.*)	**waɗànnân**	this, these
wancàn (*m.*), **waccàn** (*f.*)	**waɗàncân**	that, those
wani (*m.*), **wata** (*f.*)	**waɗansu, wasu**	a, a certain, some (*pl.*)
wannàn yārò this boy	**waɗànnân mutànē**	these people
wancàn gōnā that farm	**wani mùtûm**	a certain man

2. The specifiers **nân**, *this*, *these*, and **cân**, *that*, *those*, follow the nouns they modify. The **-n/-r** referential is suffixed to the preceding noun. The tones on **nân** and **cân** may be high, falling or low, with or without slight differences in meaning. The following are the most typical ways in which these specifiers occur :

(*a*) A falling-tone **nân/cân** following a low-tone syllable or a low-tone **nàn/càn** following a high-tone syllable is the most common way in which these words occur. The meaning is typically non-emphatic, e.g. :

ɗākìn nân	this hut	**mùtumìn cân**	that man
àbincin nàn	this food	**gōnar càn**	that farm

(*b*) A high-tone **nan/can** may be employed to indicate

previous reference. If the tone of the syllable preceding the specifier is high, it becomes falling, e.g. :

rìgân nan [1]	this gown (previously referred to)
aikìn nan	this work (previously referred to)
kujèrâr can	that chair (previously referred to)

3. The specifier **nân** can optionally precede the noun it modifies when the reference of such a noun is locative :

Nā gan shì nân gàrī.   I saw him (here) (in) this town.

4. **Nân** and **cân** may also occur alone (i.e. not as modifiers), meaning *here* and *there* respectively. Only high- and falling-tone forms occur in this usage. The high-tone forms typically indicate a greater distance from the speaker than do the falling-tone forms, e.g. :

Gà Audù nân.	Here's Audu here (nearby).
Gà Audù nan.	Here's Audu here (in the vicinity).
Gà Audù cân.	There's Audu over there.
Gà Audù can.	There's Audu in the distance.

5. An **-n/-r** suffix may be used without a following noun to specify that reference is to something previously referred to or implied from the context, e.g. :

Gà rìgā, àmmā ìnā wàndôn ? There is a/the coat, but where are the trousers (that go with it) ?

If the final syllable of the suffixed noun is high, it becomes falling before **-n/-r** in this usage.[2] The suffixed

---

[1] Before **nân/nan/nàn** the feminine **-r** suffix usually becomes **-n**, but such assimilation does not, as a rule, take place before **cân/can/càn**, though it does in the compound **waccàn** (see above).

[2] We have sought to avoid the technical issue of whether *consonants* can properly carry tone. But in this case, the falling tone may be explained by the fact that this **-n/-r** suffix has a low tone, and therefore a high final vowel + low **-n/-r** gives a falling tone over the whole syllable $C\hat{V}n/C\hat{V}r$, whereas a low final vowel + low **-n/-r** remains low.

form may usually be translated by the English definite
article *the*, e.g. :

Audù yā kāwō àbinci.	Audu brought some food.
Àbincîn bâ kyâu.	The food was not good.
Gà kujèrâr.	Here is the chair (that we talked about previously).

6. The word **ɗîn,** usually meaning *the one previously
referred to*, is usable in place of the **-n/-r** described in
section 5 above and with essentially the same meaning.
It is particularly used with borrowed words, especially
those ending in a consonant.

Inà sôn fensìr ɗîn.   I want the pencil.

Note that **nan** may accompany **ɗîn.**

Yārò ɗîn nan, bài dāwō ba.   That boy has not returned.

A possessive pronoun may also be suffixed to **ɗîn.** In the
first person singular the form is **ɗīna.**

Nā kāwō kèkē ɗînkà.	I brought your bicycle (the one we were discussing).
Ìnā fensìr ɗīna ?	Where is my pencil ?

7. Rules for the employment of the English definite (*the*)
and indefinite (*a, an*) articles in translating Hausa are
not as simple as they appear at first sight. The rendering
of the Hausa nominal without either the referential
suffix **-n/-r** (see section 5, above) or the qualifying
wani/wata (see section 1, above) is a complex question
that is, unfortunately, not so cut and dried as the *the/a*
dichotomy in English.   Of the three grammatical
sentences

   (i) **yārò yā zō**
  (ii) **yāròn yā zō**
 (iii) **wani yārò yā zō**

(ii) and (iii) are quite clear. **Yàròn yā zō** is best translated
by *the boy has come*, a reference to some specified or
implied boy being unambiguously understood. Similarly,
wani yārò yā zō is best rendered by *a (certain) boy has
come*. But what of (i) ? Standard Hausa grammars have
rightly translated **yārò yā zō** as *the boy has come*, since,
though English speakers might expect the more specific
yàròn yā zō to indicate this meaning every time it is
intended, Hausa rules do not correspond to English
rules, and in Hausa, where there is no doubt of, or no
significance attached to, which ' boy ' is meant, **yārò yā zō**
does carry much of the specificity which English expresses
by means of the definite article. This definiteness is
plainly illustrated by such acceptable sentences as **sarkī
yā zō,** *the chief has come* ; **bùɗè ƙòfà,** *open the door* ;
Bàhaushè yā zō, *the Hausa man has come*—in none of
which examples is there any question of choice over
which *chief/door/Hausa man* is referred to.

While recognizing the area of uncertainty and the
difficulty of formulating watertight rules for this issue,
we do not go as far as Abraham, who is content to
recognize no difference in Hausa between the English
the/a. As basic rules of thumb, we recommend the
following when translating into Hausa :

(*a*) Where the noun clearly refers back to a previous
referent (stated or implied), *the* should ordinarily be
rendered by means of the **-n/-r** suffix described above
(section 5) : **yàròn yā zō,** *the boy (you were expecting)
has come.*

(*b*) Where the sense requires *a certain*, **wani/wata** should
be used : **wani yārò yā zō,** *a certain boy has come.*

(*c*) Where the specificity is immaterial or unmistakable,
the unqualified noun should be used : **yārò yā zō,** *the
boy has come.* When in doubt, this is the construction
most likely to be right since it is the most frequent.

VOCABULARY

Nominals

àkwàtì	box
àlmājìrī	pupil, student
bàbba	big (thing)
cōkàlī	spoon
hakà	thus, so
kògī	river
ƙàramī	small (thing)
mōtà (*f.*)/	
mātò	car, lorry
tēbùr	table
wancàn (*pl.*	
waɗàncân)	that (*pl.* those)
wata (*f.*) (*pl.*	
waɗansu)	a certain, a (*pl.* some, certain)
wuƙā (*f.*)	knife
yawà	muchness, quantity, number

Verbals

àkwai	there is, there are
fāɗì	fall
hau	mount, climb
sanì [3]	know

Particles

àmmā	but
dàgà	from
dîn	that previously referred to
kumā	also, further, and

Important Phrases

bàn sanì ba	I don't know
dà yawà	much, many
hakà nē	it is so, indeed
nā sanì	I know (it)
ruwan shâ	drinking water

[3] The student should not attempt to use this word with an object until he has covered the material in Lesson 15.

EXERCISES

Translate into English :

1. Wani yārò yā fāɗì cikin ruwā.
2. Kògin nàn, Kwârà cē.
3. Kā sâ cōkàlin nàn cikin àkwàtìn nân.
4. Ìnā kujèrā ? Gà kujèrâr.
5. Waɗànnân mutànē sun tàfi wani gàrī.

Translate into Hausa :

1. This boy is my friend.
2. You (f.) (have) put that chair here.
3. These boys. Those boys.
4. I don't know yet.
5. I went to that town.

Dialogue

Kànde :   Waɗansu mutànē sun zō gidammù.
Maryamù :   Mādàllā, nā kāwō àbinci dàgà kàsuwā yâu.
Kànde :   Dà kyâu. Àkwai ruwan shâ dà yawà kumā.
Maryamù :   Sarkin gàrī nè ya zō.
Kànde :   Hakà nē. Yā zō tàre dà wani bàbban mùtûm.
Maryamù :   Mùtumìn, sarkī nè kumā ?
Kànde :   Hakà nē, yārònsà yā kāwō wani bàbban
               àkwàtì.
Maryamù :   Tô, mènē nè cikin àkwàtì ?
Kànde :   Bàn sanì ba.

Lesson 11

Quantifiers

1. The *quantifiers* are a subclass of nouns which include the numbers and a few other words. Quantifiers typically follow the noun they modify, but without employing the **-n/-r** suffix.

gidā gōmà	ten houses
yârā nawà ?	how many boys ?
mutằnē dukà	all the people
yārinyằ biyu	two girls

With numbers it is not always necessary to use the plural form of the noun.

2. The numbers 1–22 (see Lesson 32 for a complete listing) :

1	ɗaya	10	gōmà
2	biyu	11	(gōmà) shâ ɗaya
3	ukù	12	(gōmà) shâ biyu
4	huɗu	18	àshìrin biyu bābù [1] *or* gōmà shâ takwàs
5	bìyar	19	àshìrin ɗaya bābù [1] *or* gōmà shâ tarà
6	shidà	20	àshìrin
7	bakwài	21	àshìrin dà ɗaya
8	takwàs	22	àshìrin dà biyu
9	tarà		*etc.*

Note that **shâ**, *and*, is only used with numbers 11–19. The regular word for *and*, **dà**, is used with numbers above 20. For this reason the word **gōmà** is frequently omitted from the numbers 11–19, since **shâ ɗaya** can only mean 11, **shâ biyu** 12, etc.

[1] Literally, ' 20, two/one there is not '.

3. The interrogative **nawà ?**, *how much/many ?*, is also a quantifier.

mùtûm nawà ?	how many persons ?
sàu nawà ?	how many times ?
sū nawà ?	how many of them (are there) ?
kuɗī nawà ?	how much (does it cost) ?

4. **Dukà/duk,** *all,* may also be employed as a quantifier.

yârā dukà	all the children	**yârā ukù** three children
sū dukà	all of them	**sū huɗu** the four of them

5. Quantifiers (except **nawà**) may sometimes suffix **-n** or be followed by **ɗin**.[2] In this case they precede the dependent possessive pronoun or, occasionally, an independent nominal. The meaning varies.

ɗayansù	one of them
biyunsù or **biyu ɗinsù**	twice their number
bìyar ɗinsù	five times their number
dukàn mutànē	all the people

6. *Ordinal numbers* are formed by employing the nominalizing particle **na** (feminine **ta**).

na/ta farkō/fārì	first (*lit.* of beginning)
na/ta biyu	second
na/ta gōmà	tenth
na/ta nawà ?	which (of a series) ? (*lit.* the how manyth)
kàrē na biyu	the second dog
rìgā ta takwàs	the eighth gown
littāfì na nawà ?	which (among several) book ?, which volume ?

Note that **farkō** or **fārì** is substituted for **ɗaya** in forming ordinals (except in the case of a numbered series, e.g. **littāfì na ɗaya,** *volume I*).

---

[2] Note that this high tone **ɗin** is a different word from **ɗin** (Lesson 10, section 6).

7. The word **gùdā,** *a unit of,* is frequently used with numbers, as in the following examples. When **gùdā** occurs alone it means *one.*

yârā gùdā biyu	two boys
mutànē gùdā huɗu	four persons
mōtà gùdā	one car

VOCABULARY

Nominals

Numbers 1–22 :

àyàbà	banana(s)
bàkī	mouth ; edge
daidai	correct, right
dukà, duk	all
fārì/farkō	beginning
gùdā	a unit of, one
gwēbà	guava
kuskurè	mistake, error
lèmō/lèmū	citrus fruit, citrus tree
lìssāfì	arithmetic
mangwàrò	mango
nawà ?	how many ?, how much ?
sàu	times
wùyā (*f.*)	difficulty
wuyà	neck

Verbals		*Particles*	
gānè	understand	**fà ?**	what about ?
màntā	forget	**kâi !**	Good Heavens ! wow !, oh boy !, gee ! (general exclamation)
zaunà	sit down		
		sai	only (see also Lesson 4)
		zuwà	toward, to (see also Lesson 4)

Important Phrases
bâ kyâu   that's not good
bàkin hanyà   edge of the road

EXERCISES

Translate into English :

1. **Gà mangwàrò biyu à kân tēbùr.**
2. **Lìssāfì dà wùyā nè. Àmmā nā gānè.**
3. **Yā sâ àyàbà à bàkinsà, yā ci.**
4. **Ìnā bàbban àkwàtì ? Bellò yā tàfi gidansù dà shī.**
5. **Kā kāwō gwēbà nawà ? Gùdā gōmà.**
6. **Kâi !, Audù yā mântà sūnāna. Wànnan bâ kyâu.**

Translate into Hausa :

1. The girl sat down on the chair.
2. I made a mistake in my arithmetic.
3. He took the bicycle toward his home.
4. We followed a path at the edge of the river.
5. Good Heavens, there are eight people in that car !

Dialogue
Mālàmī :   **Biyu dà ukù nawà nē ?**
Dālìbī :   **Bìyar nè.**
Mālàmī :   **Daidai nè. Shidà dà bakwài fà ?**
Dālìbī :   **Shâ ukù**
Mālàmī :   **Dà kyâu. Huɗu sàu biyu nawà ?**
Dālìbī :   **Tarà nē.**
Mālàmī :   **Bābù ! Kā yi kuskurè.**
Dālìbī :   **Hakà nē. Sai takwàs.**
Mālàmī :   **Tô. Nawà nē shidà sàu ukù ?**
Dālìbī :   **Àshìrin biyu bābù.**
Mālàmī :   **Mādàllā. Wannàn lìssāfì dà wùyā nè ?**
Dālìbī :   **Ā'à, bâ wùyā.**
Mālàmī :   **Tò dà kyâu.**

Lesson 12

Subjunctive Aspect and Commands

1. The subjunctive aspect has a wide variety of uses, though only a few of them will be treated here (see also Lesson 27). Subjunctive constructions may usually be literally translated *let one do such-and-such*.

2. The subjunctive aspect person-aspect pronouns are characterized by low tone and a short vowel. Using the verb **zō,** *come,* as a model, the p-a pronouns in the subjunctive are:

let me come	**ìn zō**	**mù zō**	let us come
come! (*m.*)	**kà zō**	**kù zō**	come! (*pl.*)
come! (*f.*)	**kì zō**		
let him come	**yà zō**	**sù zō**	let them come
let her come	**tà zō**		
let someone come	**à zō**		

3. The negative of the subjunctive aspect is formed by employing the negative particle **kadà** (this is often shortened to **kâr** in rapid speech):

kadà kà zō	do not come
kadà yārò yà tàfi	don't let (*or, in context,* lest) the boy go away
kâr kà yi hakà	don't do that

4. The second person forms of the subjunctive aspect are commonly used to express both positive [1] and negative commands.

---

[1] A positive command may be strengthened by the use of **sai,** e.g. **sai kà shìga!** may mean *you must enter* (though it has a weaker meaning as well). See Lesson 29, section 2, for a fuller treatment.

kà shìga	enter ! (*m.*)
kù kāwō yārò	bring (*pl.*) the boy
kadà kì ci àbinci	don't (*f.*) eat (the) food

5. The *imperative* employs no p-a pronoun. There is, however, a special tone pattern for the verb in this type of construction : all syllables except the final syllable in words of two or more syllables must be low tone. The final syllable typically is high, occasionally is low. The imperative is not ordinarily used to address more than one person at a time.

(*a*) One-syllable verbs may be either high (unchanged) or low :

zò/zō nân	come here !
cì/ci àbinci	eat (your) food !

(*b*) Verbs with a basic low-high tone pattern will not change :

tàfi gidā	go home !
shìga	enter !

(*c*) Verbs with any other basic tone pattern will start with a low tone. A final long vowel on the verb will usually shorten in utterance final position :

(**kāwō**) → **kàwō àbinci**	bring the food !
(**barì**) → **bàri**	leave (it alone) !

6. Note the tonal contrast between the basic forms of the following verbs (as employed with the subjunctive p-a pronouns) and their imperative forms in the following examples. The meanings of the parallel constructions are the same.

kà zaunà	sit down !	**zàuna**
kà shigō	come in !	**shìgo**
kà karàntā	read (it) !	**kàrànta**

7. In complex sentences it is often appropriate to translate a verb in a subjunctive aspect construction as a so-called English ' infinitive ' (expressing purpose). Such a construction forms the predicate of the dependent clause, e.g. :

(a) The verb of the first clause may be in a completive or subjunctive aspect construction :

Nā zō ìn gaishē kà.	I've come *to greet* you.
Yā jē gidā yà kāwō ruwā.	He went home *to bring* water.
Kù zō kù yi aikìnkù.	Come *and/to do* your work.

(b) The verb of the first clause may be in the imperative :

Zō kù yi aikìnkù.	Come *and/to do* your work.
Zàuna kà shā ruwā.	Sit down *and/to drink* water.

VOCABULARY

Nominals

dājì	' bush ' country (*i.e.* uninhabited, uncultivated area)
ƙarfī	strength
ƙōfà (*f.*)	door (way)
rānā (*f.*)	sun, day
sā'ì	time (= **lōkàcī**)
saurī	quickness
shēkaranjiyà	day before yesterday
tāgà (*f.*)	window
zāfī	hotness

Verbals		*Particles*	
barì [2]	let, allow, leave (a thing)	**kadà, kâr** . . . do not . . .	
budè	open		

---

[2] The student should not attempt to use these verbs with objects until he has covered the material in Lesson 15.

gaishē   greet (before pronoun
          objects only)
rufè   close
sāmù [3]   get, obtain
tāshì   get up, leave (from a
          place)
tsayà   stand (up), stop

Important Phrases
dà saurī   quickly
rānā tā yi zāfī the sun is hot

EXERCISES

Translate into English :

1. **Kadà kà yi aikìn nân.**
2. **Kadà yārinyà tà ci àbincin nàn.**
3. **Zō nân kì zaunà.**
4. **Kadà kù yi hakà.**
5. **Fìta kà rufè ƙōfà.**

Translate into Hausa :

1. Don't open the window.
2. Stop ! Enter ! Sit down !
3. Bring (*f.*) the food here.
4. Let him do his work.
5. Come (*pl.*) and eat your food in our home.

Dialogue
Hārūnà : **Yàƙubǔ, sàlāmù àlaikùn.**
Yàƙubù : **Yâuwā, àlaikà sàlāmù.**
Hārūnà : **Ìyālìnkà lāfiyà ?**
Yàƙubù : **Lāfiyà ƙalau. Kā zō lāfiyà ?**
Hārūnà : **Lāfiyà. Bâ kōmē.**
Yàƙubù : **Mādàllā. Shìgō mù zaunà.**

---

[3] See footnote 2 on page 63.

Hārūnà : Tò dà kyâu. Kâi, rānā tā yi zāfī yâu.
Yàƙubù : Hakà nē. Yārò, kàwō ruwan shâ !
Hārūnà : Nā zō ìn gaishē kà nē.
Yàƙubù : Mādàllā. Nā gōdè. Kā zō dàgà kàsuwā nè ?
Hārūnà : Ā'à, nā zō dàgà gidā ɗàzu.
Yàƙubù : Tò bâ lâifī. Gà ruwā, kà shā.
Hārūnà : Tò nā gōdè. Nā tàfi yànzu.
Yàƙubù : Tò bâ lâifī. Sai wani sā'ì.
Hārūnà : Yâuwā, sai wani sā'ì.

Lesson 13

Non-aspect Verbals ; 'Yes' and 'No'

1. The non-aspect verbals are a small group of very useful words of frequent occurrence which may be followed by a noun, a noun phrase or a personal pronoun. The pronouns employed are the direct object pronouns. These verbals are not preceded by person-aspect markers.

2. **Àkwai,** *there is/are,* states the existence of something.

Àkwai yârā à gidā.	There are children at home.
Àkwai aikì dà yawà.	There is much work.
Àkwai kuɗī à wurinkà ?	Do you have any money ? (*lit.* is there money in your place ?)
Àkwai (sù).	There are some.

3. **Bābù** or **bâ,** *there is/are no/not,* means the opposite of **àkwai.** The pronouns employed after **bâ** are (as with **àkwai**) the object pronouns. **Bābù,** however, is followed by the independent pronouns (e.g. **bābù shī,** *there is none of it*).

Bābù yârā à gidā.	There are no children at home.
Bâ aikì cân.	There is no work there.
Àkwai kuɗī ? Bābù !	Is there any money ? No ! (*lit.* there is none)

4. **Gà,** *here/there is/are,* is used when pointing something out.

Gà gidammù cân.	There is our house over there.
Gà littāfì à kân tēbùr.	There is the book on the table.

Gà ni [1] **nân.**	Here I am.
Gà rìgāta.	Here is my gown.

5. *Yes* is ordinarily expressed by the use of the particle **i.** The expressions **hakà nē,** *thus it is,* **gàskiyā nè,** [2] *it is the truth,* or **gàskiyarkà,** *your truth,* are frequently used as well to indicate agreement.

Kā tàfi jiyà ? Ī.	Did you go yesterday? Yes.
Kâi, rānā tā yi zāfī yâu !	Goodness, the sun is hot
Gàskiyarkà !	today ! You're right !
Àkwai yârā dà yawà à nân.	There are many children
Hakà nē.	here. You're right.

6. *No* is ordinarily expressed by the use of the particle **ā'à.** For emphasis, the verbal **bābù** may be used. [3]

Kā kāwō àbinci ? Ā'à.	Did you bring any food ? No.
Kai àbōkinsà nē ? Bābù !	Are you a friend of his ? (Emphatically) not !

7. In answering a negative question, [4] *hasn't he come ?,* in Hausa, it is necessary to note the difference in the choice of *yes* or *no.* The following example illustrates this difference :

English :   Hasn't he come ?
           No (he hasn't come).

[1] See Lesson 15, section 3, for the remaining forms of the direct object pronoun.

[2] Although after the feminine noun **gàskiyā** one would expect **cè, nè** is regularly employed in this stylized and frequently heard expression. One explanation is that the original phrase was **àbin gàskiyā nè,** *it is a true thing.*

[3] This usage, however, appears to be a recent development in Hausa (probably due to the influence of European and/or other non-native speakers of Hausa). **Kō kàɗan,** . . . (*not*) *even a little,* or **fàufau,** lit. *utterly* (*not*), are much more commonly used by native Hausa.

[4] For a fuller treatment of asking questions, see Lesson 21, section 8.

Hausa :   **Bài zō ba ?** Hasn't he come ?
      Ī.   Yes (what you say is right : he has not come).
      Ā'à. No (what you say is wrong : he has come).

Mistakes can be avoided in interpreting the answer to a negative question by mentally relating the *yes* or *no* to the accuracy of the statement made in the question, not as a direct reply to the question ; or by the use of the American response ' right '.

Examples :

Kànde bà tà dāwō ba ?	Isn't Kande back ?
Ī (bà tà dāwō ba).	Yes (she has not come back).
Ā'à (tā dāwō).	No (she has come back).

VOCABULARY

Nominals

àràhā	inexpensiveness
dànkalì	sweet potato(es), ' European ' potato(es)
dōyà (*f.*)	(large) yam(s)
gàskiyā (*f.*)	truth
kudī	price, money (see Lesson 6)
kwabò	kobo
ƙwai	egg(s)
madarā (*f.*)	milk
mânyā	big ones (*pl.* of **bàbba,** Lesson 10)
nairà	1 naira
nāmà	meat, wild animal
sīsì	5 kobos
sulè	10 kobos
tarō	$2\frac{1}{2}$ kobos
tsàdā	expensiveness
wurī	place
yunwà	hunger

Verbals		*Particles*	
dafà	cook	**kō ?**	(question particle), or
gudù	run away	**nē ?**	(question particle) (see
kōmà	return (there),		Lesson 5)
	go to another		
	place intend-		
	ing to stay		
	there		
shiryà	prepare		
tsūfa	get old		

Important Phrases

nā ji yunwà	I am hungry
yā yi tsàdā	it is expensive
yā yi àràhā	it is cheap, inexpensive

EXERCISES

Translate into English :
1. **Nā ji yunwà. Àkwai àbinci ?**
2. **Kā kāwō mùtumìn nē ? Ì, gà shi.**
3. **Bābù cōkàlī nân ? Ì.**
4. **Yârā sun tàfi makarantā, kō ? Tùkùna.**
5. **Bà kù shiryà ba ? Ā'à.**
6. **Gà littāfìn Mālàm Garbà. Ìnā nàwa ?**

Translate into Hausa :
1. Has my mother returned ? No, she has not returned.
2. Didn't Bello go to Kano yesterday ? Yes, he went.
3. Is thᴗre work ? Yes, there is much work but no money.
4. Are there eggs and milk here ? There is milk, but there are no eggs.
5. I am hungry. What about you ?

Dialogue

Mūsā : **Àkwai dànkalì à kàsuwā yâu ?**
Gàmbo : **Ā'à, àmmā àkwai dōyà dà yawà.**

Mūsā :   Tò dà kyâu. Nawà nē kuɗin dōyà ?
Gàmbo :   Sulè dà sīsì zuwà sulè biyu.
Mūsā :   Kâi, sun yi tsàdā !
Gàmbo :   Bābù ! Dukànsù mânyā nè.
Mūsā :   Tò bâ lâifī. Àkwai àyàbà kumā ?
Gàmbo :   Ī àkwai, àmmā bâ yawà.
Mūsā :   Tô, gwēbà fà ?
Gàmbo :   Dà yawà. Àkwai mangwàrò dà lèmō dà yawà
           kumā.
Mūsā :   Dà kyâu. Bàri mù jē mù sāmù.
Gàmbo :   Tò mù jē.

Lesson 14

Intransitive Verbs

1. Intransitive verbs are verbs which cannot take a direct object.[1]

Yā shìga.	He has gone in.
Kā tsayà.	You (have) stopped/stood up.
Yā fàru.	It (has) happened.

2. Intransitive verbs may be followed by expressions of place, time, manner and the like. These are not to be confused with objects of transitive verbs (see Lesson 15).

Yā tàfi gidā.	He went/has gone home.
Nā zō jiyà.	I came yesterday.
Yā tàfi dà wuri._	He went early.

3. Intransitive verbs of motion typically imply the concept of *to* or *toward* a place. Thus no special word is used for *to/toward* if the following word indicates a place.

Yā jē kàsuwā.	He has been to market.[2]
Sun tàfi Zāriyà.	They have gone to Zaria.[2]

4. If one wishes to express motion toward a person or other non-place noun, the words **wurin** or **wajen** are used.

---

[1] Many intransitives may, however, take indirect objects (e.g. **nā tsayà/tsayam masà,** *I went/stood surety for him*). See Lesson 15, section 2, for an introduction to indirect objects, section 8 and Lesson 37, section 4 (c), for further illustrations of intransitive verb forms before indirect objects. See Lessons 25 and 37 for an overall analysis of verbs.

[2] A general distinction may be made between **tàfi,** *go (away), go to a place (and not have returned yet)*, and **jē,** *go to and return from*.

Yā tàfi wurin sarkī.   He has gone to the chief.
Yā zō wurin mutànemmù.   He has come to our people.
Yā tàfi wajen itàcē.   He has gone to the vicinity
                                 of (towards) the tree.

VOCABULARY

Nominals
bakī (*f.* **bakā**)   black (thing)
dàbārà (*f.*)   scheme, plan, device
farī (*f.* **farā**)   white (thing)
hadarì   storm
inuwà (*f.*)   shade
irì (*pl.* **irì-irì**)   kind, sort ; seed
jā (*m.* or *f.*)   red (thing)
kāyā   load, implements
mài gidā   ' man of the house ', house-owner,
                                    husband
tāyà (*f.*)   tyre
uwargidā   ' woman of the house ', (senior) wife
wajē   place, region, environs
wutā (*f.*)   fire

Verbals   *Particles*
daurè   tie (up), imprison   **ai**   well, why (a mild
fàru   happen   exclamation)
sàyā [3] buy   **mài**   possessor of . . .,
wucè   pass (by/on)   characterized
                                           by . . .

Important Phrases
dà wuri   early, in good time
kāyan aikì   implements of work, tools
mài tēbùr   small market trader
nawà nawà ?   how much each ?

---

[3] The student should not attempt to use this verb with an object
until he has covered the material in Lesson 15.

EXERCISES

Translate into English :

1. Mè ya fàru à gidan Yàƙubù ?
2. Hadarì yā wucè yànzu. Bàri mù yi wàsā.
3. Kà tsayà kà ɗaurè kāyankà.
4. Dōkìnsà yā gudù dà saurī zuwà gàrī.
5. Yā tàfi wurin àbōkinsà.

Translate into Hausa :

1. She passed by the door.
2. They went to sit in the shade of the tree.
3. It happened here yesterday.
4. Audu returned home the day before yesterday.
5. She went to market early.

Dialogue

Bellò :	Nawà nē kuɗin tayàr kèkē ?
Mài tēbùr :	Ai irì ukù cē. Àkwai farā dà baƙā dà jā.
Bellò :	Tô, nawà nawà kuɗinsù ?
Mài tēbùr :	Farā, nairà ɗaya dà sulè shidà cē.
Bellò :	Kâi, tā yi tsàdā !
Mài tēbùr :	Àmmā ita cè mài kyâu.
Bellò :	Baƙā fà !
Mài tēbùr :	Nairà ɗaya dà sulè huɗu.
Bellò :	Jā fà !
Mài tēbùr :	Jā cè mài àràhā à nairà ɗaya dà sulè biyu.
Bellò :	Tô daidai nè.

(This Dialogue is continued in Lesson 15.)

Lesson 15

Transitive Verbs ; Object Pronouns

1. Transitive verbs may be followed by indirect and/or direct objects, or by no object at all.[1]

2. *Indirect objects* are introduced by the particle **ma-** before pronouns and, most frequently in Kano, **wà** [2] before nouns. With the exception of the first person singular form, it is the inseparable possessive pronouns treated in Lesson 9, section 4, to which the **ma-** is prefixed. The pronoun indirect objects are written as single words, and sometimes show one or more alternative forms. They are :

to/for me	**manì/minì, mîn**	**manà/mamù**	to/for us
to/for you (*m.*)	**makà, mā**	**makù/mukù**	to/for you (*pl.*)
to/for you (*f.*)	**makì/mikì, mā**		
to/for him	**masà, mâr**	**masù/musù**	to/for them
to/for her	**matà**		

Examples of indirect objects (see also section 8 below) :

(*a*) Pronoun indirect objects with transitive verbs :

> **Yā shiryà manà.**   He prepared (it) for us.
> **Tā dafà minì.**   She cooked (it) for me.

---

[1] As noted in Lesson 14 (section 1, footnote), intransitive verbs may also take an indirect object. Intransitives may not, however, take direct objects. See Lessons 25 and 37 for an overall analysis of verbs.

[2] With all verbs in some dialects, however (e.g. Sokoto), and with some verbs in all dialects, **mà** is used in preference to **wà**, e.g. **Nā yi mà sarkì aikì** (Sok.), *I did work for the chief* ; **Ya tāsam mà màtā tasà,** *He attacked his wife.*

(*b*) Noun indirect objects with transitive verbs :

Mun yi wà sarkī aikì.   We did work for the chief.
Nā kāwō wà mālàmī.   I brought (it) to the teacher.

3. A direct object may be a noun, a pronoun or a nominal phrase. The tone of a *direct object pronoun* is, in general, high following a low-tone syllable and low following a high-tone syllable, like **nē/cē** (see Lesson 6). The pronouns used as direct objects are as follows : [3]

me	**ni/nì**	**mu/mù**	us
you (*m.*)	**ka/kà**	**ku/kù**	you (*pl.*)
you (*f.*)	**ki/kì**		
him	**shi/shì**	**su/sù**	them
her	**ta/tà**		

4. When both indirect and direct objects are present, *the indirect object invariably precedes the direct object*,[4] and, if the *direct* object is a personal pronoun, it assumes the independent form (see Lesson 6, section 6, and example three below).

Yā kāwō manà àbinci.   He brought us food.
Nā yi wà sarkī aikì.   I did work for the chief.
Kà kai masà shī/ita.   Take it (*m./f.*) to him.

5. The verb **bā**, *give, give to*, is the commonest of a very limited number of verbs which require no indirect object indicator (**ma-/wà/mà**) before an indirect object. If the indirect object is a pronoun, the forms employed are the direct object pronouns.[5] If (as infrequently happens) the

---

[3] Note that there is no indefinite direct (or indirect) object pronoun corresponding to the **an/à** (etc.) p-a pronouns.
[4] Unless the less common (for expressing ' indirect objectivity ') **gà/gàrē** construction is employed. See Lesson 17, section 2.
[5] This fact leads some to suggest that **bā** actually governs two *direct* objects rather than one indirect and one direct (like other

direct object is a pronoun, the independent pronoun forms are employed, as in example three below.

Yā bā mù kuɗī.	He gave us money.
Nā bā shì aikì.	I gave him work.
Nā bā shì ita.	I gave her/it to him.

If the indirect object is a noun, **bā** becomes **bâ.**

Yā bâ mùtûm kuɗī.	He gave the man money.
Nā bâ Audù aikì.	I gave Audu work.

Bā/bâ must take at least one object. When only one object occurs, it is most likely to be an indirect object. If only a direct object is employed, it must be preceded by **dà.**

Yā bā nì.	He gave (it) to me.
Yā bā dà kuɗī.	He gave money.

6. The verbs **sanì,** (*get to*) *know,* **barì,** *permit, leave,* and **ganì,** *perceive, see,* are abbreviated before an object. **Sanì** and **barì** never drop more than their final vowel.

Nā san shì.	I know [6] him.
Yā bar gidā.	He (has) left home.
Yā bar manà aikì.	He (has) left us work.
Sun san Audù.	They know Audu.

Ganì drops its final vowel before a pronoun object and its whole final syllable before a noun object. Before an indirect object it becomes **ganè.**

---

verbs). The analysis here presented seems preferable to the present authors, since it focuses on a syntactic similarity of function between the complements of **bā** and those of other verbs rather than on the (from this point of view) slight formal differences between complements filling the 'indirect object' position. If, however, the student finds it easier to think of **bā** as governing two direct objects, he should feel free to do so.

[6] See footnote 7, p. 77.

Nā gan shì.	I saw/see him.[7]
Nā ga Audù.	I saw/see Audu.
Kà ganè mini kèkēna !	Keep an eye on my bike (for me) !

7. One group of verbs (often termed *changing* or *variable vowel verbs*) [8] change their terminal vowel (and their tones if they have three or more syllables) before a direct object. Transitive verbs with an initial low tone are of this type. Before a noun direct object the terminal vowel becomes **-i**. Before a pronoun it becomes **-ē**. All tones are low except for a final high-tone syllable.

(sàyā)	**Nā sàyā.**	I (have) bought (it).
	Nā sàyi àbinci.	I (have) bought food.
	Nā sàyē shì.	I (have) bought it.
(tàmbayà)	**Na tàmbayà.**	I asked.
	Nā tàmbàyi Bellò.	I (have) asked Bello.
	Nā tàmbàyē shì.	I (have) asked him.

A very few verbs with initial high tones belong to this group of verbs. Two common ones are **sāmù,** *get,* and **ɗaukà,** *take, pick up.*

Mun sàmē shì.	We got it *or* we found him.
Yā ɗauki kāyā.	He (has) picked up/carried the load.

Variable vowel verbs will be indicated in the vocabularies by the presence of **(i/ē)** following the verb thus : **sāmù (i/ē).**

---

[7] Note that the English translation of the Hausa completive aspect in contexts such as these is present (not past) tense. In the case of **nā san shì** the literal gloss would be something like *I have got to know him,* therefore *I (still) know him.* **Nā gan shì** literally means *I have/had visually perceived him,* therefore meaning either *I saw him* or *(having visually perceived him) I (still) see him.*

[8] This class of verb is Parsons' Grade II. The Parsons' classification is introduced in Lesson 25.

8. Before a pronoun indirect object variable vowel verbs
(and low-high intransitives) operate as follows :

(*a*) They may either become high-high(-high) and suffix
-r (which assimilates to **-m**), e.g. :

(nèmā) → **Yā nēmam minì aikì.**	He sought work for me.
(sāmù) → **Nā sāmam masà kèkē.**	I got a bicycle for him.
(**yàrda-**intransitive) → **Mun yardam masà.**	We allowed him (to do it).
(tàmbayà) → **Yā tambayam minì.**	He asked me.

(*b*) Or they may become high-low(-high), e.g. :

(sàyā) → **Nā sayà masà àgōgō.**	I bought him a watch.
(fàɗā) → **Sun faɗà manà làbārì.**	They told us the news.
(**yàrda-**intransitive) → **Nā yardà makà.**	I allow you (to do it).
(tàmbayà) → **Sun tambàyā manà Audù.**	They asked Audu for us.
(kwàikwayà) → **Sun kwaikwàyā manà birì.**	They imitated a monkey for us.

9. Other transitive verbs, except those ending in **-ō,** also
shorten their terminal vowel before a direct noun object
(but not before a direct pronoun object, nor before an
indirect object). These verbs likewise, if they consist of
more than two syllables, drop the tone of the final
syllable before a noun direct object.

Nā kāmà.	I (have) caught (it).
Nā kāmà shi/ta.	I (have) caught it.
Nā kāmà kīfī.	I (have) caught a fish.

Nā kāmà̀ wà̀ Mūsā kīfī	I have caught Musa a fish.
Nā karàntā.	I (have) read (it).
Nā karàntā shi.[9]	I (have) read it.
Nā karàntà̀ littāfì.	I (have) read the book.
Sun karàntā manà̀ shī.	They read it to us.
Nā kāwō.	I (have) brought (it).
Nā kāwō shì/tà̀.	I (have) brought it.
Nā kāwō kuɗī.	I (have) brought money.
An kirāwō shì.	He has been summoned.
An kirāwō Mūsā.	Musa has been summoned.

VOCABULARY

Nominals

à̀ddā (*f.*)	matchet
dà̀līlì	reason
fartanyà̀ (*f.*)	hoe
gà̀rmā (*f.*)	large hoe, plough
gà̀tarī	axe, hatchet
kōmē	everything, whatever

Verbals

bā (bâ)	give
ɗaukà̀ (i/ē)	pick up, carry
fàɗā (i/ē)	speak
ganī	see
ƙārà̀	increase, raise (price)
ragè̀	reduce (price)
sallà̀mā	agree to sell
tayà̀	make an offer (in buying)

Particles

à̀lbarkà̀	no sale ! (said by seller)
habà̀	come, come now !, nonsense !
ma-/wà̀/ **mà̀**	to, for

[9] Note that after a high-low-high verb a pronoun object does not follow the tonal polarity rule given in section 3 above; but, rather, is high toned.

Important Phrases

nā sàyā   I (agree to) buy (it)
ƙàrā minì   give me some more, increase your offer
ràgē minì   take some away, reduce the price for me

EXERCISES

Translate into English :

1. Bellò yā kāwō manà nāmà.
2. Kài masù littāfìn nân, kà dāwō dà wuri.
3. Wà ya bā kà ƙwai ? Mài tēbùr à bàkin hanyà.
4. Tā jē kàsuwā, tā sàyi dōyà mài tsàdā.
5. Kin ɗàukē sù. Kin kai sù gidan mài gidankù.

Translate into Hausa :

1. Did he see me ? Yes, but he doesn't know you.
2. He got meat. She cooked it. They ate it in a hurry.
3. We left three mangoes in his car. Go and get them.
4. She prepared food for us in the shade of the big tree.
5. He bought tools. I don't know the reason.

Dialogue
(Continuation of Dialogue in Lesson 14.)

Bellò :   Tô, nā sàyi farâr nairà ɗaya dà sulè huɗu nè.
Mài tēbùr :   Àlbarkà. Shī nè kuɗin baƙâr.
Bellò :   Tô, nawà nē kuɗintà na gàskiyā ?
Mài tēbùr :   Nā ragè kwabô ukù.
Bellò :   Nā ƙàrà sīsì.
Mài tēbùr :   Habà mālàm !
Bellò :   Fàɗi gàskiyā.
Mài tēbùr :   Kàwō nairà dà sulè bìyar dà sīsì.
Bellò :   Tô, nā tayà nairà dà sulè bìyar.
Mài tēbùr :   Nā sallàmā nairà dà sulè bìyar dà tarō.
Bellò :   Mādàllā, gà kuɗîn.

Lesson 16

The Future Aspects and Zâ

1. There are two future aspects in Hausa. The most used construction, here termed *future I*, employs the specialized verbal **zā** plus the subjunctive aspect person-aspect pronouns. Elision (including tonal) takes place in the first and third (masculine) persons singular (cf. Lesson 7, section 8 (*c*)).

I will come	**zân zō**	**zā mù zō**	we will come
you (*m.*) will come	**zā kà zō**	**zā kù zō**	you will come
you (*f.*) will come	**zā kì zō**		
he will come	**zâi zō**	**zā sù zō**	they will come
she will come	**zā tà zō**		
one will come	**zā à zō**		

2. The *future II aspect* is less used than the future I.[1] Use of this aspect sometimes tends to lend an air of indefiniteness to what is said. The use of the future I does not, though, necessarily imply more definiteness than does the use of the future II. The future II forms are :

I shall come	**nâ zō**	**mâ/mwâ zō**	we shall come
you (*m.*) will come	**kâ zō**	**kwâ zō**	you (*pl.*) will come
you (*f.*) will come	**kyâ zō**		
he will come	**yâ zō**	**sâ/swâ zō**	they will come
she will come	**tâ zō**		
one will come	**â zō**		

[1] Some Hausa dialects do not use it at all.

3. The negative of both future aspects employs the
bà ... ba negative particles.

Bà zâi zō ba.	He will not come.
Bà mâ tàfi ba.	We will not go (away).
Bà zā sù ci àbinci ba.	They are not going to eat food.

4. In sentences of a narrative type, when a string of verbs
occurs all of which require the future aspect, the first verb
is preceded by a future I or II p-a pronoun and the rest
by the appropriate subjunctive aspect p-a pronoun.[2]

**Gòbe Mālàm Audù zâi tàfi 'Yōlà, yà buɗè makarantā,
yà dāwō, yà ci àbinci, yà hūtà.** Tomorrow M. Audu will
go to Yola, open the school, return, eat and rest.

5. A widely used, specialized verbal related to **zā** is **zâ**,
will go to, am bound for. The special set of p-a pronouns
employed by this verbal *follow* rather than precede it.
They are the same forms (with the addition of **a**) as the
direct object pronouns given in Lesson 15, section 3.[3]

Zâ ni gidā.	I am going/will go home.
Ìnā zâ ka ?	Where are you (*m.*) going/will you go ?
Zâ ki Kanò.	You (*f.*) are going/will go to Kano.
Yāròn nan zâ shi	
makarantā.	This boy is going /will go to school.
Zâ ta gōnā.	She is going/will go to the farm.
Zâ a gàrī.	They (*impersonal*) are going/will go to town.
Zâ mu aikì.	We are going /will go to work.
Zâ ku kàntī.	You (*pl.*) are going/will go to the store.

---

[2] This use of the subjunctive may also be employed if the aspect
of the first clause is continuative or habitual (see Lesson 27, section
1 (*g*)).

[3] Note that in these examples the time of the action (present or
future) is more dependent than usual on the context.

Zâ su rawā.   They are going/will go to the dance/
         games.

Zâ cannot be followed directly by a nominal.
Zâ constructions are negatived by the use of either the
bà ... ba or the **bà ... ba** negative sets :

Bà/bà zâ ni
    kàsuwā ba.   I am not going to the market.
Bà/bà zâ ku
    kàntî ba ?   Aren't you (*pl.*) going to the store ?

VOCABULARY

Nominals

gyàɗā (*f.*)	groundnuts, peanuts
jībi	day after tomorrow
kàntī	store
ƙwarai	very much
màganà (*f.*)	word, talk, matter
rawā (*m./f.*)	dance, game
sābō	new (thing)
sòsai	exactly, really, for sure, that's right !
tàfiyà (*f.*)	travelling, journey
tādî	conversation
tsōhō/tsōfō	old (thing or person)
yāwò	a walk, a stroll
zanè	woman's body cloth

Verbals

gàji	become tired
gayà	tell (requires an indirect object)
hūtà	rest, relax
nèmā (i/ē)	seek, look for
sâ	wear, put (clothing) on (see Lesson 9, Vocabulary)
sayar (dà)	sell
zâ	will go (to), am going (to)

Important Phrases
ìnā zâ ka ?   where are you going ?

EXERCISES

Translate into English :

1. **Nā ji yunwà ƙwarai. Dòmin hakà zân ci àbinci yànzu.**
2. **Bà zā mù ci àbinci nân ba.**
3. **Mè zā kì yi ? Zân kōmà gàrī an jimà.**
4. **Zā kà gayà minì làbārìn tàfiyàrkà ?**
5. **Zâ ku kàsuwā yâu ? Ā'à, zâ mu gidan àbōkīna.**

Translate into Hausa :

1. We will go to the dance in the market tomorrow.
2. You won't go to school.
3. They will ask you to give them money.
4. Where are you going ? I'm going for a walk.
5. Tomorrow Malam Bello will go to Kano. He will bring his father's horse.

Dialogue
Amìnā : Ìnā zâ ki, Kànde ?
Kànde : Zâ ni kàntī ìn sàyi sābon zanè.
Amìnā : Dom mè ?
Kànde : Dòmin ìn sâ, ìn tàfi rawā dà shī jībi.
Amìnā : Dà kyâu. Kâi, zanènkì na yànzu bâ kyâu !
Kànde : Gàskiyarkì. Yā tsūfa sòsai.
Amìnā : Mài gidankù yā bā kì kuɗîn ?
Kànde : Bābù ! Nā sayar dà gyàɗā nè.
Amìnā : Tò bâ lâifì.

Lesson 17

Relaters and Relational Nouns

1. Hausa employs several particles (here termed *relaters*) and nouns to introduce (or relate) phrases, clauses and sentences in much the way English does with prepositions and conjunctions. Some of the more important of these are listed below. (See Lesson 29 for further treatment of **sai** and **dà**.)

2. *Nominal phrase introducers* (relater-head nominal phrases).

à, *at, in, on :*

Nā gan shì à Kanò.	I saw him at/in Kano.
Yā yi aikìnsà à ɗākì.	He did his work in the hut.
Yā sâ tāsà à kân tēbùr.	He put the dish on the table.

dà, *with :*

Yā tàfi dà shī.	He has gone away with it/him *or* he has taken it/him away.
Yā gudù dà saurī.	He ran fast (*lit.* with speed).
Mun ci àbinci tàre dà shī.	We ate food with him.

dàgà, *from :*

Nā dāwō dàgà Kadunà.	I have returned from Kaduna.
Yā sāmù dàgà gidā.	He got (it) from home.
Yā zō dàgà wurin sarkī.	He has come from the chief.

gà/gàrē *to, for, in the presence of,* etc. (**gà** before nouns, **gàrē** before pronouns) [1] :

---

[1] In many contexts action performed for the benefit of someone may be expressed either by an indirect object construction or by the use of **gà/gàrē**, e.g. alternative ways of expressing examples one and three on page 86 would be : **Nā kai masà su,** and **Sun kāwō wà màlàmai ruwā.**

Nā kai sù gàrē shì.	I took/have taken them to him.
Yā nềmi aikì gà Àlī.	He sought work from Ali.
Sun kāwō ruwā gà màlàmai.	They brought water to the teachers.
Sunà gàrē shì.	They are with him/at his home.
Yā sāmù dàgà gàrē nì.	He got it from me.

sai, *until, except, only* (**sai** also has uses other than as a phrase introducer—see below) :

Sai gòbe.	Until tomorrow.
Bàn ga wani àbù ba sai tàkàlmī.	I didn't see anything except shoes.
Sai ɗayansù ya tàfi.[2]	Only one of them went.

3. *Connectors* (conjunctions). **Dà** is used (as a connector) within serial nominal phrases only. **Kō** may connect words, phrases, clauses or sentences.

dà, *and* ; **dà ... dà ...** *and, both ... and ...* :

Nā ga yārò da ùbansà.	I saw the boy and his father.
Sarkī dà mutànensà sun tàfi.	The chief and his men have gone away.
Dà nī dà shī zā mù yi.	He and I [3] will do (it).

kō, *or* ; **kō ... kō ...,** *or, either ... or ..., whether* (*... or ...*) :

Bà zân ci dànkalì kō dōyà ba.	I won't eat sweet-potatoes or yams.
Kō sarkī kō wàkilì zâi jē.	Either the chief or the deputy will go.

---

[2] The use of the short voweled p-a pronoun (**ya**) will be explained in Lesson 20.

[3] Literally, ' I and he '. The Hausa custom in constructions like this one is just the opposite of the English convention. In Hausa one mentions oneself first.

| Kō zâi yi, kō bà zâi yi ba, ôhō. | Whether he will do (it) or not, I don't know (or care). |

4. *Clause introducers.*

àmmā, *but :*

| Nā tàfi Kanò àmmā bàn daɗè cân ba. | I went to Kano but I didn't stay there long. |
| Yā yi aikì àmmā bài sàmi kuɗī ba. | He worked but didn't get (any) money. |

dà, *when, as soon as :*

| Dà yā kōmà ya [4] ganī. | When he returned home he saw (it). |
| Dà yā kōmà zâi ganī. | As soon as he returns he will see (it). |

in or ìdan, *if, when* (followed by completive aspect) :

| In nā sāmù zân bā kà. | When/If I get (some) I will give (it to) you. |
| Ìdan nā gan shì zân gayà masà. | If I see him I will tell him. |

sai, *then :*

| Dà yā zō sai ìn tàfi. | As soon as he comes (then) I will go. |
| Kwabò yā fāɗì. Sai na [4] gan shì, na [4] ɗaukà. | The kobo fell. Then I saw it and picked (it) up. |

5. *Relational nouns* are not a special subcategory of nouns. They are, rather, typical nouns which are regularly used in contexts in which English-speakers expect a preposition or conjunction. Some are frequently used with relaters.

[4] The reason for the short vowel in the p-a pronouns is explained in Lesson 20.

bāyan (from **bāyā,** *back*), *behind, after :*

Ya fitō dàgà bāyan ɗākì.	He came out from behind the hut.

Bāyan wannàn lōkàcī ya [5]
  bar mù. — After this time he left us.
Bāyân dà ya [5] **tàfi bàn gan** — After he left I didn't see
  shì ba. — him.

cikin (from **cikī,** *inside* ; cf. **cikì,** *stomach*), *in* (*side*), *among :*

Yā shìga cikin ɗākì.	He went into the hut.
Mun gan shì cikin mutànē.	We saw him among the people.

gàban (from **gàbā,** *front*), *in front of, before :*

Yā fāɗì gàban sarkī.	He prostrated (himself) before the chief.
Yā gudù gàban mōtà.	He ran ahead of the car.

kàmar (from **kàmā,** *similarity*), *like, about, as if* ; **kàmar hakà** = *thus, like this :*

Audù kàmar Bellò nē.	Audu is like Bello.
Yā yi kàmar shèkarà gōmà.	He was about ten years (old).
Nà yi kàmar zân wucè.	I made as if I'd pass by.

kân (from **kâi,** *head*), *on, on top of :*

Yā sâ à kân tēbùr.	He put (it) on the table.
Yā zaunà à kân kujèrā.	He sat on the chair.

ƙàrƙashin (from **ƙàrƙashī,** *underneath*), *under :*

Nā sâ ƙàrƙashin tēbùr.	I put (it) under the table.

[5] See footnote on page 87.

wajen (from **wajē**, *place, direction*), *about, to, from* (see also Lesson 14) :

Yā sàmi wajen bakwài.	He got about seven.
Nā jē wajen sarkī.	I went to the chief.
Mun ji wajen mutànen gàrī.	We heard (it) from the townspeople.

zuwà (from **zuwà**, *coming*), *to, toward* :

Zân gudù zuwà gidā	I will run to/toward home.
Yā kāmà hanyà zuwà Kanò.	He took the road to Kano.

6. Two relational words **don/dòmin**, *because of, in order to*, and **kàfin/kàmin**, *before*, must be treated separately. These words, though they look like nouns, have no extant forms without the **-n** suffix, and function entirely as relaters.

don/dòmin, *because of, in order to* :

Kà yī shì don Allà.	Do it please (*lit.* for God's sake).
Zân jē dòmin ìn gan sù.	I will go in order to see them.
Don hakà zâi tàfi.	For this reason he will go (away).
Dom mè bà kà jē ba ?	Why (*lit.* because of what) didn't you go ?

kàfin/kàmin/kàfin/kàmin, *before* (when introducing a clause **kàfin**, *etc.*, is followed by the subjunctive aspect) :

Kà zō kàfin ìn tāshì.	Come before I leave.
Kàmin yà gan shì yā gudù.	Before he saw him he had run away.
Kàmin gòbe zân zō.	By tomorrow I will come.

7. Chart of positional relaters.

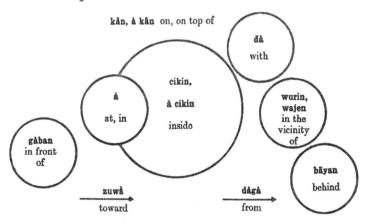

VOCABULARY

Nominals

barkà	greetings (= sànnu)
bāyā	back
cikì	stomach
dāwà (*f.*)	guinea corn
gàbā	front
kàmā (*f./m.*)	similarity
ƙàrƙashī	underneath, underside
rānā	sun, day, heat of sun
shèkarà (*f.*)	year
tàkàlmī	shoe, sandal (*or*, more frequently, a
(*pl.* tākalmà)	*pair* thereof)
tāsà (*f.*) (*pl.*	
tāsōshī)	(metal) bowl, (china) dish
wàkīlì	deputy, representative

Verbals   *Particles*
daɗè   spend a long time   dà   when

Verbals	*Particles*	
kāmà catch, seize	in, ìdan	if, when
	kàfìn/kàmìn	before
	kaɗai	only, alone
	kawài	only, merely
	òhō	what do I care ? I neither know nor care

Important Phrases

bāyan gidā	lavatory, toilet (*lit.* behind the compound)
don Allà	' please '
kāmà hanyà	take the path/road
watà mài zuwà, watàn gòbe	next month

EXERCISES

Translate into English :

1. Yā fāɗì cikin ruwā.
2. Bāyan wàsân zā mù jē wurin sarkī.
3. Ìdan yā dāwō, sai ìn tàfi.
4. Yā yi aikìnsà kàmar yārò.
5. Kàfìn ìn tàfi, zâi zō.
6. Bàkō yā sâ tàkàlminsà kàrkashin kujèrāta.

Translate into Hausa :

1. I saw Yusufu and his father in their home.
2. Either she or I will come to the school tomorrow morning.
3. I looked for the goat under the table but didn't see it.
4. When I return next month, then I will buy it.
5. If you work for me you will get money from me.

Dialogue

Mammàn : Barkà dà aikì, Dōgo.
Dōgo : Yâuwā, barkà dà zuwà.

Mammàn :   Ìnā wunì ?
Dōgo :   Lāfiyà, bâ kōmē.
Mammàn :   Mādàllā.
Dōgo :   Zâ ka gàrī nè ?
Mammàn :   Ā'à, zâ ni yāwò kawài.
Dōgo :   Tò bâ lâifī. Bàri mù zaunà, mù yi tāɗì.
Mammàn :   Tò dà kyâu. Gà inuwà mài kyâu à nân.
Dōgo :   Kâi, àkwai rānā yâu !
Mammàn :   Gàskiyarkà, lōkàcinsà nē.
Dōgo :   Hakà nē.
Mammàn :   Nā ji zā kà jē Kanò gòbe.
Dōgo :   Hakà ne. Zân tàfi cikin mōtà dà sāfē
Mammàn :   Tô, mè zā kà yi à wurîn ?
Dōgo :   Zân sayar dà dāwàtā à kàsuwā.
Mammàn :   Tò dà kyâu. Zā kà daɗè à Kanò ?
Dōgo :   Ī, zân nèmi aikì à wurîn.
Mammàn :   Tò bâ lâifī. Sai yàushè zā kà dāwō ?
Dōgo :   Sai watà mài zuwà.
Mammàn :   Tò dà kyâu. Zân tàfi yànzu.
Dōgo :   Tò bâ lâifī. Sai nā dāwō dàgà Kanò.
Mammàn :   Yâuwā, kà dāwō lāfiyà.
Dōgo :   Àmin.

Lesson 18

Continuative Aspect

1. The *continuative aspect* indicates action regarded as occurring as a process [1] rather than at a single point in time. This process may occur in present, past or future time as indicated by the context. In the absence of contextual evidence to the contrary, however, it is usually possible to assume that the reference is to a process involving present (rather than past or future) time.

2. This aspect employs the specialized verbal **nà**, *be in the process of, be at*, preceded by a high-tone, short-vowel set of person-aspect pronouns. These person-aspect pronouns are traditionally written as prefixes to **nà** rather than as separate words. A modifier (usually a noun) must follow **nà**.

I am working/ do work/ work	**inà aikì**	**munà aikì**	we are working
you (*m.*) are working	**kanà aikì**	**kunà aikì**	you (*pl.*) are working
you (*f.*) are working	**kinà aikì**		
he is working	**yanà aikì**	**sunà aikì**	they are working
she is working	**tanà aikì**		
one is working	**anà aikì**		

[1] Or, frequently, as a habit. See Lesson 26, footnote 1, and Lesson 27, section 2 (*a*).

3. The *negative* of this aspect employs a specialized verbal
bā plus a special set of low-tone, long-vowel p-a pronouns
which follow the verb.

I don't work (*etc.*)	**bā nà aikì** [2]	**bā mù aikì** [2]	we don't work
you (*m.*) don't work	**bā kà aikì**	**bā kù aikì** [2]	you (*pl.*) don't work
you (*f.*) don't work	**bā kì aikì** [2]		
he doesn't work	**bā yà aikì** [2]	**bā sù aikì** [2]	they don't work
she doesn't work	**bā tà aikì**		
no one works	**bā à aikì**		

4. A large number of nouns indicating an action,
activity, state, place, etc., may occur with **nà** in the
continuative.

yanà màganà	he is talking
yanà gidā	he is at home
yanà lāfiyà	he is well
yanà Kanò	he is at Kano
yanà nan	he is here
yanà zàune	he is sitting down/seated [3]

5. *Have* indicating possession is expressed by the use of
the continuative aspect construction plus **dà** plus the
possessed object.

---

[2] Other forms not infrequently heard are: **bā nì** . . ., *I* . . .; **bā
kyà** . . ., *you (f.)* . . .; **bā shì** . . ., *he* . . .; **bā mà/mwà** . . ., *we* . . .;
bā kwà . . ., *you (pl.)* . . .; and **bā sà/swà** . . ., *they* . . .

[3] See Lesson 19, section 7.

inà dà shī [4]	I have it
munà dà aikì	we have work
yanà dà kuɗī dà yawà	he has a lot of money

6. *Have not* is expressed in either of two ways :

(a) Employing the specialized verbal **bā** plus the set of
person-aspect pronouns listed in section 3 above.

| bā nà dà kuɗī | I haven't any money |
| bā yà dà mōtà | he doesn't have a car |

(b) Employing the specialized verbal **bâ** plus the set of
p-a pronouns listed with **zâ** in Lesson 16.

bâ ni dà shī [4]	I don't have it
bâ shi dà kyâu	it's no good (*lit.* has no goodness)
bâ ku dà hankàlī	you (*pl.*) don't have (any) sense

7. The forms **anà dà** and **bā à dà/bâ a dà** are rarely, if ever,
used.

VOCABULARY

Nominals

barcī, baccī	sleep(ing)
bùkātà (*f.*)	need(ing)
dōgō	tall, long, high (thing)
ɗan'uwā [5]	brother (*lit.* son-of-mother), *pl.*
(*pl.* 'yan'uwā)	means siblings (*i.e.* without reference to sex)
fushī	anger
gàjērē	short

[4] Note that it is the independent pronouns (see Lesson 6, section
6) which are employed after **dà** in these constructions. This is true
whenever the direct object of the verb(al) is introduced by **dà** (see
Lesson 25, sections 4–6).

[5] Note that the glottal catch which occurs (but is not written)
before every word beginning with a vowel must be written when
ɗan'uwā is written as a single word.

hankàlī	consciousness, sense, savoir-faire, circumspection, caution, slowness, care
itàcē	tree, wood
jirgī	canoe, boat
ƙasā (*f.*)	earth, ground, land, country
samà	sky
sô	wanting, desire, liking, love

Verbals		*Particles*	
dākàtā	wait (for)	kō ?	maybe ?
fi	surpass, be more/ better than	wàtàkīlà,	perhaps ? probably,
mutù	die	watakīlà	perhaps [6]
shâidā	inform, testify		
yàrda	agree, consent, accept		
yìwu	be possible		

Important Phrases

jirgin ƙasā	railway train
jirgin samà	aeroplane
kā yàrda, (kō) ?	do you agree ?
mun jimà dà yawà	(another reply to sai an jimà)
yā yìwu, yâ yìwu, yanà yìwuwā	it is possible [6]
yi fushī	get/become angry

EXERCISES

Translate into English :

1. Bâ ni dà kāyan nōmā.
2. Ùbansà yanà zuwà yànzu.

---

[6] The time reference of these expressions is determined by which aspect is employed in the following clause, e.g. **yā yìwu zâi zō** = *it is possible he will come* ; **yanà yìwuwā ya rigā ya zō** = *it is possible (that) he has already arrived.*

3. Màtātā tanà aikì dà kyâu à gōnā.
4. Sarkī yanà sô yà zō yà yi màganà dà mū gòbe.
5. Uwargidā tanà dà àbincimmù cikin d̃akìntà.
6. Mutànen gàrîn bā sù rawā.

Translate into Hausa :

1. They are talking together.
2. It is possible he is now at Lagos.
3. He has a big tree in front of his home.
4. He has three brothers and sisters (*i.e.* siblings) at home.
5. I don't have it. Please don't get angry !
6. If he is here I won't go by train.

Dialogue

Jàtau : Inà sô ìn yi màganà dà mài gidā.
Gàjēre : Mài gidā bā yà nân yâu.
Jàtau : Tô, yàushè zâi dāwō nè ?
Gàjēre : Ai, bàn sanì ba. Yā tàfi Ìkko.
Jàtau : Yā tàfi cikin jirgin samà nē ?
Gàjēre : Ā'à, cikin jirgin k̃asā.
Jàtau : Kwānā nawà zâi yi à wurîn ?
Gàjēre : Ai bà zâi fi sātī gùdā ba.
Jàtau : Tô, zâi sàyi kāyā cân nē ?
Gàjēre : Wàtàkīlà. Àmmā yā tàfi dòmin d̃an'uwansà yā mutù.
Jàtau : Tô, kō zâi dāwō sātī mài zuwà ?
Gàjēre : Hakà nē.
Jàtau : Ìdan yā dāwō kà gayà masà inà bùkātàr tàimakonsà.
Gàjēre : Tô, zân shâidā masà.
Jàtau : Dà kyâu. Sai an jimà.
Gàjēre : Tô, mun jimà dà yawà.

Lesson 19

Verbal Nouns [1]

1. Frequently, the noun employed after the continuative
nà is a nominalized form of a verb, commonly termed a
verbal noun. Most verbs have one or more verbal nouns
corresponding to them.

2. Verbal nouns of transitive one-syllable verbs almost
always [2] have a falling tone.

(sō, *want*)	inà sôn kuɗī	I want (some) money.
(yi, *do*)	yanà yî/yînsà	he is doing/making (it)
(ji, *sense*)	munà jîn zāfī	we are warm (*lit.* we feel heat)
(ci, *eat*)	bā yà cîn nāmà	he doesn't eat meat

3. A large number of transitive verbs [3] employ a verbal
noun ending in **-wā** in the continuative. If, however,
there is an object (direct or indirect) the basic verb is
employed followed by the regular indirect and/or direct
object constructions.

(sâ, *put*)	yanà sâwā	he is putting (it) on (*i.e.* article of clothing)

---

[1] The formation of verbal nouns and their functioning is one of
the most complex aspects of Hausa grammar. The following
should, therefore, be regarded as ' helpful hints ' rather than as a
complete treatment.

[2] The only exception is **ban,** *giving, causing (of)*, whose use is
confined to set phrases.

[3] Those of Parsons' Grades I, IV, V, VI and VII. See Lessons
25 and 37.

	yanà sâwā à tēbùr	he is putting (it) on the table
	yanà sâ shi à tēbùr	he is putting it on the table
(kāmà, *catch*)	yanà kāmàwā	he is catching (it/them)
	yanà kāmàwā à dājì	he catches (them) in the bush
	yanà kāmà su	he is catching them
(kāwō, *bring*)	yanà kāwôwā [4]	he is bringing (it)
	yanà kāwō manà kāyā	he is bringing us loads
(sayar, *sell*)	yanà sayârwā [4]	he is selling (things)
	yanà sayar dà kāyā	he is selling things

4. Many intransitive verbs [5] employ this same **-wā** suffix.

(fitō, *come out*)	sunà fitôwā [4]	they are coming out
(dāwō, *return here*)	yanà dāwôwā [4]	he is returning here

5. Some common intransitives employ a slightly different suffix or no suffix at all.

(zō, *come*)	yanà zuwà	he is coming
(tàfì, *go away*)	yanà tàfiyà	he is travelling
(tsūfa, *get old*)	yanà tsūfā	he is getting old

6. The usual form of the verbal noun of a *variable vowel transitive verb* [6] is the same shape as that of the verb when no object follows.

[4] Note that before the suffixed **-wā** a high-tone syllable becomes falling.

[5] Especially of Parsons' Grade VI.

[6] Parsons' Grade II verbs.

(kàrɓā, *receive*)	yanà kàrɓā	he is (regularly) receiving (it/them)
(sāmù, *get*)	yanà sāmù	he is getting (it)
(tàmbayà, *ask*)	yanà tàmbayà	he is asking (about it)

(a) Many variable vowel verbs (including many of the commonest of them), however, have irregular verbal nouns of various types, e.g. :

Verb		*Verbal Noun*	
borrow (other than money)	àrā	arō	borrowing, a loan
marry	àurā	aurē	marrying, marriage
beat, thrash	bùgā	bugù	beating, thrashing
beat, thrash	dòkā	dūkà	beating, thrashing
shoot at	hàrbā	harbì	shooting at, hunting
throw at	jèfā	jīfà	throwing at
seek	nēmā	nēmā	seeking, looking for
till a farm	nòmā	nōmā	farming, tilling
request, beseech	ròƙā	ròƙō	requesting, a request
steal	sàtā	sātà	stealing, theft
buy	sàyā	sàyē	buying
cut off a piece of	yànkā	yankā	butchering

(b) What might (because of its English translation) be regarded as a direct object construction with variable vowel verbal nouns is actually a noun plus noun/pronoun possessive construction, e.g. :

| sāmù → yanà sāmùn kudī | he is getting money (*lit.* he is in the process of *the getting of money*) |
| tàmbayà → sunà tàmbayàta [7] | they are asking me |

[7] Note that **tàmbayà** (the verbal noun) is feminine and, therefore, requires the feminine possessive pronoun suffix.

harbì → **munà harbìn**   we are hunting wild
  nāmà   animals
sàyē → **inà sàyen àbinci**   I am buying food

(c) If an indirect object ($\pm$ a direct object) is expressed
the verb form rather than the verbal noun is employed (as in section 3 above).[8] Some speakers prefer
the verb construction to the verbal noun construction
(described in (b) above) with direct objects as well.

Examples :
  I.O. $\pm$ D.O. :

yanà sayà manà
  àbinci   he is buying us food
sunà nēmam minì   they are seeking (it) for me

D.O. only :

yanà tàmbàyē shì   he is asking him (= **yanà**
                   tàmbayàrsà)
anà bùgi yārò   the boy was/is being beaten
                (= **anà bugùn yārò**)

7. There is in Hausa, in addition to the verbal nouns, a
group of nominalized verbs sometimes termed *nouns of
state* which regularly occur with **nà**. These indicate a state
resulting from the action of the verb.

(**zaunà**, *sit down*)	**yanà zàune**	he is seated
(**tsayà**, *stand*)	**yanà tsàye**	he is standing
(**ɗaurà**, *tie up*)	**yanà ɗàure**	it is tied up; he is in prison
(**būɗè**, *open*)	**yanà bùɗe**	it is open
(**tàfi**, *proceed*)	**gà shi nan tàfe**	here he comes (*lit.* there he is proceeding)

---

[8] See Lesson 15, section 8, for a discussion of indirect objects of
variable vowel verbs.

VOCABULARY

Nominals

dādī	pleasantness
kàràtū	reading (see **karàntā,** Lesson 8)
kōwànè (*f.*	
kōwàcè)	every, any
ƙòƙarī	worthy effort (usually successful), good try, hard work
ƙwaryā (*f.*)	calabash (gourd bowl)
mōtōcī	automobiles (*pl.* of **mōtà,** see Lesson 10)
nauyī	heaviness
rùbùtū	writing (see **rubùtā,** Lesson 8)
saukī	easiness
tàtsūnìyā (*f.*)	fable
wàhalà (*f.*)	trouble, difficulty

Verbals

		Particles	
cigàba	continue, make progress (**ci + gàba**)	**mànà**	indeed
hūrà/fūrà	light (a fire), blow		
iyà	be able to . . .		
shārè	sweep		
wankè	wash		

Important Phrases

ī mànà	yes indeed!
inà sôn . . .	I want . . .
kōwànè lōkàcī	all the time, every time
sai + sub-	
junctive	one ought to . . ., one must . . . [9]
yā fī makà . . .	it is the most . . . for you

---

[9] See Lesson 29, section 2, for a fuller treatment of this construction.

EXERCISES

Translate into English :
1. Tanà shân ruwā.
2. Yanà būɗè ƙōfà ? Ī, yanà būɗèwā.
3. Sunà sayar dà mōtōcī ? Ī, sunà sayârwā.
4. Àkwàtìn nân yanà dà nauyī.
5. Aikìn nân bâ shi dà wùyā.

Translate into Hausa :
1. The door is open. Close it.
2. She is bringing a calabash.
3. Is he buying food ? Yes, he is.
4. Didn't she light a fire ? Yes, she did.
5. He is standing with a heavy load on his head.

Dialogue

Mālàmī :   Cikin aikìn makarantā mè ya fī makà wùyā ?
Dālìbī :   Ai lìssāfì kawài yanà bā nì wàhalà.
Mālàmī :   Àshē ? Tūrancī fà ?
Dālìbī :   Tô, Tūrancī yanà dà wùyā sòsai, àmmā lìssāfì
           yā fī shì.
Mālàmī :   Kàràtū bā yà dà wùyā ?
Dālìbī :   Ī. Yanà dà sauƙī. Kàràtū yanà dà dāɗī kumā.
Mālàmī :   Tò dà kyâu. Kanà kàràtū dà yawà nē ?
Dālìbī :   Ī mànà ! Kōwànè lōkàcī.
Mālàmī :   Àmmā bà kà iyà lìssāfì ba ?
Dālìbī :   Ā'à, nā iyà mànà. Àmmā yanà dà wùyā.
Mālàmī :   Tò bâ lâifī. Sai kà cigàba dà ƙòƙarinkà.

Lesson 20

The ' Relative ' Aspects ; Relative Constructions

1. One completive and one continuative aspect in Hausa are known as *relative* aspects because of the fact that these aspects, not their counterparts, are employed in *relative* constructions (see sections 4–7 below for illustrations of the contexts in which these aspects are employed). The meanings of the relative aspects are essentially the same as their non-relative counterparts (see Lessons 7 and 18) and they share the negative constructions described for their counterparts (Lessons 7 and 18).

2. The *relative completive aspect* person-aspect pronouns are characterized by a high-tone, short-vowel syllable with, in some cases, a **-kà** suffix.[1] With, for example, the verb **kāwō** the forms are :

... I brought [2]	... na kāwō [2]	... mukà kāwō	... we brought
... you (*m.*) brought	... ka kāwō	... kukà kāwō	... you (*pl.*) brought
... you (*f.*) brought	... kikà kāwō		
... he brought	... ya kāwō	... sukà kāwō	... they brought
... she brought	... ta kāwō		
... one brought	... akà kāwō		

---

[1] Note that the **-kà** suffix is employed with the same persons as have the **-n** suffix in the non-relative completive aspect (see Lesson 7).

[2] See footnote 3 on page 105.

The negative of the relative completive aspect is indistinguishable from the negative of the completive aspect. See Lesson 7, sections 6 and 7, for the forms.

3. The *relative continuative aspect* employs the same high-tone, short-vowel person-aspect pronoun (minus the **-kà** suffix) plus the specialized verbal **kè,** *be in the process of, be at.*

. . . I want [3]	. . . **na kè sô** [3]	. . . **mu kè sô**	. . . we want
. . . you (*m.*) want	. . . **ka kè sô**	. . . **ku kè sô**	you (*pl.*) want
. . . you (*f.*) want	. . . **ki kè sô**		
. . . he wants	. . . **ya kè sô**	. . . **su kè sô**	. . . they want
. . . she wants	. . . **ta kè sô**		
. . . one wants	. . . **a kè sô**		

The negative of the relative continuative aspect is indistinguishable from the negative of the continuative aspect. See Lesson 18, section 3, for the forms.

4. *Relative constructions* are usually modificational constructions which typically consist of an entire clause but are employed within nominal phrases as modifiers.

Such constructions are common in English. Each of the following English nominal phrases is divisible into a head nominal (labelled *Head*) and a modificational construction (labelled *Modifier*). Note that each of the

---

[3] Since these forms occur in contexts too long to conveniently list here, the student is asked to supply in place of the three dots some such context as **àbìn dà** . . . = *the thing that* . . ., or **mutằnên dà** . . . = *the people that* . . .

modifiers introduced by *relative* words such as *that,
which, who, when,* etc., includes a whole clause. These
clauses are the relative constructions.

Non-relative Constructions :

Head	*Modifier*
the home	of the chief
the boy	of Malam Yahaya

Relative Constructions :

Head	*Modifier*
the home	that the chief built
the boy	that Malam Yahaya gave the money to
the knife	that I dropped by the road
the man	who comes to see us
the time	when we had no work

5. Relative constructions in Hausa are usually introduced by **dà** or **wandà/wândà** (*f.* **waddà, wâddà** ; *pl.*
wadàndà) meaning *that, which, who, the one which/who,*
etc. The final syllable of the nominal preceding **dà** takes
the **-n/-r** referential suffix (see Lesson 8).[4] If the final
syllable of this nominal is on a high tone, it becomes
falling before **dà**. Neither the referential nor the tone
change is necessary before **wandà**.

Non-relative constructions :

Head	*Modifier*
gidan	**sarkī**

   the home of the chief

yāròn	**Audù**

   Audu's boy

---

[4] Consideration is here confined to the commonest type of relative
clause, often termed ' restrictive relative clauses ', i.e. those in which
the clause serves to define or particularize one of a class of objects.
Actually there are in Hausa, as in English, a number of other types
of relative clauses as well.

Relative constructions :

Head	Modifier
gidân	dà sarkī ya ginà (= gidā wandà ...)

the home that the chief built

yāròn   dà Audù ya aikà (= yārò wandà ...)

the boy that Audu sent

wuƙâr   dà ta fādi à bàkin hanyà (wuƙā waddà ...)

the knife that fell by the side of the road

mùtumìn   dà ya kè [5] zuwà yà gan mù (= mùtûm wandà ...)

the man who comes to see us

lōkàcîn   dà mukà tàfi Kanò

(the time) when we went to Kano

dōkì   wandà na kè hawā (= dōkìn dà ...)

the horse which I ride

mutànē   wadàndà bà mù sani ba (= mutànên dà ...)

people whom we don't know

wurîn   dà sukà tàfi

the place where they went

àbîn   dà ya bā nì

the thing that (= what) he gave me

6. **Wan-** occasionally serves by itself as the head of a nominal phrase containing a relative construction. In each example the **wan-, wadàn-, wad-** part of the first word is the head, the relative construction introduced by **-dà** is the modifier :

wandà ya sāmù	the one which he obtained
wadàndà mukà gani	those that we saw
waddà ki kè sô	the one (*f.*) that you (*f.*) want

7. The relative aspects are employed in the following contexts :

---

[5] In the third person the person-indicator (ya, ta, sukà) is frequently omitted : mùtumìn dà kè zuwà ...

(a) In *relative constructions*. See above (sections 5 and 6) for illustrations.

(b) When a construction that characteristically occurs after the predicate in a clause is shifted to pre-predicate position for *emphasis*. Common instances of inversion for emphasis are :

  (i) *Adverbial nominals* indicating time, place, manner, etc. :

jiyà mukà tàfi	we went away *yesterday*
à gidā mu kè aikì	we work *at home*
cikin mōtà sukà zō	they came *in a car*
ran Tàlātà yârā sukà jē	the children went *on Tuesday*
lāfiyà su kè	they are *well*

  (ii) *Interrogatives*, whether adverbial or not, whenever they precede the verb :

mè sukà yi ?	what did they do ?
mè ka kè sô ?	what do you want ?
yàushè sarkī ya dāwō ?	when did the chief return ?
wà ya sanì ?	who knows ?
inā ka kè ?	where are you ?

  (iii) *Objects* (usually a direct object, occasionally an indirect object) :

sarkī mukà bi	it is the *chief* (that) we followed
aikì mu kè yî	we are doing *work* (not something else)
shī na gayà wà [6]	*he is* the one I told (it to)

---

[6] Note that when an indirect object is moved into the emphasis position the indirect object marker (always **wà**) is left behind.

(iv) Emphasis constructions involving **nē** which have been moved back into the emphasis position from either the post or the pre-predicate position. Virtually all the examples under (i) and (iii) above may alternatively involve a **nē**.

sarkī nè̄ ya tàfi	it is the *chief* (who) went away
jiyà nē sukà dāwō	it was *yesterday* they came
aikì nē mu kè̄ yî	it is *work* (that we are doing
cikin mōtà̄ nē mukà̄ zō	it is *by car* (that) we came

(c) In *narrative*. The relative completive aspect is used in preference to the completive aspect throughout a narrative or extended 'chronological' account. See the fable at the end of this lesson for an illustration. Typical introducers of narrative or 'chronological' accounts (and, therefore, of these aspects) are **rân nan,** *one day*; **sai,** *(just) then, so . . .*; and **sā'àn nan,** *then.*

(d) The relative aspects are always used after **dà,** *when* (referring to a single act in the past): **bāyân dà,** *after*; **kō dà,** *when, though*; **sai dà,** *only when, (not) until*; and **tun dà,** *since.*

VOCABULARY

Nominals

dâ	(in) the past, formerly
dūniyà̄ (*f.*)	world
kūrā (*f.*)	hyena
ƙàdangarè̄	lizard
màmākì	surprise, amazement

nēmā	seeking, looking for
ràbō	one's lot, destiny, luck (in life)
rāmì	hole
sātà	stealing
tsòrō	fearfulness, fearing
wākē	beans
yî	doing, making
zāmànī	period of time

Days of the week (are all feminine)

Lahàdì/Lâdì	Sunday
Lìttìnîn	Monday
Tàlātà	Tuesday
Làràbā	Wednesday
Àlhàmîs	Thursday
Jumma'à	Friday
Àsabàr, Sātī	Saturday

Verbals		*Particles*	
aikà (i/ē)	send (on errand)	àshē	well!, why!, is
cê, cè	say		that so ?
ginà	build		

Important Phrases

rân nan	a certain day, one day
ran Tàlātà	Tuesday
zāmànin dâ	long ago, in ancient times

EXERCISES

Translate into English :

1. Mutànên dà su kè zuwà zā sù dafè nân.
2. Wandà ya zō yâu yā tāshì dà wuri.
3. Bâ wândà su kè tsòrō.
4. Mè akà yi à Kanò shēkaranjiyà ?
5. Bàn ga wafàndà ka kè sô à wurîn ba.

Translate into Hausa :

1. It was the *teacher* we saw.
2. That woman works here.
3. When did you (*f.*) come ?
4. There are the children who will go in the car.
5. We will meet them at the place where we saw them yesterday.

Fable

Kūrā dà Kàdangarè dà Kàrē [7]

Zāmànin dâ àkwai wata kūrā. Rân nan ta ji yunwà ƙwarai. Sai [8] ta tāshì, ta fìta. Tanà nēman àbinci sai gà [9] ƙàdangarè, yanà sātàr wākē. Dà ta ga ƙàdangarè ta kāmà shi. Zā tà cī shì sai ta ga kàrē.

Sai ta cè, ' Bàri ìn kai ƙàdangarè gidā kàmìn ìn dāwō ìn kāmà kàrē.'

Sai ta tàfì gidantà dà ƙàdangarè.

Dà ta dāwō bà tà ga kàrē ba. Lōkàcîn dà ta kè tàfiyà dà ƙàdangarè kàrē yā gudù zuwà dājì.

Dà kūrā ta kōmà gidā bà tà ga ƙàdangarè ba. Lōkàcîn dà ta kè nēman kàrē ƙàdangarè yā bar rāmìn kūrā yā shìga dājì.

Kūrā ta yi màmākì, ta cè, ' Àshē, kōmē ka nèmā à dūniyà, in bà ràbonkà ba nè, bà zā kà sāmù ba ! '

---

[7] See *Ka Kara Karatu,* page 1, and Abraham, R. C., *Hausa Literature,* page 35, for another version of this story.

[8] **Sai** commonly means *then* or *so* . . . in narrative contexts.

[9] **Sai gà** is an idiomatic phrase used to introduce the appearance of a new character in a story.

Lesson 21

Interrogative and Indefinite Nominals

1. The various Hausa interrogatives (and the indefinite nominals formed from them) belong to several of the subclasses of nominals. The majority of them are adverbial nominals, three are independent nominals, one is a quantifier and one is a specifier.

2. The indefinite nominals are formed by prefixing **kō** to any of the interrogative nominals. In Hausa printed literature, some of the indefinite nominals are written as single words (e.g. **kōmē,** *whatever, anything,* **kōwā,** *whoever, everyone*). Others are officially [1] written as two words (e.g. **kō inā,** *wherever, everywhere,* **kō yàushè,** *whenever*). It seems preferable to be consistent and to write them all as single words. This will be the practice throughout this book. Indefinite nominals, when (as frequently) used to introduce relative clauses, are followed by the 'relative' aspects. Note that they do not (as do regular nouns) require a following **dà** to introduce the relative clause, e.g. **kōmē ka sāmù,** *whatever you get,* as opposed to **àbîn dà ka sāmù,** *what(ever) you get.*

3. *Adverbial* interrogative and indefinite nominals.

inā, *where?, how?* (see also Lesson 4) :

Ìnā ya kè ?	Where is he ?
Ìnā mutànemmù ?	Where are our people ?

---

[1] By decision of the Hausa Language Board. But this convention is subject to change from time to time.

Ìnā na sanì ?   How should I know ?

Yā tàfì ìnā nè ? [2]   Where did he go ?

kō'ìnā,[3] *wherever, everywhere :*

Kō'ìnā ka tàfì cùtā zā tà Wherever you go illness will
  sàmē kà.   befall you.

Yârā sunà cân kō'ìnā. Children are there every-
          where.

ƙàƙà, *how ?* (not as widely used as yàyà below) : [4]

Kàƙà zā kà yi ?   How will you do (it) ? What
          will you do ?

Kàƙà sukà sanì ?   How do they know ?

kōƙàƙà, *however, any way possible :*

Anà sāmùn kuɗī kōƙàƙà. People get (their) money
          any way possible.

À yī shì kōƙàƙà.   Do it any way possible.

yàushè, yàushe, *when ? :*

Yàushè nē ya zō ?   When was it he came ?

Sai yàushè zā sù dāwō ? (By) when will they return ?

kōyàushè, kōyàushe, *whenever, all the time :*

Sunà nan kōyàushè. They're here all the time.

Kōyàushè mu kè Kanò sai Whenever we're in Kano we
  mù zìyàrcē shì.[5]   visit him.

---

[2] Note that the regular (not the relative) completive aspect p-a pronoun is used here since the regular (i.e. non-emphatic) word order is employed which places the interrogative word in the regular object position after the verb.

[3] Note that the glottal catch which occurs (but is not written) before any word beginning with a vowel must be written when kō'ìnā is written as a single word (see also ɗan'uwā, Lesson 18).

[4] Indeed in some dialects (e.g. Zaria) its use is considered impolite !

[5] See Lesson 29, section 2, for a discussion of this usage of sai plus subjunctive.

yàyà, *how?, what?* (referring, for example, to actions) :

Yàyà mu kè ?   How are you ? (*lit.* how are
                            we ?)
Yàyà zā à yi dà shī ?   What should be done with
                            it ?

kōyàyà, *however, any way possible* :

Kōyàyà zā à gyārà shi bà   However it is fixed it (still)
zâi yi aikì ba.   won't work.
Kōyàyà akà sāmù zân   No matter how it was ob-
sàyā.   tained I'll buy it.

4. *Independent interrogative and indefinite nominals.*

mè, *what?* (introduced in Lesson 5, Vocabulary) :

Mè ya fàru ?   What happened ?
Mè ka kè sô ?   What do you want ?
Mè ya yi ? *or* Yā yi mè ? [6] What did he do ? *or* He did
                            what ?
Mènē nè ? *or* Mēcē cè ?   What is it (*m.* or *f.*) ?

komènē nè, *whatever it is* :

Zân sàyā kōmènē nè   I'll buy (it) whatever you
màganàrkà.   say (*lit.* whatever your
                            word is).

Kōmènē nè ya kè yî bâ shi   Whatever he does is not
dà kyâu.   good.

kōmē[7] *anything, everything, whatever* :

Bài kāwō kōmē ba.   He didn't bring anything.
Allà yā san kōmē.   God knows everything.

---

[6] See footnote 2 on page 113.
[7] Note that in these compounds, which are always written as
single words, the interrogatives (mè and wà) change to high tone.

Tā shiryà kōmē dà kōmē.	She (has) prepared everything (necessary).
Kōmē ka sāmù ràbonkà nē.	Whatever you get is your lot.

wà (*pl.* **su wà**), *who?* (introduced in Lesson 6, Vocabulary) :

Wà ya yi?	Who did it?
Wànē nè? *or* **Wàcē cè?**	Who is it (*m.* or *f.*)?
Su wànē nè sukà zō?	Who (*pl.*) came?

kōwànē nè, *whoever it is* :

Kōwànē nè ya zō kà kàrɓē shì.	Whoever comes accept him.

kōwā,[8] *anyone, everyone, whoever* :

Kōwā yā tàfi gidā.	Everyone has gone home.
Bài ga kōwā ba.	He didn't see anyone.
Kōwā dà kōwā sukà zō.	Everyone came.

wànnē (*f.* **wàccē**; *pl.* **wàɗànnē**), *which one?* :

Wànnē akà kāwō?	Which one was brought?
Wàccē ta dafà wannàn nāmà?	Which one (*f.*) cooked this meat?

kōwànnē (*f.* **kōwàccē**; *pl.* **kōwàɗànnē**), *whichever, everyone, anyone* :

Kōwànnē ya bā kà kà ɗaukà.	Whichever he gives you take (it).
Kōwàɗànnensù sukà bar mù.	Everyone of them left us.

5. Interrogative and indefinite *quantifiers* (see also Lesson 11).

nawà, *how much?, how many?* :

Kuɗinsà nawà nē?	How much does it cost?
Kā sàyi gōrò nawà?	How many kolanuts did you buy?

[8] See footnote 7 on page 114.

kōnawà, *however much, however many* :

| Kōnawà ya bā nì, yanà dà kyâu. | However much/many he gives me it's okay (with me). |
| Kà sàyā kōnawà kuɗinsà. | Buy it whatever its price. |

6. Interrogative and indefinite *specifiers*.

wànè (*f.* wàcè; *pl.* wàɗànnè), *what (one)?, which (one)? :*

Wànè aikì zâi yi ?	What work will he (*or* is he to) do ?
Wàcè hanyà zā mù bi ?	Which path shall we follow?
Wàɗànnè mutànē sukà zō ?	Which people came ?

kōwànè (*f.* kōwàcè; *pl.* kōwàɗànnè), *every (one), any (one), whatever :*

| Kōwànè mùtûm yanà dà mōtà à ƙasarmù. | Everyone has a car in our country. |
| Àkwai maròƙā à kōwàcè kàsuwā. | There are beggars in every market. |

7. The interrogative and indefinite specifiers are often followed by **irì**, *kind, sort.* In this context the gender and number of the specifier is determined not by **irì** but by the nominal following **irì**. **Irì** retains its masculine singular form.

Wànè irìn aikì zā mù yi ?	What kind of work will we do ?
Wàcè irìn fìtilà ka sàyā ?	What kind of lantern did you buy ?
Wàɗànnè irìn mutànē nè waɗànnân ?	What kind of people are these ?
Zâi kāwō kōwàcè irìn rìgā.	He will bring every kind of gown.
Àkwai kōwànè irìn àbinci à wurîn.	There is every kind of food in that place.

Note : This rule applies also with the specifiers **wani,** **wannàn** and **wancàn** introduced in Lesson 10.

Wani irìn tsuntsū nè.	It's a certain kind of bird.
Nā ga wata irìn rìgā à cân.	I saw a (different) kind of gown there.
Irìn wadànnân [9] **mutànē bâ kyâu.**	These kinds of people are no good.

8. There are several ways of *asking a question* in Hausa :

(a) By using an interrogative nominal (plus interrogative intonation) :

Ìnā gàrī ?	Where is the town ?
Mēnē nè wannàn ?	What is this ?

(b) By using the particles **kō** [10] or **nē,** or the expression **kō bà hakà ba ?,** *or isn't it so ?,* at the end of a sentence (plus interrogative intonation) :

Kanà dà kudī kō ? [10]	Have you any money ?
Yārò yā zaunà nē ?	Has the boy sat down ?
Yārò yā tàfi kàsuwā nè ?	Has the boy gone to market ?
Gàskiyā nè, kō (bà hakà ba) ? [10]	It is true, isn't it ?

(c) The particle **shin/shìn,** *could it be ?* (plus interrogative intonation) is also common in interrogative contexts such as the following : [11]

[9] Hausa prefers to reverse the normal order of *specifier* + **irì** with **wannàn** and **wancàn,** although **wadànnân irìn mutànē** would also be understood.

[10] **Kō** used as a question word is actually an abbreviated form of **kō bà hakà ba.** Note the parallel expression in English, *Are you coming or . . . ?* for *. . . or aren't you ?*

[11] The use of this particle is similar to that of *say* or *look (here)* as question introducers in English, e.g. *Say, are you coming ?, Look, can you prove that ?*

Shin kā san shì ?	Do you (by any chance) know him ?
Shîn dà aikì à wurinkà ?	Say, do you have a job (for me) ?

(d) A change of the intonation pattern of the utterance as described in Lesson 3, section 6, is frequently employed by itself to change an utterance from a statement to a question and, in addition, is regularly employed with each of the above question words by most speakers. A partial exception to this rule is that some speakers will not employ interrogative intonation at all times with interrogative nominals (category (a) above).

VOCABULARY

Nominals

àllūrà (*f.*)	needle, inoculation
bàɗi (*f.*)	next year
bana (*f.*)	this year
bàra (*f.*)	last year
cīwò	illness, injury
fātā	hope, hoping that
kō'ìnā	everywhere, anywhere
kōwā	everyone, anyone
kōwànnē	whichever, everyone, anyone
kōyàushè, kōyàushe	whenever
kōyàyà	however, in whatever way
likità	doctor
māgànī	medicine
maròƙī (*pl.* maròƙā)	beggar
muryà (*f.*)	voice

wànnē (*f.*
  wàccē ; *pl.*
  wàɗànnē)   which one ?
yàyà   how ?
zàzzàɓī   fever, malaria

Verbals		*Particles*	
bā dà	give (when no indirect object follows)	**shin/shîn**	could it be ?
dūbà	look at, look around		
gwadà	measure, test, try to do		
kashè	kill		

Important Phrases

cīwòn kâi	headache
cīwò yā kāmà ka	you have become ill (*lit.* sickness (has) caught you)
shā māgànī	take medicine
(yanà) dà saukī *or* **yā yi saukī**	it (illness) is (a bit) better
zàzzàɓī yā kāmà ni	I have a fever (*lit.* a fever has caught me)

EXERCISES

Translate into English :

1. **Ìnā kuɗîn dà na bā kà jiyà ?**
2. **Wàcè mōtà zā kà tàfi à cikī ?**
3. **Nā ga wani irìn wàsân dà bàn ganī ba dâ.**
4. **Kōyàushè zâi zō bā nà sô ìn gan shì.**
5. **Yâu bà zân sàyi kōmē à kàsuwā ba.**

Translate into Hausa :

1. Do you know him ? He's got malaria.
2. Where did you go with our car ?

3. What kind of gown did you bring from the store ?
4. I have a lot of work everywhere in this town.
5. There I saw the chief who came to town yesterday.

Dialogue

Sulè :   Uwargidā tā gayà minì bâ ka dà lāfiyà.
Būbà :   Hakà nē.
Sulè :   Mè̀ ya dàmē [12] kà ?
Būbà :   Cīwòn kâi nē.
Sulè :   Kâi, sànnu ! Kā shā māgànì nè̀ ?
Būbà :   Ì. Likità yā yi minì àllūrà.
Sulè :   Tò dà kyâu. Àkwai zàzzàɓī kumā ?
Būbà :   Àkwai dâ, àmmā yànzu yā yi saukī.
Sulè :   Mādàllā. Yàushè ya kāmà ka ?
Būbà :   Ai, jiyà nē, lōkàcîn dà na kè̀ nōmā.
Sulè :   Tô, inà fātā Allà zâi bā dà saukī.
Būbà :   Àmin.

[12] From dàmā (i/ē), *bother*.

Lesson 22

Noun Plurals

1. Noun pluralization is a highly complex feature of Hausa grammar. It is usually advisable simply to memorize the most common plural form of a given noun. It is, however, possible to classify Hausa noun plurals, and to arrange them in four major and several minor classes. Some nouns employ more than one plural, but usually a single plural form will be more prominent in a given area than any of the other forms. See Lesson 38 for further treatment of noun plurals.

2. *Class I* plurals are characterized by all high tones and an -ō . . . ī ending. The -ō . . . ī replaces the final vowel of the singular form, with the final consonant of the singular form reappearing between the ō and the ī.[1] Class I is the largest class of plurals and includes most of the recent

---

[1] Here, as a rule (note two exceptions below—both recent borrowings from English), as throughout the language, the following consonants occurring before **a, o** or **u** change before a final i or **e** as follows:

t	becomes **c,**	e.g. :	**mōtà**	car, lorry	**mōtōcī** (Class I)
d, z	become **j,**	e.g. :	**gidā**	home	**gidàjē** (Class III)
			ōdà	order	**ōdōjī** or **ōdōdī** (Class I)
s	becomes **sh**	e.g. :	**tāsà**	bowl	**tāsōshī** (Class I)
w	*often* becomes **y**	e.g. :	**kàsuwā**	market	**kàsuwōyī** (sometimes **kàsuwōwī**) (Class I)

Illustrations of these changes in verbs are :

yā sàtā	he stole (it)	**yā sàci rìgāta**	he stole my gown
yā cìzā	it (*i.e.* snake) bit (it)	**yā cìjē nì**	it bit me
yā fànsā	he redeemed (it)	**yā fànshē shì**	he paid the ransom for him
canjì	(a noun) change	**yā canzà/ canjà (shi)**	he changed (it)

loanwords from English. The singular forms of most (but
by no means all) of Class I nouns end in **-ā**.

hanyà (*f.*)	path, road	**hanyōyī**
tēbùr	table	**tēburōrī**
tàmbayà (*f.*)	question	**tambayōyī**
fartanyà (*f.*)	hoe	**fartanyōyī**

3. *Class II* plurals are characterized by a **-u...à**
ending with all tones high except the final **-à**.[2] The
-u...à replaces the final vowel of the singular, the
consonants **n, w** or **k** being the most common ones
appearing between the **u** and the **à**. Class II is the second
largest class of plurals and includes many recent loan-
words. Most of the disyllabic nouns with a low-high tone
pattern in the singular and many with a high-low pattern
(ending in a vowel other than **a**) belong to this class.
Some nouns reduplicate their final syllable before the
plural suffix, like the third and fourth examples below.

kèkē	bicycle	**kēkunà**
ɗākì	hut, room	**ɗākunà**
àbù	thing	**abūbuwà**
sulè	shilling	**sulūlukà** [3]

4. *Class III* plurals are characterized by a **-à...ē**
ending with a high-low-high tone pattern. The consonant
appearing between the **à** and the **ē** is typically either **y** or,
where the first syllable of the root consists simply of a
consonant plus a short vowel, the consonant introducing
the final syllable of the singular form. Many of the oldest

[2] Note that these Class II plurals are virtually the only plurals in
the language with a low final tone.
[3] Several shilling (10k) coins ; in computing money the singular
form is used with a number, e.g. seven shillings (70k) is **sulè** (*not*
sulūlukà) **bakwài**.

and commonest nouns in the language—especially those
with a high-high tone pattern —belong to Class III.

sūnā	name	**sūnàyē**
tsuntsū	bird	**tsuntsàyē**
birnī	(walled) city	**birànē**
wuƙā (*f.*)	knife	**wuƙàƙē**
wurī	place	**wuràrē**
gidā	home	**gidàjē**

5. *Class IV* plurals are characterized by a **-ai** (infrequently **-au**), **-ī** or **-ū** suffix with all tones but that of
the suffix low. Many nouns whose singulars consist of more
than two syllables belong to Class IV. Some nouns reduplicate their final syllable before this plural suffix. Note
that derived nouns of place and implement introduced
in Lesson 30, sections 4 (*b*) and (*c*), belong in this class.

àbōkī	friend	**àbòkai**
làbārì	news	**làbàrai** *or* **làbàrū**
mālàm(ī)	teacher	**màlàmai**
kwabò	penny	**kwàbbai** (see note 3 on page 122)
tsōhō/tsōfō	old (thing)	**tsòfàffī**
bàƙō	guest	**bàƙī**
gōnā	farm	**gònàkī**
kujèrā (*f.*)	chair	**kùjèrū**
màganà (*f.*)	word	**màgàngànū**
makarantā (*f.*)	school	**màkàràntū**

6. Among the minor classes of noun plurals are :

Class V—those with terminal **-à** ... **ā/ū** :

sirdì	saddle	**siràdā**
ƙarfè	metal	**ƙaràfā**
dūtsè	rock, stone	**duwàtsū**
idò	eye	**idànū**
ƙafà (*f.*)	leg	**ƙafàfū**

Class VI—those with terminal **-ā** or **-ä** in the plural from singulars with terminal **-ī** or **-ē** :

(*a*) Plurals of **mā . . . ī** derived nouns signifying *agent*, etc. (see Lesson 30, section 4 (*a*)) :

maɗìnkī	tailor	maɗìnkā
maƙèrī	blacksmith	maƙèrā
maròƙī	beggar	maròƙā

(*b*) Plurals ending in **-ä** with high-high-low tones (with, on occasion, a change of penultimate vowel) :

cōkàlī	spoon	cōkulà
ƙànƙanè	small (thing)	ƙanānà
tàkàlmī	shoe(s)	tākalmà

(*c*) Plurals ending in **-ā** with high-high tones :

| màcè | woman, wife | mātā |
| mijì | male, husband | mazā |

Class VII—other plurals ending in **ā** :

(*a*) Those with falling-high plurals :

bàbba	big (thing)	mânyā
yārò	boy	yârā
zōbè	ring	zôbbā

(*b*) **āwā** plurals (usually pluralizing ethnic designations whose singulars involve a **bà-** prefix—see Lesson 30, section 2) :

Bàtūrè	European	Tùràwā
talàkà	peasant	talakāwā
Bàkanè	Kano person	kanāwā
bàdūkù	leather worker	dùkàwā

Class VIII—**akī/ākī** plurals :

àkwiyà	goat	awākī
dōkì	horse	dawākī
kāyā	loads	kāyàyyakī
tunkìyā	sheep	tumākī

Class IX—those with terminal -ū and all high tones :

māshì	spear	māsū
nāmà	animal (wild)	nāmū
sâ, sānìyā	bull, cow	shānū
yātsà	finger	yātsū

Class X—*reduplicative* plurals : [4]

irì	kind	irì-irì
en'è	Native Administration	en'è-en'è

7. Among the common plurals not classifiable as 'regular' in terms of the above classes are the following :

(*a*) The specifiers (see Lessons 10 and 21, section 6) e.g. :

wannàn	this	waɗànnân
wani	a (certain)	waɗansu
kōwànè	every(one)	kōwàɗànnè

(*b*) Kinship terms (see also Lesson 35) :

ɗā	'yā (màcè)	'yā'yā
son	daughter	children, offspring
		'yā'yā mazā
		sons
		'yā'yā mātā
		daughters
ùbā	uwā	iyàyē
father	mother	parents
ɗan'uwā	'yar'uwā	'yan'uwā
brother	sister	brothers and sisters, siblings
ɗan'ùbā	'yar'ùbā	'yan'ùbā
half-brother	half-sister	half-brothers and half-sisters

[4] See Lesson 28, section 9, for another reduplicative construction sometimes regarded as pluralization.

wâ	yâ	yâyyē
elder brother	elder sister	elder siblings
ƙanè	ƙanwà	ƙânnē
younger	younger	younger siblings
brother	sister	

'yam mātā (employed
as a plural of
yārinyà, *girl*, or of
bùdurwā, *unmar-
ried, young woman*)

Plurals of previous vocabulary words not listed as examples above.

Class I

kàsuwā (*f.*)	market	kàsuwōyī/kàsuwōwī
ƙōfà (*f.*)	door(way)	ƙōfōfī
lâifī	fault	laifōfī (*or* Class II laifuffukà)
likità	doctor	likitōcī
muryà (*f.*)	voice	muryōyī
nāmà	animal (wild)	nāmōmī (*or* Class VII nāmū)
tāgà (*f.*)	window	tāgōgī
tàtsūnìyā (*f.*)	fable	tàtsūniyōyī
tāyà (*f.*)	tyre	tāyōyī

Class II

àddā (*f.*)	matchet	addunà
aikì	work	ayyukà
gàrī	town	garūruwà *or* garurrukà
itàcē	wood, tree	itātuwà
jàkī	donkey	jākunà
kàntī	store	kantunà
kàrē	dog	karnukà
kògī	river	kōgunà
māgànī	medicine	māgungunà

rāmì	hole	rāmunà *or* rāmummukà
rìgā (*f.*)	gown	rìgunà
sarkī	chief	sarākunà
zanè	body cloth	zannuwà

Class III

baƙī	black (thing)	baƙàƙē
6ērā	mouse, rat	6ēràyē
dōgō	long (thing)	dōgàyē/dōgwàyē
farī	white (thing)	faràrē
jirgī	boat	jiràgē
ƙasā	country	ƙasàshē
mùtûm	man	mutànē
uwā (*f.*)	mother	uwàyē, iyàyē

Class IV

àkwàtì	box	àkwàtai (*or* Class II akwātunà)
àllūrà (*f.*)	needle	àllùrai
bùkātà (*f.*)	need	bùkàtai *or* bùkàtū
dàlīlì	reason	dàlìlai
fìtilà (*f.*)	lamp	fìtilū (*or* Class I fìtilōlī)
gàjērē	short (thing)	gàjèrū *or* gàjèjjèrū
kuskurè	mistake	kùskùrai *or* kùràkùrai
littāfì	book	lìttàttàfai *or* lìttàfai
sābō	new (thing)	sàbàbbī
shèkarà (*f.*)	year	shèkàrū
wàkīlì	representative	wàkìlai

EXERCISES

Translate into English :

1. Mōtōcī sun kashè mutànē dà yawà bàra.
2. Anà sô likitōcī sù yi aikìnsù dà kyâu.
3. Mazā sun fi mātā ƙarfī.
4. Ìnā gidàjên dà mukà bar kāyammù à cikī jiyà ?

5. Yā àikē nì wurin mânyan mutànen gàrī dòmin sunà sô
   ìn yi musù màganà.

Translate into Hausa :

1. There are many schools in African countries.
2. Hausa have many chairs in their homes.
3. Certain books have fables in them.
4. There are not many cars in some countries.
5. The beggars that were here yesterday are not here
   today.

Dialogue

Sùlèmānù :   Mè a kè yî à gàrîn ?
Ishāƙù :   Ai sunà wàsā — wàsan ran kàsuwā.
Sùlèmānù :   Tò dà kyâu. Wànè irìn wàsā su kè yî ?
Ishāƙù :   Kōwànè irì. Bâ irìn dà bà zā sù yi ba.
Sùlèmānù :   Mutànē dà yawà sunà wurîn nē ?
Ishāƙù :   Sòsai !   Àkwai mazā dà mātā, yârā dà
                   tsòfàffī.
Sùlèmānù :   Zā sù yàrda ìn jē ìn ganī ?
Ishāƙù :   Ai zā sù yàrda mànà ! Bàri mù jē tàre.
Sùlèmānù :   Tò dà kyâu. Zā kà yi rawā nè ?
Ishāƙù :   Kâi ! Nī, bā nà rawā yànzu.   Nā tsūfa
                   ƙwarai !
Sùlèmānù :   Tò bâ lâifī.
Ishāƙù :   Kai fà ? Zā kà gwadà wàsân ?
Sùlèmānù :   Ā'à. Nī, bàn iyà irìn nākù rawân ba.
Ishāƙù :   Tô, bàri mù tsayà mù dūbà kawài.
Sùlèmānù :   Tò dà kyâu.

Lesson 23

Adjectival Nominals ; Comparison

1. *Adjectival* nominals are distinguishable as a subclass of nominals primarily by the fact that, when they are employed as modifiers, they ordinarily precede rather than follow what they modify. Adjectival nominals (with the exception of the quantifiers—see Lesson 11) also typically have both masculine and feminine as well as plural forms.

2. It is important to recognize that adjectival nominals are true nominals, not simply adjectives called by a more technical name. There is no separate category of words in Hausa corresponding to what are termed ' adjectives ' in European languages. An adjectival nominal in Hausa is a noun which designates basically *a person or thing characterized by the particular quality indicated*—not merely the quality itself.

Adjectives in European languages cannot stand alone (with an article) as sentence subjects or objects. Sentences like the following are not correct in English :

> The big went home.
> He hit the red.

In Hausa, however, since the words which translate English adjectives are nouns and can stand alone as sentence subjects or objects, it is perfectly proper to say :

Bàbba yā tàfi gidā.	The big (one) went home.
Yā bùgi jân.	He hit the red (one).
Tsōhuwā tā dāwō.	The old (woman) has returned.
Mânyā sun zō gàrimmù.	Important (people) have come to our town.

3. The referential **-n/-r,** when employed to join two nominals, is always suffixed to the first. When the first nominal is an àdjectival nominal, this means that the referential is suffixed to the modifier (the adjectival nominal) rather than to the head nominal of the phrase, e.g. :

Modifier	*Head*	
bàbban	**gidā**	the large home
dōguwar	**hanyà**	the long road

Note that this is a slightly different usage of the referential in Hausa ; ordinarily the **-n/-r** is suffixed to the head nominal rather than to the modifier, e.g. :

Head	*Modifier*	
gidan	**sarkī**	the home of the chief
màtar	**Bellò**	Bello's wife

The reason for this is that ordinary nouns (technically known as *independent nominals*) when employed as modifiers follow the noun (the head of the phrase) that they modify. Adjectival nominals ordinarily precede the noun that they modify. The referential is in either case suffixed to the first nominal.

4. The most common adjectival nominals are :

Masculine	*Feminine*	*Plural*	*Meaning*
bàbba	**bàbba**	**mânyā**	a big thing
ƙàramī	**ƙàramā**	**ƙanānà**	a small thing
ƙànƙanè	**ƙànƙanùwā**	**ƙanānà**	a small thing
gàjērē	**gàjerìyā**	**gàjèrū**	a short thing
dōgō	**dōguwā**	**dōgwàyē**	a tall/long thing
sābō	**sābuwā**	**sàbàbbī**	a new thing
tsōhō/tsōfō	**tsōhuwā/**		
	tsōfuwā	**tsòfàffī**	an old thing
mūgù	**mūgùwā/**	**miyàgū/**	
	mugunyà	**mûggā**	an evil thing

Masculine	Feminine	Plural	Meaning
jā	jā	jājàyē	a red thing
baƙī	baƙā	baƙàƙē	a black thing
farī	farā	faràrē	a white thing
kōrè	kōrìyā	kwârrā	a (light) green thing
shūɗì	shūɗìyā	shûɗɗā	a (light) blue thing
ràwayà	ràwayà	ràwàyū	a yellow thing

5. Adjectival nominals may also be employed appositionally as modifiers. The referential -n/-r is not used in appositional constructions.

> **gidā bàbba**   a large house (*lit.* a house, a big one)

This type of construction is, however, less common than that described in section 3 above for nearly all the adjectival nominals except the quantifiers and **ƙànƙanè** :

> **Yārò ƙànƙanè yā zō.**   A small boy has come.
> **Sarkī biyu sunà nân.**   Two chiefs are here.

6. A more common type of appositional modification involves the particle **mài** (*pl.* **màsu**), *possessor of . . .*, *characterized by . . .* (see Lesson 14). Many independent nominals, and even nominal and verbal phrases, may be converted into modifiers by adding **mài** as a prefix or introducer.

> **Yā bā mù àbinci mài dāɗī.**   He gave us (very) good food.
> **Yanà dà kuɗī mài yawà** (*or* **dà yawà**).   He has a lot of money.
> **Yā yi manà aikì mài kyâu.**   He did good work for us.
> **Àkwai dawākī màsu girmā** [1] **à wurîn.**   There are (very) large horses there.

The word **maràs** (*pl.* **maràsā**), *lacking*, is employed to introduce appositional constructions as the negative of **mài** :

[1] Only **girmā** (never **bàbba**) can be used with **mài, maràs,** or in comparison, to mean *big/large*.

Wani yārò maràs [2] hankàlī yā zō.	A certain senseless boy has come.
An bā mù abūbuwà maràsā àmfànī.	They have given us useless things.

Constructions introduced by **mài** and **maràs** are frequently employed independently (not as modifiers) as well :

Mài gidā bài dāwō ba tùkùn.	The head of the house has not returned yet.
Ìnā mài mōtà ?	Where is the owner/driver of the lorry ?
Bā à sôn maràs [2] kyâu.	No one wants a poor (quality) one.
Màsu dawākī sun dāwō.	The horsemen have returned.

7. Doubling of the colour terms indicates less intensity than the original forms. The final vowel of the colour term shortens in both occurrences.

Hannūnā yā kōmà baƙi-baƙi.	My hand has become blackish.
Wàndonsà shūdì-shūdì nē.	His trousers are bluish.
Fātàrsà tā zama ràwayà-ràwayà.	His skin was yellowish.

8. *Comparison* in Hausa involves the use of the verbs **fi,** *surpass,* and **kai,** *reach, arrive at,* e.g. :

A surpasses B in . . .

Bellò yā fi Mūsā girmā.[3]	Bello is bigger than Musa.

[2] It is common for the first consonant of the following word to replace the -s of **maràs** in pronunciation (though the -s is ordinarily written). Thus the pronunciations here would be **maràh hankàlī, maràk kyâu.**

[3] See footnote 1 on page 131.

Yārò yā fi ùbansà wàyō.	The boy is cleverer than his father.
Rìgā tā fi wàndō tsàdā.	A gown is more expensive than trousers.
Sulè yā fī sù dukà ƙarfī.	Sule is stronger than all of them.

A does not reach B in . . .

Bellò bài kai Mūsā girmā [4] **ba.**	Bello is not as big as Musa.
Talàkà bài kai sarkī arzìkī ba.	A peasant is not as rich as a chief.

A is the same as B in . . .

Audù yā kai ùbansà tsawō.	Audu is as tall as his father.
Wutā tā kai rānā zāfi.	Fire is as hot as sunshine.

A surpasses all in . . .

'Yarsà tā fi dukà kyâu.	His daughter is the most beautiful of all.
Jirgin samà yā fi dukà gudù.	An aeroplane is the fastest of all.
Aikìn lēbùrà yā fi dukà wùyā.	Working as a labourer is the most difficult (work) of all.

VOCABULARY

Nominals

àmfànī	usefulness
arzìkī	wealth
fātà (*f.*) (*pl.* **fātōcī** *or* **fātū**)	skin, hide
girmā	bigness
gudù	running, speed
hàƙurī	patience

[4] See footnote 1 on page 131.

jìkī	body
kàɗan	a small amount
kibiyà (*f.*) (*pl.* kibiyōyī *or* kìbau)	arrow
kōrè (*f.* kōrìyā ; *pl.* kwârrā)	a (light) green thing
kūkā	a cry
ƙànƙanè (*f.* ƙànƙanùwā ; *pl.* ƙanānà)	a small thing
lēbùrà (*pl.* lēburōrī)	labourer
mahàrbī (*pl.* mahàrbā)	hunter
mūgù (*f.* mūgùwā ; *pl.* miyàgū)	an evil thing
ràwayà (*pl.* ràwàyū)	a yellow thing
shāhò (*pl.* shāhunà)	hawk
shūɗì (*f.* shūɗìyā ; *pl.* shûɗɗā)	a (light) blue thing
talàkà (*pl.* talakāwā)	peasant, commoner
tsawō	length, height
tsūtsà (*f.*) (*pl.* tsūtsōtsī)	worm, grub
wàyō	cleverness
'yā	daughter

Verbals			*Particles*	
gàmu (dà)	meet (with)		maràs (*pl.* maràsā)	lacking, without
ƙi	refuse, hate		màsu	possessors of . . ., doers of . . . (plural of mài)
sàkā (i/ē)	release			
sākè	change, repeat			
sàuka	get off, descend, land, arrive, lodge			
zama	become			

Important Phrases

an jimà kàɗan (*or* jìm kàɗan)   a little while later

EXERCISES

Translate into English :

1. Waɗansu mânyan jiràgen samà sun sàuka à Kanò.
2. Màsu nēman àbinci sun sàmi kàɗan.
3. Wannàn ƙàramin littāfì yā fì wancàn bàbba dāɗin kàràtū.
4. Kanānàn yârā sunà wàsā à gidan tsōhō.
5. Yā sâ bàbbar rìgā àmmā bài yi rawā ba.

Translate into Hausa :

1. Kano is not as big as Lagos.
2. His gown is reddish.
3. His horse is as fast as mine.
4. Many short people are seated in the hut.
5. The white ones are prettier than the black ones.

Fable

Kōwā Yanà Dà Wandà Ya Fì Shì Karfì [5]

Wata rānā wani ƙàramin tsuntsū ya kāmà tsūtsà. Zâi cī tà, sai tsūtsà ta yi kūkā, ta cè, ' sàkē nì mànà ! '

Tsuntsûn ya cè, ' Ā'à, ai zân cī kì, don nā fì kì ƙarfì.'

Sai ya ɗàuki ƙàramar tsūtsà, ya cī tà.

Dà ya gamà cîntà sai wani shāhò ya gan shì. Sai shāhòn ya kāmà ƙàramin tsuntsū. Zâi cī shì, sai tsuntsûn ya yi kūkā, ya cè, ' Kà yi minì hàƙurī, kà sàkē nì ! '

Shāhòn ya ƙi, ya cè, ' Ai kai nè àbincīnā yâu, don nā fì kì girmā.'

Sai shāhòn ya ci tsuntsûn dà ya ci ƙàramar tsūtsà.

Kàfìn shāhòn yà gamà cîn tsuntsûn sai gà wata mīkìyā [6] ta fāɗì à kânsà. Sai shāhòn ya fārà kūkā, àmmā mīkìyâr bà tà sàkē shì ba dòmin tā fì shì ƙarfì.

---

[5] See *Ka Kara Karatu*, page 18, and Abraham, R. C., *Hausa Literature*, page 43, for another version of this story.

[6] A large bird of prey whose ornithological name is Ruppell's griffon.

An jimà kàɗan mīkìyâr ta tāshì samà. Bà tà daɗè ba
sai ta ji kibiyà à jìkintà. Àshē wani mahàrbī yā gan tà, ya
kashè ta.

Mīkìyâr tā gàmu dà wandà ya fī sù dukà ƙarfī kè̀ nan.

Lesson 24

Adverbial Nominals and Ideophones

1. Adverbial nominals, though they regularly occur in positions occupied by nominals (and, therefore, must be classified as nominals), differ from other subclasses of nominals in several ways :

(a) They do not have plural forms.
(b) They rarely occur as subjects or objects.[1]
(c) They rarely end in a long vowel.
(d) Many adverbial nominals are derived from independent nominals (see section 2 (b) below).
(e) They cannot be preceded by **mài/màsu.**
(f) They do not ordinarily take the referential (**-n/-r**) suffix.[2] Modifiers of these nominals are, therefore, typically introduced by a relater (usually **dà**).

2. Adverbial nominals are divisible into two major subclasses :

(a) Those which are not derivable from independent nominals. Some of the more important of these words are :

bàɗi	next year	**dàban**	different
bana	this year	**daidai**	exactly
banzā	worthlessly	**dōlè**	of necessity
bằra	last year	**dằzu**	just now
dâ	previously	**gabàs**	east

---

[1] When they do occur as subjects they usually take *feminine* concords (see the next to last example under 2 (a) below).

[2] Except when followed by **nàn/nân**, e.g. **banan nàn** = *this (very) year.*

gòbe	tomorrow	ƙwarai	very much
hakà	thus	lallē	certainly
jībi	day after	nēsà	far away
	tomorrow	sànnu	slowly
jiyà	yesterday	sòsai	really
kàɗan	a small amount	tīlàs	of necessity,
kawài	only		perforce
kullum	always	yànzu	now
kusa	close	yâu	today

Bā yà sô yà yi aikì à banzā.	He doesn't want to do work that is not worthwhile *or* work for nothing
Nā kāwō wani àbù dàban.	I have brought something different.
Lìssāfìnsà bà daidai ba nè.	His arithmetic is not correct.
Zâi yàrda nè ? Ai, tīlàs nē.	Will he agree ? Why, of necessity (=he'll have to).
Yanà zuwà wurimmù kullum.	He regularly comes to (see) us.
Dà ya zō kusa mukà gan shì.	When he came close we saw him.
Lallē zâi zō.	He will come for sure/he is sure to come.
Sànnu bā tà hanà zuwà.	(Going) slowly doesn't prevent (one's) arriving.
Tīlàs nē à yī shì.	It must be done.

(*b*) Those which are derivable from independent nominals. The majority of the nominal relaters listed and illustrated in Lesson 17, section 5, are suffixed forms of many of the same independent nominals. The adverbial nominal form is typically the same as the independent nominal form except that the final vowel is short. Sometimes there is a change of tone as well. Some of the more important of this type of adverbial nominal are :

arèwa	northwards	kudù	southwards
bāya	backwards	ƙasà	downward
cikī	inside	nīsa	far away
dāma	to the right	samà	upward
gàba	in front (of)	wàje	outside
hagu/hagun	to the left	yâmma	westward

Yā tàfi arèwa dà Kanò.	He has gone north of Kano.
Mun bi hanyàr dāma.	We followed the road to the right.
Yā fāɗi ƙasà.	He fell down to the ground.
Tsuntsū yā tāshì samà.	The bird took wing.
Sun fìta wàje.	They have gone outside.

3. Certain adverbial nominals may be intensified or made more definite by doubling, e.g. :

Dâ dâ akà ginà wannàn bangō.	A long long time ago this wall was built.
Anà yayyafī kàɗan kàɗan.	It's drizzling a (very) little bit.
Mun yi kusa kusa (or kurkusa) dà shī.	We got very close to him.
Kùnkurū yanà tàfiyà sànnu sànnu.	The tortoise is walking very slowly.
Zâi yī shì yànzu yànzu.	He will do it right now.
Zâi yī shì yâu yâu.	He will do it today (for sure).
Jirgin samà yā yi ƙasà ƙasà.	The aeroplane began to descend.
Yā yi samà samà.	It went right up.

4. A large number of relater phrases and stylized phrases

of other types function adverbially in Hausa. Most, but
by no means all, of these are introduced by the relater **dà**.
A few of the more common expressions of this type are :

(**à hankàlī**)	**Sai kà rik̃è shi à hankàlī.**
	You must hold it carefully.
(**an jimà**)	**Zâi zō an jimà.**
	He will come after a while.
(**bâ làbārì**)	**Bâ làbārì ya kāmà shi.**
	Without warning he caught it.
(**bâ shakkà**)	**Bâ shakkà zā kà san shì.**
	Without a doubt you will know him.
(**dà dàmunā**)	**Anà ruwā dà yawà dà dàmunā.**
	It rains a lot in the rainy season.
(**dà kyar**)	**Dà kyar na fid dà shī.**
	With difficulty I got (= I hardly got)
	it out.
(**dà k̃arfī**)	**Yā yi kūkā da k̃arfī.**
	He cried loudly (*lit.* strongly).
(**dà fārì**)	**Dà fārì zā mù nèmi tashà.**
	First of all we will look for the station.
(**dà rānī**)	**Dà rānī bā à ruwā.**
	It doesn't rain during the dry season.
(**dà saurī**)	**Yā iyà gudù dà saurī.**
	He can run fast.
(**dà wuri**)	**Zō nân dà wuri.**
	Come here in good time !
(**gàba ɗaya**)	**Sun tāshì gàba ɗaya.**
	They left all together (and at one
	time).
(**har yànzu**)	**Bài zō ba har yànzu.**
	He still hasn't come.
(**nan dà nan**)	**Nan dà nan sukà gudù.**
	At once they ran (away).
(**tun dà daɗèwā**)	**Yanà nan tun dà daɗèwā.**
	He has been here for a long time.

(tun dà wuri)   **Nā zō tun dà wuri.**
                I came early/in good time.
(tun dâ)   **Anà yînsà hakà tun dâ.**
                It has been done this way from olden
                times.

5. *Ideophones* are a large group of very specialized
particles varying widely from each other and, very
often, from all other words in the language. A given
ideophone is, typically, restricted in its usage to occurrence in quite a limited number of contexts (often as a
modifier of but a single word) :

(*a*) Ideophones modifying nominals.
     Each colour term (and many other nominals) has
     one or more ideophones which occur with the term to
     intensify what it indicates :

jà [3] wur ; jà [3] jir ; jà [3] zur	red as red can be, scarlet, blood-red
baƙī ƙirin ; baƙī sidiƙ ; baƙī sil	jet-black, black as pitch
farī fat ; farī kal	snow-white
kōrè shar	bright green
arèwa sak	due north
kudù sak	due south
mutànē tìnjim	people beyond number, people galore
lāfiyà lau	completely well
sābō ful	brand new
ɗaya tak	one and only one
ƙarfè gōmà cif	exactly ten o'clock

(*b*) Ideophones modifying verbals.
     A number of ideophones are employed as verb
     modifiers. Some of these are onomatopoeic. :

---

[3] Note that with **wur/jir/zur** the tone of **jà** drops to low.

tā sàuka jirif	it (*e.g.* a vulture) landed 'kerplunk'
yā cìka fal	it's chock full
yā ƙōnè ƙùrmus	it's completely burnt up, burnt to ashes
yi maza !	be quick !
yā yi tsit	he kept silence, kept mum
yā yi but	he suddenly 'popped out' (from hiding)
yā fitō ɓutuk	he emerged stark naked
an kullè kam	it was locked securely
sun yi jùrum	they stood despondently
kà yi farat	do (it) at once
yanà zàune sùkùkù	he's sitting despondently
sun bī sù wōhò wōhò	they followed them, booing
kà yi shirū	be quiet !, shut up !

6. Three particles of frequent occurrence which are usually labelled 'adverbs' are **wàtàkīlà/watakīlà/kīlà,** *probably, perhaps,* **tùkùn(a),** *not yet, first,* and **ainù(n),** *very much.*

Wàtàkīlà zâi zō gòbe.	Probably he will come tomorrow.
Bài dāwō ba tùkùn.	He hasn't returned yet.
Bàri ìn shiryà kāyānā tùkùna.	Let me prepare my loads first.
Yanà gudù dà saurī ainù.	He is running very fast.

VOCABULARY

Nominals

arèwa	northward
bangō (*pl.*	
bang(w)àyē)	wall, book cover
banzā	worthlessly, useless thing, *etc.*
dàban	different

dāma	to the right
dàmunā (*f.*)	rainy season
dōlè	of necessity, perforce
gabàs	east
hagu/hagun	to the left
kudù	southwards
kullum/kullun	always
kusa	close
lallē	certainly
nēsà	far away
rānĭ	dry season
shakkà (*f.*)	doubt
tashà (*f.*)	(railway) station
tīlàs	of necessity, perforce
wàje	outside

Verbals		*Particles*	
cìka	become full	ainù(n)	very much
cikà	fill, complete, fulfil	dà kyar	with difficulty
fitar (dà)/		har	to the extent
fid dà	put out, take out		that, until
hayè	cross over (*e.g.* a	maza	quickly
	river)	tun	since
rìƙè	hold (on to), keep		

EXERCISES

Translate into English :

1. Dà dàmunā wannàn kògĭ ya cìka fal dà ruwā.
2. Dukàmmù mukà tāshĭ gàba ɗaya, mukà fitar dà shī wàje.
3. Dà na gan shĭ sai bâ làbārĭ ya hau dōkĭ, ya gudù.
4. Dâ dâ àkwai wani tsōhō wandà ya shiryà gōnarsà à bàkin wannàn hanyà.
5. Tīlàs nē sù sàmi aikĭ dà wuri. Zā kà bā sù ?

Translate into Hausa :

1. The tyre that I saw was brand new.
2. Run quickly and bring water.
3. She will prepare the food today for sure.
4. I want to go to my home first.
5. After a little while we will return to our homes.

Dialogue

Lawàl : Kâi, dàmunā tā yi sòsai !
Hasàn : Gàskiyarkà. Nā jē kògī dà sāfē. Bàn iyà ìn
        hayè ba.
Lawàl : Tô, yā cìka nè ?
Hasàn : Yā cìka fal ! Har ƙarfin gudùnsà yā bā nì tsòrō.
Lawàl : Lallē àbin tsòrō nè. Yanà gudù dà saurī ainùn.
Hasàn : Sòsai ! Har wani sā'ì zâi tàfi dà mùtûm.
Lawàl : Hakà nē. Ìdan wani yā fāɗì à cikī sai yà mutù.[4]
Hasàn : Sòsai ! Irìn wannàn kògī mūgùn àbù nē.
Lawàl : Tô, yàyà zā mù yi ?
Hasàn : Ai, sai mù bi wata hanyà dàban.[4]
Lawàl : Àmmā wata hanyà zā tà yi nīsā. Kō bà hakà ba ?
Hasàn : Hakà nē. Àmmā bâ wata dàbārà.
Lawàl : Gàskiyarkà. Ai dōlè nē mù bi dōguwar hanyà kè
        nan.
Hasàn : Tô, mù tàfi.

[4] See Lesson 29, section 2, for usages of **sai** plus subjunctive.

Lesson 25

Verb Forms

1. The intricacy of the Hausa verb system is one of the more fascinating aspects of Hausa grammar. The most adequate overall classification of verbs to date is that of F. W. Parsons.[1] The major features of this system and the vast majority of Hausa verbs are organizable into seven categories (called ' Grades ' by F. W. Parsons) on the basis of their terminal vowels and tone patterns.

Of these seven grades, the first three may be termed ' basic ', while the remaining four may be termed ' derived '. That is, though there are several verbs which have derivative forms in more than one of the first three grades, the basic form of the majority of Hausa verbs will be either a Grade I, a Grade II or a Grade III form. From this basic form, however, may be derived up to four additional forms distinctive in both shape and meaning from the basic form. These derived forms are labelled Grades IV–VII, e.g. :

Basic Grades

I	gamà[2]	tārà	II	sàyā	kàrɓā	III	shìga	sàuka

Derived Grades

IV	gamè	tārè		sayè	karɓè		shigè	saukè
V	gamar	tārar		sayar	—		shigar	saukar
VI	gamō	tārō		sayō	karɓō		shigō	saukō
VII	gàmu	tàru		sàyu	kàrɓu		shìgu	sàuku

---

[1] See his *The Verbal System in Hausa* listed in the Bibliography of which the following is a summary. We are deeply grateful to Mr. Parsons both for the privilege of incorporating his analysis here and in Lesson 37, and for his detailed amplifications and corrections of this summary.

[2] See section 2 below for the meanings of these forms.

With many verbs certain of the forms do not occur.
This is usually either because such forms would be
meaningless or because the meaning that would be
conveyed is already covered by some other word, making
such a form unnecessary.

2. The characteristic patterns of the grades are as
follows. Irregular forms and patterns of low frequency
are not dealt with :

Grade	Terminal Vowel	Tone Pattern	General Meaning
I	-ā	high-low(-high/ low)	Basic : most Grade I verbs transitive, a few intransitive (**gamà**, *join together, finish* ; **tārà**, *gather together*)
II	-ā	low-high(-low)/ (low-)low-high	Basic : *always transi*tive (**sàyā**, *buy* ; **kàrɓā**, *receive*)
III	-a [3]	low-high(-low) [3]	Basic : intransitive (**shìga**, *enter (there)* ; **sàuka,** *descend*)
IV	-ē	high-low(-high/ low)	Derived : most transitive, some intransitive. Signifying more complete or thorough action than basic (**tārè**, *gather all* ; **sayè**, *buy all* ; **karɓè**, *take away* ; **shigè**, *go through* ; **saukè**, *put down a load*)

[3] A few Grade III verbs end in -i (e.g. **tàfi, gàji**) and a few have a
high-low tone pattern (e.g. **tāshì, fādì**).

Grade	Terminal Vowel	Tone Pattern	General Meaning
V	-ar	high-high(-high)	Derived : transitive (requiring **dà** before direct object). Often a causative meaning, sometimes more specialized (**gamar,** *cause to become complete* ; **sayar,** *sell* (lit. *cause to buy*) ; **shigar,** *put inside* ; **saukar,** *lower*)
VI	-ō	high-high(-high)	Derived : most transitive, some intransitive. Typically signifying action completed in vicinity of speaker (**gamō,** *finish and come* ; **tārō,** *gather here* ; **sayō,** *buy and bring* ; **karɓō,** *receive and bring* ; **shigō,** *enter here* ; **saukō,** *come down*)
VII	-u	(low-)low-high	Derived : intransitive. Usually passive meaning (**gàmu,** *have met* ; **tàru,** *have gathered together* ; **sàyu,** *has been (well), bought* ; **kàrɓu,** *has been collected in full* ; **shigu,** *be crowded* ; **sàuku,** *be comfortably settled in*)

Note that, in general, monosyllabic verbs (e.g. **ci, bi,** etc.), high-high toned verbs ending in -ā (e.g. **kirā, jirā, biyā**) and certain other verbs (e.g. **gudù, mutù, sanì, ganì**), including some of the commonest in the language, do not fall within this system and may, therefore, be termed irregular, though even most of these have several derived grade forms.

3. The *Grade IV* or -ē form has, in addition to its -ē termination, a high-low or falling-high tone pattern for two-syllable verbs and a high-low-high pattern for three-syllable verbs.[4] If (rarely) the verb has more than three syllables, the final two syllables are low-high and all preceding syllables high. The -ē forms frequently indicate more complete, extensive or thorough action than the basic form of the verb.[5] With many verbs, however, the -ē form has virtually replaced the basic form in common usage so that very little, if any, difference in meaning remains between the -ē form and the basic form of those verbs. With a great many verbs, further, the -ā form is transitive and the -ē form intransitive.

open	**būdà**	**būɗè**	open (and leave open)
beat	**bugà/**		
	bùgā	**bugè**	knock over/out
blow	**būsà**	**būshè**	get dry
eat	**ci**	**cînyē**	eat all of
fill	**cikà**	**cikè**	fill completely
increase	**daɗà**	**daɗè**	spend a long time
pick up	**ɗaukà**	**ɗaukè**	remove (completely)
tie up,			
tie on	**ɗaurà**	**ɗaurè**	tie up, imprison
sew, make			
by sewing	**ɗinkà**	**ɗinkè**	sew up (completely)

[4] Subject to the changes noted in Lesson 15, section 9.
[5] Also often connoting excessive or destructive action.

go out	fīta	wucè̱/	
		fīcè̱ [6]	pass by
chat (con-			
fidentially)	gānà̱	gānè̱	understand (completely)
rub (on)	gōgà̱	gōgè̱	rub (completely), rub off
go around	kēwàyā	kēwàyē	go around, surround
dip out	kwāsà̱	kwāshè̱	collect and remove all
increase	k̇ārà̱	k̇ārè̱	finish
step over	k̇ētà̱rā	k̇ētà̱rē	cross (*e.g.* river, road)
reduce			
(price)	ragà̱	ragè̱	reduce (anything)
cover	rufà̱	rufè̱	cover, close
buy	sàyā	sayè̱	buy all of
enter	shìga	shigè̱	pass by, (event) come and go
(basic form		warkè̱	recover completely
apparently lost)			(from illness)
cut up	yankà̱	yankè̱	cut off, sever
pour	zubà̱	zubè̱	spill

4. The *Grade V* or -ar form (often termed *causative*) also has, in addition to its -ar termination, all high tones. The meaning of the -ar form of a given verb typically indicates that the performer of the action caused the action of the verb to come about.[7] The relater dà̱ is required to introduce a direct object following an -ar verb. When a direct object follows, therefore, the final -r of the verb often ·becomes -d, e.g. fītad dà̱. Some dialects and individual speakers regularly employ -s in place of the final -r, especially in sentence-final position, e.g. yā sayas.

[6] Note the change from -t- (before -a) to -c- (before -è̱). See footnote 1, Lesson 22.

[7] But there are other meanings as well, and these cannot always be readily deduced from that of the basic form of the verb (e.g. gayar).

eat	ci	ciyar (dà)	feed (animal)
go out	fìta	fitar (dà)	take out, remove
tell	gayà	gayar (dà)	greet
return	kōmà	kōmar (dà)	take back (something)
lie down	kwântā	kwantar (dà)	put down, lay down
take the place of	màyā	mayar (dà)	put back, restore
dismount, descend	sàuka	saukar (dà)	set down, lower
buy	sàyā	sayar (dà)	sell
drink	shā	shāyar (dà)	water (an animal)
be sure	tabbàtā	tabbatar (dà)	confirm (a fact)
stand, stop	tsayà	tsayar (dà)	cause to stand, stop, detain
get well	warkè	warkar (dà)	heal
sit down, live	zaunà	zaunar (dà)	seat (someone), settle (people in a place)
pour, throw (away) [8]	zubà	zubar (dà)	throw away,[8] pour/ spill out

5. If an indirect object is employed, it follows the **-ar** form immediately, e.g. :

Yā fitar minì.   He removed (it) for me.
Nā sayar masà.   I sold (it) to (*or* for) him.

If a direct object follows an **-ar** form (whether or not there is an indirect object), it is introduced by **dà**. If a pronoun object is employed, it takes the independent form (just as it would elsewhere after a relater).

Sun mayar dà kēkunànsù.   They returned their bicycles.

---

[8] I.e. a number of things simultaneously.

An zaunar dà mū.	We were (caused to) sit down/settle.
Tā kwantar dà yārò.	She laid the boy down.

If both indirect and direct objects occur, the order is verb + indirect object + **dà** + direct object,[9] e.g. :

Yā sayar minì dà mōtà.	He sold me a car.
Nā saukar masà dà kāyansà.	I set his loads down for him.
Sun shāyar manà dà shānū.	They watered the cattle for us.
Kà gayar minì dà shī.	Greet him for me.

6. Several **-ar** forms have a shortened form which is commonly employed when a direct object, but no indirect object, follows. A **-shē** form may also be employed before a pronominal direct object with no following **dà**. The direct object pronouns are used with this form.

(ciyar)	**Yā cī dà shī.**	He fed it.
	Yā cīshē shì.	He fed it.
(fitar)	**Nā fid dà yārò.**	I expelled/extricated the boy.
	Nā fisshē shì.	I expelled/extricated him.
(gayar)	**Mun gai dà sarkī.**	We greeted the chief.
	Mun gaishē shì.	We greeted him.
(mayar)	**Yā mai dà shānū.**	He returned the cattle.
	Yā maishē sù.	He returned them.
(sayar)	**Yā sai dà jàkinsà.**	He has sold his donkey.
	Yā saishē shì.	He has sold it.
(shāyar)	**Yā shā dà dōkì.**	He watered the horse.
	Yā shāshē shì.	He watered it.

[9] Where the indirect object is a noun, Kano speakers frequently omit the **dà**, e.g. **yā sayar wà Audù mōtà** (rather than ... **dà mōtà**), *he sold Audu a car.*

(tsayar)	**Mun tsai dà mōtà.**	We stopped the car.
	Kadà kà tsaishē nì.	Do not detain me.
(zubar)	**Sun zub dà tàkàrdū.**	They threw the papers away.

7. The longer **-ar** forms may occur with no object at all. In this case the **dà** does not occur.[10]

Wancàn mùtûm yā kōmar.	That man returned (it).
Wancàn mùtûm yā fitar.	That man took (it) out.
Ìnā mōtàrkà ? Ai, nā sayar.	Where's your car ? Oh, I've sold (it).

8. The *Grade VI* or **-ō** form has, in addition to its **-ō** termination (whatever the tonal pattern of the basic form of the verb), all high tones. The meaning of the **-ō** form of a given verb typically indicates that the action performed had reference to, or was completed in, the vicinity of the scene of the conversation or (in a story) the centre of interest at the time.

send (out)	**aikà**	**aikō**	send here
pick up, take	**ɗaukà**	**ɗaukō**	pick up and bring here, fetch
(basic form apparently lost)		**dāwō**	return (here)
go out	**fìta**	**fitō**	come out
go (and return)	**jē**	**zō** [11]	come
carry, convey, reach (there)	**kai**	**kāwō**	bring, reach here
catch	**kāmà**	**kāmō**	catch and bring here
return (there)	**kōmà**	**kōmō**	return (here)
seek	**nèmā**	**nēmō**	seek and bring

[10] Nor does the **dà** occur when, as in a relative clause, the object precedes the verb, e.g. **jàkîn dà na sayar,** *the donkey that I sold.*

[11] Note the change from **j-** (before **-e**) to **z-** (before **-o**). See Lesson 22, footnote 1.

get	sāmù	sāmō	get and bring
arrive (there), get down	sàuka	saukō	arrive (here). come down
enter (there)	shìga	shigō	enter (here)
go (away)	tàfi	tafō/ tahō	arrive, come
leave (on journey hence)	tāshì	tāsō	leave (and arrive from journey hither)

9. The *Grade VII* or -u form has, in addition to its -u termination, a low-high tone pattern (all tones low except the final syllable which is high). The meaning of the -u form of a verb is typically passive, often with the added connotation of thoroughness or potentiality.

fall in, collapse	aukà	àuku	happen, befall
cook	dafà	dàfu	be cooked (thoroughly)
bother	dàmā	dàmu	be worried
begin	fārà	fàru	happen
join, finish	gamà	gàmu	(people) meet
rub	gōgà	gògu	be experienced
repair (thing)	gyārà	gyàru	be repaired (completely)
put on, wear	jità	jìtu	(people) get along well
establish	kafà	kàfu	be established
increase (thing)	ƙārà	ƙàru	be increased
squeeze	matsà	màtsu	be under pressure
wind, appoint	nadà	nàɗu	be wound, appointed,
cause to meet	sādà	sàdu	(people) meet
get, obtain	sàmā/ sāmù	sàmu	be obtainable/ available, occur
gather (*trans.*)	tārà	tàru	(group) gather (*intr.*), assemble
do, make	yi	yìwu	be possible

VOCABULARY

Nominals

àsīrī (*pl.* **àsìrai**)	secret
bàtun	concerning (from the noun **bàtū** = *conversation, matter, affair*)
hàsārà/àsārà	loss due to some unlucky incident, misfortune
kwānò (*pl.* **kwānōnī**)	basin, bowl, headpan, corrugated iron sheeting
ƙarfè	iron
tsàmmānì	thinking, thought
wāƙà (*f.*) (*pl.* **wāƙōƙī**)	song, poem, hymn
zūcìyā (*f.*) (*pl.* **zūciyōyī** *or* **zūkàtā**)	heart

Verbals

àuku	happen
bugà	beat
būshè	get dry
dàmu	be worried
gōgà	rub
gyārà	repair, fix
jìta	(people) get along well
kafà	set up, establish, erect
kēwàyē	go around, go roundabout
kwântā	lie down
kwāshè	collect and remove
ƙārè	finish
ƙētàrē	cross over
matsà	squeeze, press
naɗà	appoint (*e.g.* a chief), wind (*e.g.* a turban), fold (a cloth)
shigè	pass by (= **wucè**)

tabbàtā	be sure
tārà	gather together (*trans.*)
warkè	get well (from illness)
zubà	pour, throw (a number of things)
zubar/zub (dà)	pour (out), throw away
zubè	(something) spilled

Important Phrases

bà sù jìtu ba	they don't get along with each other/ 'hit it off'
(kà) gai dà shī!	greet him!
(kà) gayar minì dà shī	give him my greetings, remember me to him
kadà kà dàmē ni!	don't bother me!
kâr kà dàmu!	don't worry (about it)!
mè ya fàru?	what has happened?
mun sàdu dà shī	I (*lit.* we) met him
sàukad dà shī!	let it down! lay it down!
sun tàru	they (a group) have gathered
kà zub dà shi!	throw it away!

EXERCISES

Translate into English:

1. **An fisshē tà dàgà aikìn.**
2. **Kà sayar minì dà shī don Allà.**
3. **Kadà kù dàmu, bà àbîn dà ya àuku tùkùna.**
4. **Zùbà shi cikin kwānò. Bāyan hakà kù shāyar dà dōkì.**
5. **Dom mè bà zā kà fid dà àsīrinkà dàgà cikin zūcìyarkà ba?**

Translate into Hausa:

1. Don't throw it away! Catch it and go inside.
2. They bought some wood and brought it back.
3. Are you sure she drank it all up? Yes, she did.

4. Put it down here. Now lay it down (flat).
5. We took it out and stood it up.

Dialogue

Ùmarù : Kā dāwō dàgà birnī ?

Bàlā : Ī. Nā dāwō shēkaranjiyà dà sāfē.

Ùmarù : Tô. Àmmā nā ji wàhalà tā àuku à wurîn.

Bàlā : Sòsai ! Kâi ! Wutā tā kāmà waɗansu gidàjē, tā
ƙōnè su ƙùrmus !

Ùmarù : Kâi ! Mutànē sun yi hàsārà ƙwarai ! Kai fà ?

Bàlā : Ai, lāfiyà na kè. Àbîn bài zō kusa dà wurîn dà
na kè zama ba.

Ùmarù : Mādàllā ! Dâ nā yi tsàmmānì kō wàtàkīlà tā zō
wurinkù nē.

Bàlā : Ā'à. Bà tà dàmē mù ba kō kàɗan. Àmmā
waɗansu sun shā wàhalà dà yawà.

Ùmarù : Lallē.

Bàlā : Ai, rân nan na gàmu dà àbōkīnā, na tàmbàyē
shì bàtun wutâr. Ya cê, gidansù duk yā ƙōnè.

Ùmarù : Tabɗì ! Mè ka yi ?

Bàlā : Ai, dōlè nē ìn shiryà masà wurī à ɗākìna.

Ùmarù : Tô, àmmā mè ya fàru gà ìyālìnsà ?

Bàlā : Ai sun sàuka à gidan wani.

Ùmarù : Mādàllā ! Sai yàushè kàmìn sù kafà sābon
gidā ?

Bàlā : Bà zā sù daɗè ba. Zā sù tārà kāyà sù fārà dà
wuri.

Ùmarù : Tò dà kyâu. Allà yà tàimàkē sù.

Bàlā : Āmin !

Lesson 26

The Habitual Aspect ; ' Auxiliary ' Verbs ; Exclamations

1. The habitual aspect is employed to indicate action that occurs intermittently, customarily or habitually.[1] The habitual aspect person-aspect pronouns are formed from a high-tone, short-vowel set of p-a pronouns prefixed to the particle **-kàn.** Since, however, these forms are traditionally written as two words (e.g. **na kàn,** etc.) they will be so represented here. With the verb **zō** the forms are :

I regularly come	**na kàn zō**	**mu kàn zō**	we regularly come
you (*m.*) regularly come	**ka kàn zō**	**ku kàn zō**	you (*pl.*) regularly come
you (*f.*) regularly come	**ki kàn zō**		
he regularly comes	**ya kàn zō**	**su kàn zō**	they regularly come
she regularly comes	**ta kàn zō**		
one regularly comes	**a kàn zō**		

[1] It must, however, be pointed out that customary or habitual activity in Hausa is more frequently expressed by employing the continuative aspects than by the use of the habitual (see also Lesson 27, section 2 (*a*)). For example, if a Hausa person wanted to say *he comes every day*, he would be more likely to say **yanà zuwà kōwàcè rānā** than to say **ya kàn zō kōwàcè rānā,** though either would be correct. Sometimes, however, a distinction is indicated by the contrast between continuative and habitual aspects, e.g. **yanà shầ** = *he is a (habitual) drinker* ; **ya kàn shā** = *he takes a drink from time to time.*

2. This aspect, even more than the others, must often be reinforced by the use of an adverbial nominal to indicate the time of the action.

Dâ su kàn zō kōwànè mākò.	They used to come every week.
Su kàn zìyàrci Kanò lōtò-lōtò.	They visit Kano from time to time.

3. The negative of the habitual aspect employs **bà . . . ba.**

Bà na kàn zō ba.	I don't regularly come.
Bà su kàn ci àbincimmù ba.	They don't eat our (kind of) food (very often).

4. There are in Hausa a number of verbs which are often termed *auxiliary* verbs because the meaning of the utterance in which such verbs occur is determined not so much by the verb itself as by that which immediately follows the verb. Several of these are treated below.

5. The verb **rigā/rìgāyà** = *have already done* . . . (generally in the regular completive aspect) : [2]

Yā rigā yā tàfi.	He has already gone.
Nā rìgāyà nā tàmbàyē shì.	I have already asked him.
Sun rigā sun fārà.	They had already begun.

6. The verbs **rìkà** and **dingà** followed by a noun or verbal noun = *regularly do* . . ., *keep on doing* . . : [3]

---

[2] Unlike the other verbs here illustrated, **rigā** is followed not by a verbal or other noun, but by another *verb construction* in the same aspect as itself. These two verbs are closely co-ordinated—even to the extent that in the negative the final **ba** always comes after the *second* verb construction which ordinarily takes a positive, *not* a negative, p-a pronoun, e.g. **bài rigā yā tàfi ba,** *he had not yet gone* (though **bài rigā bài tàfi ba** is also possible).

[3] They differ slightly in meaning in that **dingà** usually implies that the thing being continued is already being done, whereas **rìkà** may be applied to something not yet started.

Sai kà rìƙà shân wannàn māgànī.	You must regularly drink this medicine.
Yā dingà zuwà gidammù.	He kept on coming to our home.
Kadà kà rìƙà cîn bāshì.	Don't always borrow (**ci bāshì** = *incur a debt*).

7. The verb **taɓà**, *touch*, followed by certain types of nouns or verbal nouns = *have ever* . . . :

Kā taɓà zuwà Kanò ?	Have you ever been to Kano ?
Bàn taɓà ganinsà ba.	I have never seen him.
Nā taɓà cî.	I have eaten it (at some time in the past/once or twice).

8. The verbs **ƙārà, daɗà** and **sākè** = *repeat* . . ., *do* . . . *again* :

Bàn sākè ganinsà ba.	I didn't see him again.
Yā ƙārà zuwà.	He came again.

9. The verbs **ƙārà** and **daɗà** = *increase* . . ., *add* . . . *to* :

Nā ƙārà masà kuɗī.	I increased his pay.
Yā daɗà ƙòƙarī.	He tried harder.

10. The verbs **cikà** and **fayè** = *be full of* . . ., *be characterized by* . . . :

Yā cikà kàràmbànī.	He's extremely meddlesome, a big nuisance.
Àbîn yā fayè minì wùyā.	The thing was too difficult for me.
Bàn cikà sô ba.	I don't really like (it).

11. The verb **iyà** = *be able to do* . . . :

Yā iyà Hausā.	He can speak Hausa well.
Yanà iyà aikìn.	He can do the work.
Bà zân iyà zuwà ba.	I won't be able to come.

12. The verb **yi,** *do,* may be translated in a variety of
ways according to what follows (or precedes) it, e.g. :

Yā yi aikì mài kyâu.	He did good work
An yi ruwā.	It (has) rained.
Yā yi girmā.	He's big. *Or* He grew up.
Mun yi yāwò.	We wandered about.
Àbinci yā yi.	The food is ready.
Yā yi ƙaryā.	He lied.
Yā yi barcī.	He slept.
Nā yi masà màganà.[4]	I talked to him (about a specific topic).

13. Hausa, like other languages, has its share of excla-
matory utterances.   These expressions are usually
specialized particles, though certain nominals, verbals
and stylized phrases may also be employed as exclamations.   The following exclamations have already been
introduced :

Particles:

ā'à	no	Lesson 13
ai	why!, well!	Lesson 18
àlbarkà	no sale !	Lesson 15
àmin	may it be so, amen	Lesson 4
àshē	well !, is that so ?	Lesson 20
habà	nonsense, come now !	Lesson 15
ī	yes	Lesson 13
mādàllā	fine, praise God !	Lesson 4
mànà	indeed	Lesson 19
tabdì	(utter amazement)	Lesson 25 (Dialogue)
tô/tò	well, okay	Lesson 4
yâuwā/yâuwa	fine, okay	Lesson 4

Nominals :

kâi	wow ! Good Heavens !	Lesson 11
sànnu	greetings !	Lesson 4

---

[4] Note that the -**i** of **yi** does not lengthen before an indirect object.

Verbal :

bābù	no ! (emphatically)	Lessons 4, 13

Phrases :

don Allà	please	Lesson 25
shī kè̀ nan	that's that !	Lesson 6

14. Several additional exclamations to listen for and learn to use are listed below. There are many more. Though it is very difficult adequately to illustrate in writing the usage of exclamations, it is hoped that the examples below will be found helpful.

a'a	exclamation of (real or feigned) amazement
a'àhā	expression of concern at hearing of misfortune
af/ap	expression of surprised recognition
allà ?	really ?
allà	it is true (reply to **allà ?**)
m'm̀	expression of sympathetic concern
na'àm	expression of interest or agreement (*e.g.* in a story or account which is being narrated)
nà'am	yes ? (in reply to one's name being called)
wâyyô̂	(exclamation of despair), alas !
wâyyô̂ Allà	alas !
wâyyô̂ nī	woe is me !

Examples :

(**a'a**) After the tortoise has made the statement to the hare that he can outrun him in a race, the hare might reply :

> **A'à ! Kai, zā kà cī nì dà gudù ? Habà !** The thought of it ! You, you will beat me in a race ? Nonsense !

(a'àhà)   In the dialogue in Lesson 25 where **Ûmarù** used the comparatively neutral **tabdî** to express his amazement he might alternatively have used **a'àhā,** since the subject of the discussion was a misfortune.

(af/ap)   When two visitors come to the home of someone who knows one of the visitors well and the second of them less well, the householder and the visitor he knows well will commonly exchange greetings between themselves only, at first. Then the householder will typically turn to the second visitor (whom we will call Bello) with feigned surprise (as if he had not seen him standing there until this moment) saying :

> **Af Bellò ! Kā zō nè ? Barkà dà zuwà.** Why, Bello ! Have you come (too) ? Greetings at (your) coming.

(allà)   If a person relates a remarkable incident, it is very common for either of the two following exchanges to take place :

> Person A : **Allà ?**   Did that really happen ?
> Person B : **Allà (kùwā)** Every word of it is true.

> *Or*

> Person A : **Hakà nē ?** *Or* **Gàskiyā nè ?** Is it a fact ?
> Person B : **Allà.** It certainly is.

(m'm̀)   If a story is being related in which someone gets into difficulty (usually, though not necessarily, minor), it would be common for a listener to express his concern by the use of this particle.

(na'àm)   As a longish story (such as a fable) is being narrated by one person, it is appropriate for the listener(s) fairly frequently to interject a casual **na'àm** (*or* **tô**) to signal to the narrator continued interest in and/or agreement with what he is saying.

(nà'am)   If a person is called by name, he will commonly answer by using this particle, e.g. :

Audù :	**Mammàn !**	Mamman !
Mammàn :	**Nà'am ?**	What ?, Yes ?
Audù :	**Zō nân !**	Come here !

(wâyyô)   This cry of utter despair is reserved for real emergencies.   One Hausa fable relates the story of a careless fisherman casting his hook too near to other people and before long hooking the ear of one of the others.   This situation seemed appropriate for the story-teller to put the exclamation **wâyyô Allà** in the mouth of the unfortunate person who had been hooked.   See the fable at the end of this lesson for another illustration.

VOCABULARY

Nominals

allà	it is true, is it true ?
bāshì	debt, loan
ganī	seeing (verbal noun of **ganī**, *see*)
jàkā (*f.*)	
(*pl.* **jakunkunà**)	(small) bag, ₦200
kàràmbànī	nuisance/putting one's nose in someone else's business
ƙaryā (*f.*)	a lie
lōtò	time (= **lōkàcī**)
mafàshī	
(*pl.* **mafàsā**)	highway robber

mākò	week (= **sātī**)
sā'à (*pl.* **sā'ō'ī**)	luck, good fortune ; time, hour
sabò dà/sabòdà	because of
sātī	week (= **mākò**)
zìyārà	visiting, a visit

Verbals		*Particles*	
daɗà	repeat . . ., do . . . again	**a'a**	(exclamation of amazement)
dingà	keep on doing . . .	**a'àhā**	(exclamation of concern over misfortune)
fāɗà	fall upon, fall into (*cf.* **fāɗì**)	**af/ap**	(exclamation of surprised recognition)
fayè	be characterized by . . .		
rigā/rìgāyà	have already done . . .	**dai**	(emphasis particle), on the other hand, for my part
rìƙà	keep on doing . . ., do regularly and repeatedly	**m'm̀**	(exclamation of sympathetic concern)
taɓà	touch ; have ever . . .	**na'àm**	(exclamation of interest or agreement)
zìyartà (i/ē)	visit	**nà'am**	(reply to a call), yes ?, what ?
		wâyyô	(exclamation of despair), alas !

Important Phrases

Allà yà bā mù . . .	may God give us . . .
Allà yà sâ	may God bring (it) about
baƙin dājì	forest (*lit.* dark bushland)
ci bāshì	incur a debt
duk dà hakà	in spite of this, nevertheless, yet

lōtò-lōtò   from time to time
zūrà dà gudù break into a run

EXERCISES

Translate into English :

1. Allà yà sâ mù yi sā'à cikin cìnikimmù. In bà hakà ba
   dōlè nè mù ci bāshì.
2. Bàri in daɗà ƙòƙarīnā cikin aikìn nân. Af, bà kà gàji
   ba ? Bà zā kà barì ba tùkùna ?
3. Bàn taɓà ganin irìn wannàn rawâr ba. Bàri in gwadà
   yîntà. A'a ! Kâi, bà zā kà iyà ba !
4. Nā yi màganà dà shī mākòn dà ya wucè àmmā bài ƙārà
   zuwà sātin nàn ba.
5. Dâ a kàn hau dōkì àmmā yànzu an fi sôn mōtà. Allà ?
   Allà kùwā.

Translate into Hausa :

1. I visited the chief's home but he had already gone
   away.
2. Gosh!, that man is a terrible liar (*translate*, is full of
   lying)! Because of this I don't like him.
3. It rains a lot during the rainy season. That's so.
4. He hasn't been in Nigeria long but he speaks Hausa
   fluently (*translate*, like a Kano donkey).
5. I want to take out a loan in order to buy a new car.

Fable

Audù dà Àlī [5]

Audù dà Àlī sunà cikin tàfiyà. Zā su kàsuwā dà kāyā.
Sai gà wani àbù à bàkin hanyà. Àlī ya ɗaukà, ya dūbà.
Àshē jàkar kuɗī cè.
 Sai Audù ya cê, ' Kâi, yâu mun yi sā'à.'

[5] See *Ka Kara Karatu*, page 12, and Abraham, R. C., *Hausa Literature*, page 41, for another version of this story.

Àlī ya cê, ' A'a ! Mū mukà yi sā'à nē ? Kō dai nī, na yi sā'à ? '

Audù ya cê, ' Tò shī kè nan, Allà yà bā mù lāfiyà.'

Sukà cigàba dà tàfiyàrsù har sukà shìga wani bakin dājì. Sai waɗansu mafàsā sukà fāɗà musù. Audù dà Àlī sukà zūrà dà gudù. Su mafàsā sukà bī sù.

An jimà sai Àlī ya gàji sabòdà nauyin kāyansà. Ya cê, ' Wâyyô. Yâu mun yi hàsārà.'

Audù ya cê, ' A'a ! Mū mukà yi hàsārà nē ? Kō dai kai, ka yi hàsārà ? '

Lesson 27

Uses of Aspects

1. The *subjunctive aspect* has a wider variety of uses than any other aspect in Hausa. In addition to its use to express commands (see Lesson 12), the subjunctive is commonly employed :

(a) In a large number of contexts that may in English be translated by the infinitive, notably in subordinate clauses (see also Lesson 12, section 7) :

Nā tàfi ìn gan shì.	I went to see him.
Zā sù jē sù hàrbi nāmà.	They will go to/and shoot (some) meat.
Inà sô kà zō nân.	I want you to come here.
An cê masù sù zō.	They were told to come.
Yā yàrda yà yī shì.	He agreed to do it.
Yā fi kyâu à dākàtā kàɗan.	It would be better to wait a little.
Yā yìwu à biyā kà gòbe ?	Is it possible to pay you tomorrow ?
Inà jirànsà yà dāwō.	I'm waiting for him to return.

(b) In many contexts that may be translated by ' in order to ' (see also some of the examples above) or, negatively (with **kadà**), ' lest ' :

Yā zō (don) yà tàimàkē mù.	He came (in order) to help us.
Sun gudù (don) kadà à kāmà su.	They ran so that they would not be caught.

(c) In some contexts that may be translated by *that* (which does not in Hausa always require a special word) :

Munà fātā kà dāwō lāfiyà.	We hope (that) you will come back safely.
An cè manà (wai) mù dākàtā.	We were told (that) we should wait.

(d) In contexts relating to seeking, denying or assuming permission :

Tô mù jē !	Well, let's go !
In shìga kō ?	May/shall I (am I to) enter ?
Kadà kōwā yà shā wannàn.	Nobody is to drink this.

(e) Following certain relaters :

kàmin/kàfin, *before* :

Kàmin in tāshì sun rigā sun zō.	Before I left they had already come.
Zā mù hūtà kàɗan kàmin mù ci àbinci.	We will rest a little before we eat.

dòmin/don (see also above, section (b)), *in order to/ that* :

Yā kāwō shì dòmin in ganī.	He brought it so I could see it.

har, *until* (future) :

Bàri mù dākàtā nan har sù isō.	Let's wait here until they come.

Note : **har,** in contexts indicating action in the past, requires the relative completive or the regular completive p-a pronouns :

Mun dākàtā har sukà isō.	We waited till they came.

gāra/gwàmmà, *it is better that* :

Gāra mù yi hakà.	It is better that we do thus.
Dà tàfìyà banzā gwàmmà à zaunà à gidā.	It is better to stay home than to travel without purpose.

saurā, *there remain (only), all but* :

Saurā mintì gōmà sù isō.	They will be here in ten minutes.
Saurā kàɗan yà fāɗì.	He nearly fell.

(*f*) **Ìn ji...** (lit. *let me hear*) is a stylized expression employing the subjunctive which means ... *says* or *according to* ... : [1]

Zâi zō gòbe, ìn ji Audù.	He will come tomorrow, according to Audu.
Ìn ji wà ?	Who says so ?
Kadà kà sākè zuwà, ìn ji sarkī.	The chief says don't come again.

(*g*) In an utterance describing future (or habitual) action and involving several predicate constructions, only the first verb need be preceded by the future (or habitual) p-a pronouns—the remaining predicates are typically subjunctive (see also Lesson 16, section 4) :

Gòbe Mālàm Ùsmân dà Mìnistà na Ilmì zā sù tàfì Sakkwato, sù būɗè makarantar 'yam mātā, sù zìyàrci asìbitì, sù dāwō Gùsau, sù bā dà laccà dà yâmmā.

---

[1] **Ìn ji** is also used whenever the verb *says/said* comes at the end of, or in the middle of, a quotation. **Cê,** *say,* cannot be used in such positions. See paragraph 4, line 1, of the fable at the end of this Lesson for an example.

Tomorrow Mr. Usman and the Minister of Education will go to Sokoto, (will) open a girls' school, (will) visit a hospital, (will) return to Gusau, (and will) give a (political) speech in the evening.

2. The *continuative aspect*, in addition to expressing simple continuative action (see Lesson 18), has the following more specialized uses :

(*a*) The continuative is employed to express customary or habitual action, natural abilities or disabilities, and the like :

Yanà zuwà kōwàcè rānā.	He comes every day.
Bā yà aikì sòsai.	(It is characteristic of him that) he doesn't work hard.
Àladè bā yà tāshì.	Pigs can't fly.

(*b*) The continuative is often employed in a subordinate clause after a main clause employing a completive or continuative aspect to indicate an action occurring simultaneously with the action of the main clause :

Nā gan shì yanà aikì.	I saw him working.
Yā tāshì inà barcī.	He got up (while) I was (still) asleep.
Munà zuwà yanà ganimmù.	(As) we were coming he watched us.
Inà aikì yanà ta sùrūtù.	(As) I worked he chattered foolishly.
Yā daɗè yanà aikì.	He has been working for a long time.

3. The *future aspects* and the specialized verbal **zâ,** in a ddition to expressing simple future action (Lesson 16), are frequently employed to express :

(*a*) Intent :

Dà zuwànsà zâi yi màganà sai . . .	When he arrived he intended to say something but . . .
Mwâ zō.	We intend to come.
Dâ zâ ni gidā . . .	I had originally planned to go home . . . . I *was* going home (but . . .).
Dâ mā zân kōmà, . . .	I was planning all along to return . . .

(*b*) To be about to :

Zâ shi Ingìlà sai ùbansà ya mutù.	He was about to leave for England when his father died.
Dà na shiryà, zân hau kèkēnā, gà shi bābù iskà.	When I was ready, (and) was about to climb on to my bicycle, why! there was no air (in the tyre).

(*c*) Conditional action :

Bàn sàmi wandà zâi yī shì ba.	I didn't find anyone who would do it/to do it.[2]
Dà yā nūnà minì dà zân sàyā.	Had he showed (it) to me I would have bought (it).

4. The *completive aspect* may be employed within a sequence of relative completive clauses to express a more remote past (the English pluperfect) than that indicated by the relative completive predicates :

Dà sukà shiryà sukà tàfì. Màkānìkì yā gyārà masù mōtàrsù.

---

[2] Another meaning could be ' I didn't find the (particular) man who was going to do it '.

When they had got ready they left. The mechanic had
(previously) repaired their lorry for them.

**Sā'àn dà mātā sukà dāwō dàgà kàsuwā, ya tàmbàyē tà, ya
cê, 'Yàyà cìnikī? Yā yi kyâu?' Sai ta amsà, 'Yā yi
kyâu.'**

When the women returned from market, he asked her,
he said ' How was the trading ? Did (completive) it go
well ? ' Then she answered, ' It went (completive) well.'

VOCABULARY

Nominals

asìbitì (*pl.* asibitōcī)	hospital
cêwā	saying (verbal noun of cê)
dabbà (*f.*) (*pl.* dabbōbī)	animal
dàriyā (*f.*)	laughter
fādà	chief's residence
fiffìkè (*pl.* fìkàfìkai)	wing
haƙōrī (*pl.* haƙòrā)	tooth
hannū (*pl.* hannàyē)	arm (including hand), hand
hàrājì	tax
ilmì, ilìmī	knowledge, book-learning
iskà (*f.* or *m.*) ³	wind, air
jēmāgè (*pl.* jèmàgū)	fruitbat
kàshègàrī	on the following day
laccà	political speech, lecture
màkānīkì (*pl.* màkànìkai)	mechanic
màmā	breast, mother, mother's milk
mìnistà (*pl.* ministōcī)	minister (of government)
ōfìs/ōfìshī (*pl.* ōfìsōshī)	office
râi (*pl.* rāyukà)	life
saurā	remainder
sùrūtù	(senseless) chatter

³ The plural iskōkī means (*evil*) *spirits.*

tùnằnī	reflecting, thinking
tsakà/tsakiyà (*f.*)	centre
tsàkānī	between
wàkīlì	representative

Verbals

amsà	answer
haifù (i/ē)	give birth to
hàrbā (i/ē)	shoot
isō	arrive (here)
kàrɓā (i/ē)	receive, accept
kirā	call, summon
ƙyālè	not bother with, ignore
saurā	be left over, remain

Particles

gāra	it is better that
gwàmmà	it is better that
mā	(emphasis particle), even, too, actually
wai	quote, they say

Important Phrases

dâ mā	it has been planned that, it is well known that, already
ìn ji ...	... says, according to ...
kuɗin ƙasā	taxes (*lit.* money for the land)
nan dà nan	immediately
rânkà yà daɗè [4]	may you live long ! (said to a chief or other social superior)
tsakàr-tsàkānī	betwixt and between
yā fi kyâu (plus subjunctive)	it is better/best (that ...)
yanà ta ...	he continuously ...

[4] Often heard as **rânkài daɗè.**

EXERCISES

Translate into English :

1. Dâ mā zâ ni gidansà ìn gaishē shì, sai na ji làbārì, na cê, yā fi kyâu ìn gayà masà.
2. Kàmìn yà fārà zuwà nā dadè inà aikì à nân.
3. Dà na sàmē shì, nan dà nan sai ya zūrà dà gudù.
4. Àbincimmù yā ƙārè nē ? Ā'à, dà⁵ saurā kàɗan. Kanà sô ìn dafà wani ?⁶
5. Mìnistàn Màkàràntū zâi yi laccà à Gùsau ? Ī, bàri mù shiryà, mù jē.

Translate into Hausa :

1. Certain highway robbers wanted me to tell them the news of the town.
2. I came upon him while he was working. He is a mechanic. He has been repairing automobiles for a long time.
3. Originally he had agreed to wait here until I came, but now I don't know what⁷ he will do.
4. The chief says don't ever come to his home again. It is better that you meet him at his office.
5. He can speak Hausa, but it is very difficult for him.

Fable

Jēmāgè Bā Yà Biyàn Hàrājì⁸

Wata rānā sarkin dabbōbī ya kirā wàkīlìnsà, ya cê masà, ' kà kēwàyē cikin ƙasātā kà jē gidàjen dabbōbī dukà kà kàrɓi kuɗin ƙasā à hannun kōwànnensù.'

Wàkīlì ya cê, ' Rânkà yà daɗè, nâ yi nan dà nan.'

---

⁵ In this context dà = àkwai (see Lesson 37, section 3).
⁶ In contexts such as this wani means *some more*.
⁷ Translate *what* as *the thing which* (àbìn dà . . .).
⁸ See *Littafi Na Karantawa*, page 8, for another version of this story.

Sai wàkīlì ya kēwàyē cikin ƙasâr, ya kàrɓi hàrājì à kōwànè gidā. Àmmā dà ya isō gidan jēmāgè, jēmāgè ya ƙi biyàn kuɗîn.

' Ai, nī bà dabbà ba cè,' in ji jēmāgè. ' Kō cikin talakāwan sarkin dabbōbī àkwai mài fīkàfīkai kàmar nī ? Àkwai wandà ya iyà tāshì samà kàmar nī ? Ai, bā nà biyàn hàrājì gà sarkin dabbōbī ! '

Shī kè nan. Wàkīlìn sarkin dabbōbī ya bar shì, ya kōmà fādà, ya shâidā wà sarkinsù. Sarkī dai, ya yi tùnànī, ya cè, ' Lallē, gàskiyarsà. Jēmāgè bà irìmmù ba nè, à ƙyālè shi.'

Kàshègàrī sarkin tsuntsàyē ya kirā nāsà wàkīlì, ya àikē shì yà kàrɓi kuɗin ƙasā à hannun kōwànè tsuntsū. Dà wàkīlìn ya isō gidan jēmāgè, ya tàmbàyē shì kuɗin ƙasā, sai jēmāgè ya yi masà dàriyā, yanà cêwā, ' Nī, bā nà biyànsà hàrājì.'

Wai, ' Kō kā taɓà ganin tsuntsū mài haƙōrā ? ' ' Kō wandà ya kàn hàifi 'yā'yansà dà râi, yà bā sù màmā ? Kâi ! Nī bà talàkàn sarkin tsuntsàyē ba nè ! '

Dà wàkīlìn ya kōmà fādà ya shâidā wà sarkin tsuntsàyē, sai sukà yàrda cêwā jēmāgè bà tsuntsū ba nè.

Sabòdà hakà jēmāgè yanà tsakàr-tsàkānī, bā yà cikin dabbōbī, bā yà, kùwā, cikin tsuntsàyē.

Lesson 28

Reduplication

1. Hausa employs various types of reduplication for various purposes. Sometimes only a syllable is reduplicated, sometimes the whole word. Examples of the most frequent types of reduplication follow.

2. Reduplication of the first syllable of a *verb* gives it an *intensive meaning* (e.g. *keep on . . ., do . . . time after time, do . . . in succession*). Typically, the first syllable is reduplicated with accompanying duplication of the initial consonant of the original verb (which has now become the first consonant of the second syllable). If the original first syllable has a final consonant, it may remain or may be assimilated as a doubled consonant.[1] The great majority of reduplicated verbs have at least three syllables and their tones follow the regular patterns for three- and four-syllable verbs. Thus :

(*a*) High-low verbs become high-low-high :

beat	**bugà**	**bubbùgā**	keep on beating
cook	**dafà**	**daddàfā**	keep on cooking
look	**dūbà**	**duddùbā**	look everywhere

(*b*) Low-high verbs [2] become low-high-low :

| go out | **fìta** | **fìffìtà** | keep going out |

---

[1] When, for example, the first syllable ends in a nasal, assimilation does not take place, e.g. **tàntàmbayà** (not **tàttàmbayà**), and it is optional where the first syllable ends in some other consonants, e.g. **fìffìtà** or **fìrfìtà**, **sàssayà** or **sàisayà**, **kakkāwō** or **kankāwō**.

[2] If the base verb is a variable vowel (Grade II) verb, the derived intensive verb will also be a *v.v.* verb. Thus the rules for final vowel and tone change before direct objects (as well as all other *v.v.* verb rules) apply, e.g. **sun nànnèmi shānunsù, sun nànnèmē sù,** *they looked all over for their cattle/them.*

look for	nềmā	nànnềmà [3]	look all over for
buy	sàyā	sàssayà	buy a variety of things

(c) Verbs with all tones high remain all high :

bring	kāwō	kakkāwō	keep on bringing
call	kirā	kikkirā	call various people
sell	sayar	sassayar	keep on selling

(d) Three-syllable verbs [4] merely reduplicate the first syllable (tone and all) [5] while retaining the original tone pattern on the original three syllables :

read	karàntā	kakkaràntā	read in succession
ask	tàmbayà	tàntàmbayà	keep on asking

3. An *adjectival nominal* may be formed from most transitive and certain intransitive verbs by reduplicating and doubling the final consonant of the original word, while replacing the final vowel with an **-aCCē** suffix (**CC** = doubled final consonant of the original word). The meaning of such a form is typically *something which has been . . ., something characterized by. . . .* These, like other adjectival nominals, have feminine as well as plural forms (the examples below list the forms in the order : masculine, feminine, plural).

(a) These forms *derived from two-syllable words* have the initial syllable low toned, with all following syllables

---

[3] When the original verb has an -ē- or an -ō- in the root, this becomes -a- in the reduplicate syllable, if this -ē- or -ō- is preceded by a *velar* consonant (**k, g, ƙ**), it becomes **-ya-** and **-wa-** respectively, e.g. **kḕtà,** *tear,* **kyakkḕtā,** *tear to shreds* ; **gògā,** *rub (against)*, **gwàggōgà,** *rub vigorously (against)*.

[4] See footnote 2 on page 176.

[5] Some verbs, in addition to a form which shows first syllable reduplication, have an alternative form (with the same meaning) in which it is the second syllable that is reduplicated, e.g. **ajìyē,** *put down/aside→* **ar'ajìyē/a"ajìyē** or **ajìjìyē,** *put down/aside a number of things.*

high except for the plural form, in which all syllables
are low except the final one, e.g. :

(cikà,	cìkakkē cìkkakkiyā,[6] cìkàkkū
fill)	(something) filled, complete
(dafà,	dàfaffē, dàfaffiyā, dàfàffū
cook)	(something) cooked
(fārà,	fàrarrē, fàrarriyā, fàràrrū
start)	(something) started
(ganī,	gànannē, gànanniyā, gànànnū
see)	(something) seen
(mântā,	màntaccē, màntacciyā, màntàttū
forget)	(something) forgotten
(nēmā,	nèmammē, nèmammiyā, nèmàmmū
look for)	(something) sought)
(sanì,	sànannē, sànanniyā, sànànnū
know)	(something) known

(*b*) These forms *derived from three-syllable words* have the
first two syllables low, with all following syllables
high except for the plural form, in which all syllables
are low except the final one, e.g. :

(ajìyē,	àjìyayyē, àjìyayyiyā,[6] àjìyàyyū
set aside)	(something) set aside
(fàhimtà,	fàhìmtaccē, fàhìmtacciyā, fàhìmtàttū
understand)	(something) understood
(lāfiyà,[7]	làfìyayyē, làfìyayyiyā, làfìyàyyū
health)	healthy (person or thing)
(tabbàtā,	tàbbàtaccē, tàbbàtacciyā, tàbbàtàttū
be sure)	(something) certain
(tàfasà,	tàfàsasshē, tàfàsasshiyā, tàfàsàssū
boil)	(something) boiled

---

[6] There is an alternative feminine form in **-aCCā**, which is not
uncommon, especially with the longer words, e.g. **tàfàsassā**.

[7] This form is derived from a noun rather than a verb. It is
apparently the only such exception in the whole language.

Examples :

Mūjìyā sànanniyā cè à ƙasarmù.	The owl is well-known in our country.
Dàfaffen àbinci nè mu kè sô.	We want *cooked* food.
Zīnārìyā nèmammiyar àbā cè.[8]	Gold is a sought after (*i.e.* valuable thing).
Mu kàn shā tàfàssasshen ruwā kawài.	We drink only boiled water.
Tàbbàtaccē nè.	It is certain.

4. Certain *nouns indicating a quality* have a derivative adjectival nominal which is formed by reduplicating the first syllable and changing the final vowel to **-ā**. The tone pattern of the new form is low-high-high in the singular. The plural form (which duplicates the final consonant in an **-àCā** suffix) has a high-low-high pattern. The meaning is usually intensive.[9]

(**ƙarfī,** *strength*)	**ƙà k̃ƙarfā, ƙarfàfā** (*pl.*)	very strong thing/ person
(**kyâu,** *goodness*)	**kyàkkyāwā, kyāwàwā** (*pl.*)	excellent (looking) thing/person

Examples :

Màcè kyàkkyāwā cè.	The woman is beautiful.
Sū ƙarfàfā nè.	They are very strong.
Kyāwàwā na sàyā.	I bought very good looking ones.

5. *Adverbial nominals and ideophones* may be intensified by reduplicating the whole word (see also Lesson 24, section 3).

---

[8] Where the noun to which it refers is feminine **àbù,** *thing,* has a feminine form **àbā.** Many Hausa, however, would say **Zīnārìyā nèmammen àbù nè.**

[9] I.e. more so than a simple **mài** compound, e.g. **mài zurfī,** *deep* ; **zùzzurfā,** *very deep.*

(maza,
  quickly) **Kù zō maza-maza !**   Come very quickly !
(shirū,   **Audù shiru-shirū**   Audu is very soft
  silence)   **nè.**   spoken.
(sànnu,   **Yanà tàfiyà sànnu-**
  slowness)   **sànnu.**   He is walking slowly.

6. Complete reduplication of *adjectival nominals of colour* and some others lessens their intensity (see also Lesson 23, section 7). Note that the final vowel becomes short in both the second and (with few exceptions, like **jā-ja** below) the first occurrence of the reduplicated word.[10]

(farī, *white*)   **Nā sàyi fari-fari.**   I bought the whitish
                                            one.
(baƙī, *black*)   **Baƙi-baƙi yā fi kyâu.** The blackish one is
                                            best.
(jā, *red*)   **Wannàn, jā-ja nè.**   This is reddish/pink.
                 Waɗànnân jājàye-   These are reddish/
                 jājàye nè.   pink.
(tsōfō, *old*)   **Tsōfuwa-tsōfuwa cè.**   She is rather elderly.

7. Complete reduplication of quantifiers and monetary terms is employed to give the sense of, for example, ' two each '.[11]

Sīsì sīsì nē.   They are 5 kobos each.
Bà su gōmà gōmà.   Give them each ten.
Nawà nawà nē waɗànnân ?   How much apiece are these ?
Màsu ƙafà huɗu huɗu.   Quadrupeds.

---

[10] In a few cases the vowel remains *long* and the meaning is *intensive*, e.g. **Sū mânyā-mânyā nè**, *They are very large/important* (*of people*).

[11] If the quantifier is a compound only the last word is repeated, e.g. **yā bà sù nairà shâ ɗaya dà sī-sīsì**, *he gave them* ₦11·6 *each*: **kuɗinsù sulè bâ kwabò kwabò**, *they cost nine pence apiece.*

8. The plurals of certain nouns are formed by reduplication (see also Lesson 22, section 6).

en'è, *pl.* en'è-en'è   Native Administration
àkàwū, *pl.* àkàwū-àkàwū   clerk (other plurals also occur)

9. Complete reduplication plus final -e and a low-high tone pattern is employed with many *nouns denoting an activity* to indicate (frequently) something like *varieties of* . . ., *various kinds of* . . . or simply *a number of instances of this kind of activity*, e.g. :

gudū, running → gùje-gùje, running (various types of) races
tsallē, jumping → tsàlle-tsàlle, (various kings of) jumping [11]
tādì, chatting → tàɗe-tàɗe, (various) chattings
shāwarà, advising → shàwàrce-shàwàrce, advisings (of various kinds).

10. Complete reduplication of *certain nouns* may be employed to indicate . . . *like*. Note that the final vowels are short.

ruwa-ruwa   watery, liquid (*i.e.* water-like)
gàri-gàri   powdery (*i.e.* flour-like)
gishiri-gishiri   salty (in taste)

VOCABULARY

Nominals
àkàwū (*pl.* akāwunà *or*
    àkàwū-àkàwū)   clerk
ɗanyē (*f.* ɗanyā, *pl.* ɗànyū)   raw, uncooked, unripe
firāmàrè   primary school

---

[12] Thus the term for *track and field competition* is gùje-gùje dà tsàlle-tsàlle.

giyà (*f.*)	beer (local brew)
gwangwan (*pl.* **gwangwàyē**)	tin can
jarràbâwā (*f.*)	test, examination
kwalabā/kwalbā (*f.*) (*pl.* **kwalàbē**)	glass bottle
kyàkkyāwā (*pl.* **kyawàwā**)	excellent (looking), hand-some, beautiful
ƙārā (*f.*)	a complaint (*e.g.* in court), cry, noise
ragì	reduction (as in trading)
sakandàrè	secondary school
simintì/sumuntì	cement
tàbbàtaccē	(something) certain
takàrdā (*f.*) (*pl.* **tàkàrdū**)	paper, letter
Tūrai	Europe
yādì	European cloth, a yard (measurement)
zīnārìyā (*f.*)	gold

Verbals

ajìyē	put (thing) down, set (aside), give (thing to someone else to keep for you)
fàhimtà (i/ē)	understand
tàfasà	boil (intransitive)

Particles

câ	thinking (from **cêwā**; see *Important Phrases* below)
shirū	silence (ideophone)

Important Phrases

àbin màmākì	an amazing thing
àbin shâ	something to drink, a drink
àbin shâ na kwalabā	bottled drink

bâ ragì	no reduction (of price—in trading)
bàbban àkàwū	head clerk
bā dà màmākì	cause amazement, wonder
câ na kè	I thought (*lit.* thinking I was)
ci jarràbâwā	pass an examination
nan ƙasā	(in) this country
yi jarràbâwā	take an examination

EXERCISES

Translate into English :

1. Ai, nā mântā ìn kāwō àbinci dàfaffē. Nā kāwō shì ɗanyē.
2. Gwàmmà kà dākàtā nân tùkùn. Kàfìn kà sākò dāwôwā lōkàcin àbinci yā yi.
3. Mun tàntàmbayà kō'ìnā cikin gàrī àmmā bà mù sàmi làbārìnsà ba.
4. Kâi! Wani àbin màmākì yā fàru jiyà—ƙarar jirgin samà tā bā nì tsòrō har saurā kàɗan ìn gudù!
5. Zâ ni kàntī ìn sàyi àbincin gwangwan dà giyà ta kwalabā dà sauran abūbuwàn dà na kè bùkātà.

Translate into Hausa :

1. How much apiece are guavas ? A penny apiece, no reduction.
2. I thought you would come tomorrow but you came yesterday.
3. There are many wonderful things in the world today.
4. You should eat cooked food and boiled water lest you get ill.
5. If I don't take the examination I won't pass it.

Dialogue

Talle :   Daudà !
Daudà : Nà'am.

Talle :   Ìnā zâ ka ?
Daudà :   Zâ ni gidā. Yànzu nè na tāsō dàgà aikì.
Talle :   Tò bâ lâifī. À ìnā nè ka kè aikì ?
Daudà :   Ai, nī àkàwū nè à kàntī.
Talle :   Àshē ? Câ na kè kanà makarantā.
Daudà :   Â'à. Bàra nè na fita firāmàrè. Bàn sàmi shìgar
           sakandàrè ba.
Talle :   Bà kà ci jarràbâwā ba nè ?
Daudà :   Ì, tā yi minì wùyā ainùn. Àmmā bâ kōmē, tun
           dà na sàmi aikì.
Talle :   Tò dà kyâu. Wànè irìn aikì nē ka kè yî ?
Daudà :   Ai, inà dà ayyukà irì-irì : wani sā'ì na kàn
           shisshìryà kāyā, wani sā'ì na kàn sayad dà kāyā,
           wani sā'ì mā, bàbban àkàwū yanà bā nì aikìn
           takàrdā ìn yi.
Talle :   Tô. Yawancin kāyankù dàgà ƙasàshen Tūrai nè
           a kè kāwō sù ?
Daudà :   Ì. Àmmā yànzu an fārà yîn waɗansu abūbuwà
           nan ƙasā—kàmar su tākalmà, dà yādì, dà
           simintì, dà àbin shâ na kwalabā.
Talle :   Mādàllā ! Gàskiyā nè sai dà tàfàsasshen ruwā
           a kè yîn àbin shâ na kwalabā ?
Daudà :   Sòsai ! Bà kàmar irìn tāmù giyàr ba !
Talle :   Àbincin gwangwan fà—dukànsà dàfaffē nè ?
Daudà :   Hakà nē. Wai, sā'àn dà a kè shirìnsà anà
           daddàfâwā.[13]
Talle :   Tabdì. Àbin màmākì nē yaddà yā yìwu à dafà
           àbinci dà yawà à rufè shi cikin gwangwan à
           ajìyē shi har shèkarà bìyar !
Daudà :   Gàskiyarkà. Ai, hakà nē dūniyà yànzu—cìke
           ta kè dà abūbuwà màsu ban [14] màmākì.
Talle :   Lallē, hakà nē.

---

[13] Verbal noun from daddàfā.
[14] See Lesson 19, footnote 2.

Lesson 29

The Relaters Sai and Dà

1. The relaters **sai** and **dà** (the spelling of which actually represents several different words) are among the most frequently occurring words in the Hausa language. They each have a wide variety of usages, the more important of which, not already noted in Lesson 17, section 2, are treated below.

2. **Sai** as a clause introducer is often followed by the subjunctive aspect. There are two kinds of meaning indicated by this construction :

(*a*) The weaker (and more common) meaning is to indicate a regular contingent habit or an inevitable contingent consequence, e.g. : [1]

In nā tāshì dà sāfē sai in shā tî	When I get up in the morning I (always) have a cup of tea.
In bà kà bâ ganyên nan ruwā ba, sai yà mutù	If you don't water that plant, it will surely die.
Ìdan yā zō, sai mù gaishē shì.	When(ever) he comes we will (certainly) greet him.

(*b*) The stronger meaning, often limited to shorter contexts, is as a strong command, typically meaning *must*, *ought to* or the like, e.g. :

Sai kà tàfi.	You ought to go, *or* Get away !

[1] See Lesson 24, dialogue (footnoted phrases), for two additional examples.

Bài zō ba tùkùna. Sai mù   He hasn't come yet. We'll
kirā shì.   have to call him.

3. Stylized utterances such as **sai kà cê**, *as if*, and (less
frequently) **sai kà ganī**, *you ought to see it*, are frequently
interjected for emphasis.

Yanà tàfiyà, sai kà cê sarkī.   He goes around as if he
                                     were a chief.
Aikìnsà, sai kà cê bài iyà ba.   His work (is) as if he
                                     doesn't know how.
Wannàn àbù, sai kà ganī,   This thing—you'll have to
àbin màmākì nē.   see it (to believe it)—is
                                     really amazing.

4. **Sai** often introduces a nominal phrase which indicates
an exception to the preceding statement. (See also
Lesson 17, section 2.)

Bâ mài iyàwā sai kai.   There is none able to do it
                                     except you.
Bā à sāmùn ilmì sai dà   One doesn't get knowledge
ƙò ƙarī.   without (a lot of) effort.
Nī kàm, sai àbîn dà ka cê.   As for me (I'll do) only
                                     what you say.

5. **Sai** meaning *until* often introduces clauses in the completive, sometimes in the continuative.[2]

Bà zân tàfi ba sai nā gamà.   I won't go until I finish.
Bà zân tàfi ba sai inà sôn   I won't go until I want to
tàfiyà.   go.
Sai kā dāwō.   See you when (*lit.* until) you
                                    return.

[2] Quite often, though not invariably, the **sai**-introduced clause is
a dependent clause following an independent clause in the negative
(see the first two examples).

Sai nā shiryà tùkùna.	(Don't bother me.) Let me get ready first.
Sai yā zō zā mù ci.	We won't eat until he comes (*lit.* Only when he has come will we eat).

6. **Sai** and **har** each often mean *until*. When, as often, a contrast is intended, **har** focuses on the completion or fulfilment of the action at the end of the prescribed time, whereas **sai** may simply refer to the action in general or focus on the start of it, e.g. :

Bà zân tàfi ba sai gòbe.	I won't go until tomorrow.
Bà zân tàfi ba har gòbe.	I won't go (at least) until tomorrow (has come).
Bàn yi barcī ba sai dà gàrī ya wāyè.	I didn't get to sleep until dawn.
Bàn yi barcī ba har gàrī ya wāyè.	I didn't get a wink of sleep all night.

7. **Sai** is frequent in narrative as a clause (sentence) introducer indicating sequence and translatable as *then* or *so*. (See also Lesson 17, section 4.)

Mun gan shì nan dà nan. Sai mukà gaishē shì.
We saw him immediately. Then/so we greeted him.
Sun zō. Sai sukà zaunà. Sai sukà hūtà sòsai.
They came. (Then) they sat down. (Then) they rested well.

8. **Dà . . . sai** is commonly used for *when . . . then*, with reference to events in the past.

Dà na gan shì (sai) nā jē wurinsà.	When I saw him (then) I went to him.
Dà zuwànsà [3] **sai aikì.**	When he comes (then) (there's a lot of) work.

---

[3] **Dà zuwànsà**, lit. *on his coming.* A verbal noun may usually be substituted for a finite verb in this construction.

Dà ya shìga (sai) mukà   When he entered (then) we
tsayà.   stopped.

9. **Dà** meaning *with* or *and* is amply illustrated in Lesson
17, sections 2 and 3. The use of **dà** as introducer of the
direct object after the **-ar** form of a verb is treated in
Lesson 25, section 4 and following. **Dà** meaning *when* is
illustrated above. **Dà** as introducer of the thing possessed
after the continuative is illustrated in Lesson 18,
sections 5 and 6.

10. **Dà** (or **wandà**) is employed to introduce relative
clauses. It may mean *that, whom,* etc. (See also Lesson 20,
sections 5 and 6.)

àbîn dà na ganī   the thing that I see
lōkàcîn dà zâi tàfi   when (= the time that) he
                               will go
an kòri mùtumìn dà akà   they chased away the man
   aikō   that was sent
yārò wandà bâ shi dà
   hankàlī   a boy who has no sense

11. **Dà** is employed as an auxiliary with certain other
relaters.

Tun dà bài bā mù ba bâ   Since he didn't give it to us
   kōmē.   it doesn't matter.
Kō dà bài gan mù ba munà   (Even) though he didn't see
   wurîn.   us, we were there.

VOCABULARY

Nominals
àgōgō (*pl.* **agōgunà**)   watch, clock
àlāmà/hàlāmà (*f.*) (*pl.*
   àlàmū, alāmōmī)   indication, sign
àlkalàmī (*pl.* **alkalumà**)   pen

àlmakàshī (*pl.* **àlmàkàsai**)	(pair of) scissors
awà (*f.*)	hour
bukkà (*f.*) (*pl.* **bukkōkī**)	grass hut ; market stall
cìyāwà (*f.*) (*pl.* **cìyàyī**)	grass
dinkì	sewing
hūtū	vacation, rest
kàkī	khaki cloth
kirkì	excellence of character **or** quality
madinkī (*pl.* **madinkā**)	tailor
sàna'à (*f.*) (*pl.* **sana'ō'ī**)	trade, occupation, profession
tufāfì (*sing.* **tufà**)	garments, clothes
wàhalà (*f.*)	trouble, difficulty
wàndō (*pl.* **wandunà**)	trousers

Verbals

dinkà	sew, make by sewing
hanà [4]	prevent, hinder, keep from, refuse, forbid
jirā	wait for
kau/kawad (**dà**)	move to another place, alter position of
nūnà [5]	point out, show
tàimakà (**i/ē**)	help, assist
yankà	cut (up), slaughter

Particles

kàm	(emphasis particle) at least, at any rate, as for . . .

---

[4] Typical examples of the way **hanà** is employed are : **yā hanà ni/ minì aikì** = *he kept me from working* or *he kept me from getting a job ;* **kadà kà hanà masà àbinci** = *don't refuse him food ;* **an hanà shân giyà** = *beer drinking is proscribed.*

[5] An indirect object is very frequent with **nūnà**, e.g. **yā nūnà minì** = *he showed me ;* **nā nūnà masà hanyà** = *I showed him the road ;* **tā nūnà wà yārò àbincinsà** = *she showed the boy his food* ; but **yā nūnà ƙarfinsà** = *he showed his strength.*

wàtò   that is, . . . (the preceding
                              statement is then re-
                              phrased to clarify it),
                              namely, viz.

Important Phrases
kèken ɗinkì   sewing machine
sai kà cê   like, as if
sai kà ganī   you have to see it (to believe
                                  it)
shā wàhalà   have (*lit.* drink) difficulty,
                                  suffer

EXERCISES

Translate into English :

1. Yā kàmātà in yankà wannàn yādì. Ɗàuki àlmakàshī
   kà tàimàkē nì.
2. Shī bà mùtumìn kirkì ba nè. Yanà sô yà hanà àbōkīnā
   aikì.
3. Dà ya shiga bukkàrsà sai ya zaunà, ya fārà ɗinkì.
4. Zân jirā shì. Wàtò, zân dākàtā nân sai yā dāwō.
5. Àkwai àlāmà zā kà shā wàhalà nân idan bà kà kawad
   dà kāyankà dà wuri ba.

Translate into Hausa :

1. Sew me a good (looking) gown. I am going to the
   dance tomorrow.
2. I want you to help me to move my sewing machine to
   another stall.
3. As for me I will wait for him here—perhaps he will
   come after a while.
4. I didn't show him your watch. They say he saw it on
   your wrist (arm).
5. He hasn't eaten yet. Why ? Because I refused him
   food until you arrived.

Dialogue

Hārūnà : Sànnu maɗinkì !

Gàmbo : Af Hārūnà ! Barkà dà yâmmā.

Hārūnà : Barkà kàdai. Ìnā aikì yâu ?

Gàmbo : Aikì, ai bā yà ƙārèwā.

Hārūnà : Mādàllā. Hakà a kè sô.

Gàmbo : Gàskiyarkà. Kanà yāwò à kàsuwā nè ?

Hārūnà : Ā'à. Dâ mā inà nēman bukkàrkà.[6]

Gàmbo : Tô. Rân nan na kau dà kāyānā zuwà nân.

Hārūnà : Dà kyâu. Dâ kanà cikin bukkà ta ciyāwà àmmā wannàn ta kwānò[7] cē.

Gàmbo : Hakà nē. Nā yi sā'à kè nan.

Hārūnà : Mādàllā. Zā kà iyà kà ɗinkà minì waɗansu tufāfì nē ?

Gàmbo : Ai sàna'àtā cè. Wànè irì nē ka kè sô ?

Hārūnà : Inà bùkātàr gàjēren wàndō gùdā biyu dà bàbbar rìgā kumā.

Gàmbo : Tò bâ lâifì. Kā zō dà yāɗì nē ?

Hārūnà : Ì. Gà kàkì na yîn wandunà dà farin yāɗì na yîn rìgā. Nawà nē kuɗin ɗinkì ?

Gàmbo : Dukà zâi kai sulè àrbà'in dà biyar—wàtò, nairà huɗu dà sulè biyar kè nan.

Hārūnà : Kâi, yā yi yawà ! In bà kà yàrda dà nairà huɗu ba, sai in nèmi wani.

Gàmbo : Tò nā yàrda. Àjiyè yāɗin càn.

Hārūnà : Dà kyâu. Sai yàushè zân zō in kàrɓā ?

Gàmbo : Sai gòbe ai. Bà zân iyà gamà ɗinkìnsù dukà yâu ba.

Hārūnà : Tô, sai gòbe kè nan.

Gàmbo : Yâuwā, sai gòbe.

---

[6] The addition of **mā** to **dâ** completely alters the meaning from *formerly (but no longer)* to *formerly too*, i.e. *anyway, in any case, all along*.

[7] I.e. made of corrugated iron or aluminium roofing materials.

Lesson 30

Prefixes and Suffixes

1. Hausa employs a number of prefixes and suffixes to change basic forms of words into words with more specialized meanings. Certain prefixes and suffixes have already been described (see Lessons 25 and 28), but several others are common enough to warrant mention here.

2. **Bà-** = *place of origin, profession.*

(a) Certain nouns may be prefixed with **bà-** in the singular with the resultant form indicating the *place of origin* of the person referred to. The masculine forms usually end in -**è** with initial and final low tones (all other tones high). These words have feminine and plural forms as well, as illustrated below.

(Kanò)	Bàkanè̀/Bàkanò̀, Bàkanùwā, Kanāwā	Kano person
(Hausā)	Bàhaushè̀, Bàhaushìyā, Hàusàwā	Hausa person
(Tūrai)	Bàtūrè̀, Bàtūrìyā, Tùràwā/ Tūrāwā	European person
	Bàfàransì̀, Bàfàransìyā, Fàrànsâi	Frenchman
	Bàfilācè̀, Bàfilātà̀, Filànī	Fulani person

(b) Other nouns may be prefixed with **bà-** in the singular to form nouns indicating the *occupation* of the person referred to. The tone rules are usually the same as those above, but the final vowel of the masculine form varies. Feminine forms are not common (nor are women who have these occupations).

	bàdūkù, dùkàwā [1]	leatherworker
(fādà, *chief's* palace, *court*)	bàfādà/bàfādè, fàdàwā	courtier
(sarkī, *chief*)	bàsarākè, sarākunà/ sàràkai [2]	office-holder under a chief

3. The noun ɗā, *son*, is widely used (in the form ɗan ; *f.* 'yar ; *pl.* 'yan) as a prefix (although it is written as a separate word) in the following senses :

(*a*) To indicate *place of origin :*

ɗan Kanò, 'yar Kanò, 'yan Kanò	Kano person
ɗan ƙasā, 'yan ƙasā	local inhabitant(s) of a country, son(s) of the soil

(*b*) To indicate *occupation :*

ɗan kàsuwā, 'yar kàsuwā, 'yan kàsuwā	market trader
ɗan tēbùr, etc.	petty market trader (who displays his goods on a table)

(*c*) As a *diminutive :*

ɗan yārò	little boy
'yar kàsuwā	small market
'yan kāyā	small belongings
cikin ɗan lōkàcī	in a short time

---

[1] These may have originated from a place called **Dūkù**.

[2] These plurals are also employed for **sarkī**, but there is seldom any confusion of meaning since any given town or region has only one **sarkī**.

(d) In certain *stylized expressions* :

ɗan sàndā, 'yan sàndā	Government policeman (*lit.* son of a stick)
ɗan dòkā, 'yan dòkā	N.A. (= Native or Local Authority) policeman (*lit.* son of an order)
ɗan Adàm, 'yan Adàm	human being (*lit.* son of Adam)
'yar cikī	type of gown

(e) 'Dan (never 'yar or 'yan) is used with verbs (with or without kàɗan) signifying *a little (bit)* :

Nā ɗan dākàtā (kàɗan).	I waited a bit.
Yā ɗan tūrè shi.	He pushed it a little.
Sai kà ɗan ragè kuɗinsà.	You should lower the price a bit.

4. Various types of nouns may be formed from verbs by employing a **ma-** prefix with or without an **-ī** suffix :

(a) Nouns signifying the *agent or doer of an action* are formed by prefixing the **ma-** and (usually) suffixing an **-ī**. The tones on the masculine form are high-low for two-syllable words, high-low-(low-)high for three- and four-syllable words. Feminine (sometimes) and plural (usually) forms of these words also occur. Forms having the **-ī** (high tone) suffix take a ' referential ' **-n** before a modifying noun or pronoun, e.g. **masòyin Sāratù, masòyinkà**; the others do not, e.g. **majì dādī**.

(fi,	mafì/mafìyī, *pl.* mafìyā	
surpass)	surpassing, exceeding, e.g. :	
	Wannàn mafì kyâu nē.	This is the best one.
	mafì tsàdā	more expensive

| (sŏ, *want,* | masŏ ³/masòyī, masōyìyā, masòyā |
| *love*) | one who likes or loves, e.g. : |

Masòyinkà bā yà	Your close friend
ganin aibùnkà.	doesn't see your
	faults.

| masòyin Sāratù | one who loves Sarah |
| masòyin shìnkāfā | one who likes rice |

| (ji, *hear,* | majì/majìyī, majiyìyā, majìyā |
| *feel*) | hearer, feeler, e.g. : |

| majì dādī | happy person |

| (rasà, | maràs/maràshī, marashìyā, maràsā |
| *lack*) | lacking in . . ., e.g. : |

| maràshin hankàlī, | senseless |
| (See also Lesson 23, section 6.) |

| (àikā, | ma'àikī, ma'àikā |
| *send*) | messenger ⁴ |

| (aikàtā, | ma'àikàcī, ma'aikacìyā, ma'àikàtā |
| *do work*) | worker |

| (ɗinkà, | maɗìnkī, maɗinkìyā, maɗìnkā |
| *sew*) | tailor |

| (fàutā, *cut* | mahàuci, mahàutā |
| *up meat*) | butcher, meat-seller |

(haifù	mahàifī, mahaifìyā, mahàifā
give	parent
birth)	

| (haukàcē, | mahàukàcī, mahaukacìyā, mahàukàtā |
| *go mad*) | madman |

| (ƙerà, | maƙèrī, maƙèrā |
| *forge*) | blacksmith |

---

³ The short form **masŏ** is regularly employed with the meaning *tending toward* to denote the intermediate points of the compass, e.g. **arèwā masŏ gabàs** = *north-east,* **kudù masŏ yâmma** = *south-west,* etc.

⁴ The meaning here is passive, i.e. one who is sent (compare **maciyī** = (i) *glutton,* (ii) *dependent* (i.e. *one fed by you*)). The word is mainly used of the Prophet in the expression **Ma'àikin Allà,** *God's Messenger.*

(b) Nouns signifying a *place* where the activity indicated
by the original verb is performed are also formed by
prefixing **ma-**. The ending may be either **-ā** or **-ī**.
The tones on the singular form are all high.

(**aunà,** *measure, weigh*)	**ma'aunā, mà'àunai**	place where corn is sold
(**ajìyē,** *set aside*)	**ma'ajī, mà'àjìyai**	storehouse
(**dafà,** *cook*)	**madafā/madafī, màdàfai**	kitchen, cooking-place
(**fàutā,** *cut up meat*)	**mahautā, màhàutai**	place where meat is sold
(**karàntā,** *read*)	**makarantā, màkàràntū**	school
(**sàllàtà,** *perform a* **sallà**)	**masallācī, màsàllàtai**	mosque, place of Muslim prayers

(c) Nouns signifying a *tool* or *implement* involved in the
action indicated by the original verb are formed by
prefixing **ma-** and suffixing **-ī**. The tones on the
masculine form are all high.

(**aunà,** *measure, weigh*)	**ma'aunī, mà'àunai**	any measure, scales
(**būɗè,** *open*)	**mabūɗī, màbùɗai**	key
(**gìrbā,** *reap*)	**magirbī, màgìrbai**	type of harvesting tool
(**gwadà,** *measure*)	**magwajī, màgwàdai**	measuring rod
(**kaɗà,** *beat a drum*)	**makaɗī, màkàɗai**	drum stick

5. A **-ancī** (sometimes **-cī**) suffix is employed with ethnic terms to indicate the *language (and customs) of* .... All tones are high.

(**Tūrai,** Europe)	**Tūrancī**	European language (in Nigeria this usually means English)
(**Kanò,** Kano)	**Kanancī**	language (dialect) of Kano
(**Zazzàu,** Zaria)	**Zazzagancī**	language (dialect) of Zaria
(**Bàlārabè,** Arab)	**Lārabcī**	Arabic language

A rather humorous (but acceptable) term to designate the mixture of Hausa and English in which many bilinguals converse has recently come into currency.

It is :

      mālamancī   (from **mālàm,** *educated person*)

So, too :

      bībīsancī   (from B.B.C., *the Hausa of the B.B.C. Hausa broadcasts*).

6. Certain abstract nouns may be formed from more definite nouns by using the following suffixes :

(*a*) **-ntakà, -antakà** = *the quality of being* .... The tones are low-low-high-low :

(**bēbē,** *deaf mute*)	**bèbàntakà**	deaf-muteness
(**mùtûm,** *person*)	**mùtùntakà**	human nature (with its frailties)
(**gwaurō,** *wifeless man*)	**gwàuràntakà**	state of wifelessness

| (shḗgḕ, *bastard*) [5] | shḕgàntakà | impudence, rascality |
| (yārò, *boy*) | yàràntakà | childishness |

(b) **-ntà, -ncì, -tā, -ntā** = *that possessed by* . . . :

(gwànī, *expert*)	gwànintà	skill
(ƙanƙanè, *a little*)	ƙanƙantà	smallness
(mùtûm, *man*)	mutuncì	manliness, self-respect, integrity
(bāwà, *slave*)	bàutā	slavery
(gàjērē, *a short thing*)	gajartà	shortness
(angò, *bridegroom*)	angwancì	state of being a bridegroom
(ādàlī, *just person*)	ādalcì	justness, righteousness
(mūgù, *evil thing*)	mùgùntā [6]	wickedness

7. Nouns may be formed from certain verbs by using the following suffixes :

(a) **-ayyà** = *repetition* and/or *reciprocity, settled attitude* :

(bùgā, *hit*)	bùgayyà	exchanging blows
(sō, *love*)	sòyayyà	mutual love
(jā, *pull*)	jàyayyà	controversy, dispute
(ji, *hear*)	jìyayyà	being on good terms, mutual trust
(àurā, *marry*)	àuràtayyà	intermarriage
(ƙi, *hate*)	ƙìyayyà	mutual hatred
(bi, *follow, obey*)	bìyayyà	obedience, loyalty

(b) **-au** = *person or thing characterized by* :

| (mântā, *forget*) | màntau | forgetful person |
| (màkarà, *be late*) | màkàrau | dilatory person |

[5] This term is used in Hausa (as in English) as a term of abuse. Note that the meaning of the derived form is taken from the figurative (rather than the literal) meaning of the original noun.

[6] Note the shortening of the first -u- here.

VOCABULARY

Nominals

dilā (*pl.* **dilōlī**)	jackal
gìndī	base, bottom, buttocks, foundation
girbì	harvest
guntū (*f.* **guntuwā**, *pl.* **guntàyē**)	short (thing)
gwànī (*f.* **gwànā**, *pl.* **gwanàyē**)	expert
gwànintà	skill, expertise
hànkākà (*m.*) (*pl.* **hànkàkī**)	crow
kallō	watching, looking at
kûnnē (*pl.* **kunnuwà**)	ear(s)
mabūdī (*pl.* **màbūɗai**)	key
macìjī (*pl.* **màcìzai**) [7]	snake (*lit.* ' biter ')
mahàucī (*pl.* **mahàutā**)	butcher, meat-seller
mahàukàcī (*pl.* **mahàukàtā**)	madman
màimakon	instead of, in return for (from **màimakō,** *substitute*)
makàɗi (*pl.* **makàɗā**)	drummer
makèrī (*pl.* **makèrā**)	blacksmith
sàndā (*pl.* **sandunà**)	stick, force
shìnkāfā (*f.*)	rice

Verbals

aunà	measure, weigh
cìzā (**i/ē**)	bite
dòkā (*v.n.* **dūkà**)	beat, strike, thrash
fāɗō	fall down (here)
gìrbā (**i/ē**)	reap, harvest
kasà	arrange in heaps, dispose (with **kûnnē** = *listen*)
màkarà	be late

[7] This plural, note, is irregular (it should be **macìzā**). Also the verb used of a snake biting is usually **sàrā,** not **cìzā.**

rasà	lack, be short of, lose
rḗrà	(with wāƙà = *compose and sing*)
sàrā (i/ē)	chop down (a tree), (snake) bite
tūrè	push, knock over

Particles

kaɗai	only
ƙùrùnƙus	the story is over!
shḗgè!	damn it! (very strong swear-word, *lit.* 'bastard')

Important Phrases

arḕwā masò yâmmā	north-west
ɗan sàndā (*pl.* 'yan sàndā)	Government policeman
kasà kûnnē	prick up one's ears, dispose one's ears to listen
nā rasà yaddà zân yi	I don't know what to do
rērà wāƙà	(compose and) sing a song
'yan ƙasā	' sons of the soil '

EXERCISES

Translate into English :

1. Macìjī yā sàri ma'àikī àmmā likità yā bā shì māgànī har yā warkè.
2. Shī bà Bàhaushè ba nè, Bàfilācè nē. Àmmā duk dà hakà yā iyà Kanancī.
3. Zāriyà kudù masò yâmmā ta kè dà Kanò. Kàtsinà, arḕwā masò yâmmā ta kè dà ita.
4. Dā zā mù yi aikìmmù tàre àmmā shī yā màkarà. Sabòdà hakà nā rasà àbîn dà zân sayar à kàsuwā.
5. Mūsā gwànī nè. Bā wandà ya iyà irìn wannàn aikì sai shī kaɗai. Yā kàmātà mù nèmē shì màimakon Audù.

Translate into Hausa :

1. He's a forgetful person. Don't tell him to do anything for you.
2. In a short time all the workers had left. I didn't know what to do.
3. Bring the key here. Let me open the door.
4. I waited a bit until the drummers began to pay attention.
5. I think if his wife sings a song the chief will be surprised.

Fable

Dilā Sarkin Dàbārà [8]

Wata rānā wani hànkākà yanà yāwò. Yanà nēman àbîn dà zâi ci. Sai ya ga wani guntun nāmà à ƙasà kusa dà wani dūtsè. Ya sàuka, ya sâ bàkī ya ɗaukà. Ya tāshì samà dà nāmàn à bàkinsà ya sàuka bisà wani itàcē.

Àshē dilā yanà kallonsà—yā ga duk àbîn dà hànkākà ya yi. Dilā, kumā, yanà jîn yunwà. Yanà sô yà sàmi nāmàn. Sai ya yi dàbāràr dà zâi sāmù.[9]

Sai dilā ya tàfi gìndin itàcē, ya gai dà hànkākà. Ya cè masà, ' Kâi, rân nan na ji kanà rērà wāƙà. Muryàrkà, kùwā, dà dāɗī ta kè ainùn. Sai yàushè zân sākè jîn wāƙà irìn tākà kumā ? '

Hànkākà, dai, ya kasà kûnnē. Àbîn dà dilā ya fàɗā ya yi masà dāɗī. Dà ya ji hakà sai ya mântā dà àbîn dà kè cikin bàkinsà. Ya būɗè bàkinsà. Zâi rērà wāƙà kè nan.

Shī kè nan ! Sai nāmàn ya fāɗō. Dilā ya ɗaukà, ya cè, ' Mādàllā '. Ya tàfi dà shī. Kùrùnƙus !

---

[8] See *Ka Koyi Karatu*, page 9, for another version of this story.
[9] ' He made a plan to get it.'

Part Three

Reference

Lesson 31

Greetings II

1. In Lesson 4 a number of the most common greetings were introduced. It is the aim of this lesson to provide the student with a much longer (though still by no means complete) list of typical greetings than was necessary earlier in the course.

2. General greetings :

Greeting		Reply	
sànnu	hello	yâuwā, sànnu	hello
		sànnu dai	hello
		sànnu kàdai	hello
sànnu-sànnu	hello	(same replies as for sànnu)	
sànnunkù	hello (to several)	(same replies as for sànnu)	
sànnunkì	hello (to a woman)	(same replies as for sànnu)	
lāfiyà ?	are you well ?	lāfiyà	all's well
		lāfiyà lau	very well
		lāfiyà ƙalau	very well
		lāfiyà dai	all's well
		lāfiyà, bâ kōmē	all's well
ìnā gàjiyà ?	how's your tiredness ?	bâ gàjiyà	all right
		bābù gàjiyà	all right
		gàjiyà dà sauƙī	it's better
		àlhamdùlìllāhì	all's well

Greeting		Reply	
		gàjiyà tā bi	the tiredness
		lāfiyà	is only
			tempo-
			rary [1]
ìnā làbāri ?	what's the	(làbāri) sai	
	news ?	àlhērì	all's well
		lāfiyà	all's well

3. Situational :

Greeting	Reply
ìnā aikì ?	aikì dà gòdiyā
how's (your) work ?	with thankfulness
	àlhamdùlillāhì
	thank God (for it)
	mun gōdè Allà
	we thank God (for it)
sànnu [2] dà aikì	
greetings at work	(same replies as for sànnu)
sànnu [2] dà zuwà	
greetings on arriving	(same replies as for sànnu)
maràbā dà zuwà	
greetings on arriving	(same replies as for sànnu)
maràbā	
welcome	(same replies as for sànnu)
sànnu [2] dà hūtàwā	
greetings at rest	(same replies as for sànnu)
sànnu dà àniyà	
greetings in (your) effort	(same replies as for sànnu)

[1] Literally, ' tiredness has alternated with well being '.

[2] **Barkà** is frequently substituted for **sànnu** in these (and other) contexts. The two words are equivalent in meaning, but **barkà** usually implies a greater familiarity between the greeters and tends to be used to the exclusion of **sànnu** between close friends. The usual reply to a greeting with **barkà** in it is **barkà dai.**

Greeting	Reply
sànnu dà ƙòƙarī	
greetings in (your) effort	(same replies as for **sànnu**)
sàlāmù àlaikùn	**yâuwā, àlaikà sàlāmù**
(on entering a compound)	(reply)
	m̀hm̂ (reply)
gāfarà	**yâuwā, barkà dà zuwà**
(woman entering	greetings on arrival
compound)	
gāfarà dai	**yâuwā, barkà dà zuwà**
(woman entering	greetings on arrival
compound)	

4. Time of day :

Greeting	Reply
ìnā kwānā ?	
how did you sleep ?	(same replies as for **lāfiyà ?**)
kwal lāfiyà ?	
how did you sleep ?	(same replies as for **lāfiyà ?**)
barkà dà kwānā	**barkà dai** greetings
greetings in the a.m.	
kā tāshì lāfiyà ?	
did you get up well ?	(same replies as for **lāfiyà ?**)
kā kwāna lāfiyà ?	
did you sleep well ?	(same replies as for **lāfiyà ?**)
ìnā wunì ?	
how's (your) day ?	(same replies as for **lāfiyà ?**)
ìnā yinì ?	
how's (your) day ?	(same replies as for **lāfiyà ?**)
barkà dà rānā	**barkà dai** greetings
greetings (at noon)	
barkà dà yâmmā	**barkà dai** greetings
greetings (in late p.m.)	
barkà dà darē	**barkà dai** greetings
greetings (at night)	

5. Personal :

Greeting	*Reply*
kanà lāfiyà ?	
are you well ?	(same replies as for **lāfiyà ?**)
ìnā gidā ?	
how's (your) family ?	(same replies as for **lāfiyà ?**)
ìnā ìyālì ?	
how's (your) family ?	(same replies as for **lāfiyà ?**)
ìnā mutànenkà ?	
how's your family ?	(same replies as for **lāfiyà ?**)
gidankà lāfiyà ?	
how's your family ?	(same replies as for **lāfiyà ?**)
ìyālìnkà lāfiyà ?	
how's your family ?	(same replies as for **lāfiyà ?**)
mutànenkà lāfiyà ?	
how's your family ?	(same replies as for **lāfiyà ?**)
ìnā yârā ?	
how are (your) children	(same replies as for **lāfiyà ?**)
yârā lāfiyà ?	
how are (your) children ?	(same replies as for **lāfiyà ?**)
yàyà yârā ?	
how are (your) children ?	(same replies as for **lāfiyà ?**)
ìnā uwargidā ?	
how's (your) wife ?	(same replies as for **lāfiyà ?**)
rânkà yà daɗè [3]	**m̀hm̂** (reply)
greetings (to social superior)	
yàyà jìkī ? [4]	**(yanà) dà saukī**
how's (your) illness ?	it's better
sànnu	**yâuwā**
greetings (in misfortune)	thanks
Allà yà bā dà saukī	**àmin**
may God make (you) well	may it be so

[3] This greeting is used especially to a chief or other important person.
[4] Literally : *how's (your) body ?*

Greeting	Reply
Allà yà sawwàk̃ē [5]	**àmin**
may God lighten (your) trouble	may it be so
Allà yà ji k̃ansà [6]	**àmin**
may God have mercy on him (may his soul rest in peace)	may it be so

6. Seasonal :

Greeting	Reply
inà gùmī ?	**lōkàcinsà nē**
how's the heat ?	it's the time for it
	kwànàkinsà nē
	it's the season for it
	kâi, yā yi yawà !
	there's a lot !
	dà sauk̃ī
	it's eased off
inà ruwā ?	(same replies as for **inà**
how's the rain ?	**gùmī ?**)
	ruwā yā yi gyārā
	the rain has helped
	(same replies as for **inà**
	aikì ? but substitute
	ruwā for **aikì** in first
	reply)
inà sanyī ?	(same replies as for **inà**
how's the cold ?	**gùmī ?**)
yàyà ka ji dà darī ?	(same replies as for **inà**
how's the cold ?	**gumī ?**)
barkà dà sallà	**barkà dai**
greetings (during holidays)	greetings

---

[5] Or, less commonly, **sauk̃àk̃ē.**
[6] Employed with reference to a dead person.

7. Parting greetings :

Greeting	*Reply*
sai an jimà [7]	**yâuwā, sai an jimà**
see you later	okay, see you later
	yâuwā, mun jimà dà yawà
	okay, we'll wait
sai gòbe	**yâuwā, sai gòbe**
see you tomorrow	okay, see you tomorrow
	tò Allà yà kai mù
	may God bring it about
sai dà sāfē	**yâuwā, sai dà sāfē**
until morning	okay, until morning
	tò Allà yà kai mù
	may God bring it about
sai dà yâmmā	**yâuwā, sai dà yâmmā**
until evening	okay, until evening
sai wani lōkàcī	**yâuwā, sai wani lōkàcī**
see you sometime	okay, see you sometime
sai wani sā'ì	**yâuwā, sai wani sā'ì**
see you sometime	okay, see you sometime
sai wata rānā [8]	**yâuwā, sai wata rānā**
see you sometime	okay, see you sometime
sai kā dāwō	**yâuwā, sai nā dāwō**
until you return	okay, till I return
sàuka lāfiyà	**tò Allà yà sâ**
may you arrive safely	may God make it so
(kà) gai dà gidā	**tò sâ ji** [9]
greet your family	okay, they'll hear
(kà) gai minì dà Audù	**tò yâ ji** [9]
greet Audu for me	okay, he'll hear

---

[7] Literally ' until one has waited a while '.

[8] **Sai wata rānā** usually implies less expectation of seeing the person again than does either of the two preceding greetings.

[9] Future 2 (see Lesson 16) is invariably used in this formula.

8. Miscellaneous expressions often employed in greeting
situations :

tô	okay, well
mādàllā	fine, splendid, thank you (*lit.* praise God)
yâuwā	(reply) okay, fine
àlbishìrinkà !	I've brought you good news !
gŏrò	(reply to **àlbishìrinkà**) = (I'll give you) a kolanut (if you tell me)
bismillāhì	(formula said before beginning an action, *e.g.* eating, starting work— *lit.* in the name of God)
bismillà !	go ahead and start (whatever is to be done) !
in Allà yā yàrda	if God wills
in shā Àllā(hù)	if God wills

Lesson 32

Numbers

1. In Lesson 11 the numbers 1-22 and several related expressions were introduced. It is the purpose of this lesson to list Hausa numbers in greater detail than in Lesson 11.

2. Cardinal numbers :

1	ɗaya	12	(gōmà) shâ biyu
2	biyu	13	(gōmà) shâ ukù
3	ukù	14	(gōmà) shâ huɗu
4	huɗu	15	(gōmà) shâ bìyar
5	bìyar	16	(gōmà) shâ shidà
6	shidà/shiddà	17	(gōmà) shâ bakwài
7	bakwài	18	àshìrin biyu bābù *or* (gōmà)
8	takwàs		shâ takwàs
9	tarà	19	àshìrin ɗaya bābù *or* (gōmà)
10	gōmà		shâ tarà
11	(gōmà) shâ ɗaya	20	àshìrin

All numbers above 20 employ **dà**, rather than **shâ**, in compound numerals, e.g. **àshìrin dà ɗaya, àshìrin dà biyu, tàlàtin dà ɗaya,** etc.

20	àshìrin	90	càsà'in [1]
30	tàlàtin	100	ɗàrī
40	àrbà'in	200	mètan/ɗàrī biyu
50	hàmsin	300	ɗàrī ukù
60	sìttin	400	ɗàrī huɗu/àrbàminyà
70	sàbà'in	500	ɗàrī bìyar/hàmsàminyà
80	tàmànin	1000	dubū/alìf/zambàr

[1] **Tàsà'in, tìs'in, tàmànin dà gōmà** and **ɗàrī bâ gōmà** are also used for 90.

3 000   dubū ukù   1 000 000   milyân, zambàr dubŭ
10 000   zambàr gōmà

When more than one term is listed above, the first is
the most common. The term zambàr is ordinarily
reserved for use in numbers above 9000.
Numbers between those listed above are formed in a
regular manner with dà, e.g. hàmsin dà biyu (52), mètan
dà shidà (206), ɗàrī biyar dà gōmà (510), ɗàrī takwàs dà
sàbà'in dà ukù (873), dubū bakwài dà ɗàrī huɗu dà
càsà'in dà ɗaya (7491), dubū ɗaya (or gùdā) dà biyu
(1002), milyân gùdā dà dubū biyar dà ɗàrī tarà dà gōmà
shâ takwàs, etc. (1005, 918).
The year 1973 is dubū ɗaya dà ɗàrī tarà dà sàbà'in dà
ukù.

3. The term for zero is siflrī.

4. See Lesson 11, section 6, for the formation of ordinal
numbers.

5. See Lesson 11, section 7, for the use of gùdā with
numbers.

6. Addition employs dà, e.g. :

Ukù dà ukù nawà (nē) ?
   Shidà nē.   3 and 3 are how many ? 6.
Shâ biyu dà àshìrin ɗaya bābù   12 plus 19 are how many ?
   nawà (nē) ? Tàlàtin dà ɗaya.   31.

7. Subtraction employs . . . bābù, dàgà or ɗēbè/fìtad dà . . .
dàgà cikin, e.g. :

Gōmà, huɗu bābù nawà (nē) ?   10 minus 4 is how many ?
   Shidà.   6.

Biyu dàgà shidà nawà (nē)? | 2 from 6 (leaves) how
Huɗu. | many? 4.

À ɗēbè bìyar dàgà cikin | Take 5 from (in) 34, how
tàlàtin dà huɗu, nawà (nē) | many remain? 29.
ya ragè? Tàlàtin ɗaya
bābù.

8. *Multiplication* employs **sàu**, *times*, e.g.:

Ukù sàu ukù nawà (nē)? Tarà. $3 \times 3 = ?$ 9.

Shâ bìyar sàu huɗu sittin nè. $15 \times 4 = 60$.

9. *Division* employs **shìga** and **sàu**, e.g. :

Shidà zâi shìga àshìrin dà huɗu | 6 goes into 24 how many
sàu nawà? Huɗu. | times? 4.

Sàu nawà gōmà zâi shìga | How many times does 10
mètan? Àshìrin. | go into 200? 20.

10. *Fractions* are expressed as follows :

$\frac{1}{2}$ is **rabì**. $\frac{1}{4}$ is **kwatà** or **rubù'ì**.

Other fractions are usually described as, e.g. :

$\frac{1}{3}$ is **sulùsī** *or* **ɗaya bisà ukù** *or* **ɗaya dàgà cikin ukù**

$\frac{2}{5}$ is **biyu bisà bìyar** *or* **biyu dàgà cikin bìyar**

$\frac{3}{8}$ is **ukù bisà takwàs** *or* **ukù dàgà cikin takwàs**

$\frac{1}{10}$ is **ushùrī** *or* **ɗaya bisà gōmà** *or* **ɗaya dàgà cikin gōmà**,
etc.

11. Percentages are expressed as follows :

$10\% =$ **gōmà bisà ɗàrī** (*lit.* 10 on/over 100), etc.

Lesson 33

Time

1. The days of the week (see also Lesson 20) are :

Lahàdì/Lâdì	Sunday
Lìttìnîn/Àttànîn	Monday
Tàlātà	Tuesday
Làràbā	Wednesday
Àlhàmîs	Thursday
Jumma'à/Jūma'à	Friday
Àsabàr/Sātì	Saturday

The words for week are **mākò** and **sātì**. Other useful expressions are :

(ran) Lìttìnîn	Monday (**ran** is optional, but frequently used)
sātì mài zuwà *or* mākòn gòbe	next week
sātì wandà ya wucè	last week
mākòn dà ya wucè *or* mākòn jiyà	last week
mākòn jìbi	two weeks hence

2. Other expressions relating to days are :

	yâu	**today**	
yesterday	**jiyà**	**gòbe**	tomorrow
day before yesterday	**shēkaranjiyà** [1]	**jìbi** [1]	two days hence
		gātà	three days hence
		città [2]	four days hence
		shēkaràn città [2]	five days hence
		rānā (ì) ta yâu	today week

---

[1] In some places these words refer simply to a vague past and future time.

[2] These words are now only used by country folk.

rānā (*f*.) [3]	sun, day
kwānā [3]	day, spending of a night
kàshègàrī/ **wàshègàrī**	the following day
yâu dà yâmmā	this evening
yâu dà dàddarē	tonight
daren yâu	last night
daren jiyà	night before last
daren jumma'à	Thursday night

last night, night before last, Thursday night } (the Hausa 'day' starts at sunset)

When days are counted **kwānā** (not **rānā**) is used, e.g. *ten days* would be **kwānā gōmà**, *three days*, **kwānā ukù**.

Kwānā biyu, though literally meaning *two days*, is most frequently used idiomatically to mean *a long time*, e.g. **yā yi kwānā biyu à gidāna** [4] = *he spent a long time at my home* ; **sai an kwāna biyu** = *see you some time* ; **yā kwāna biyu (à dūniyà)** = *he's no (spring) chicken, he's lived a long life.*

The term **wàrhakà** means . . . *at the same time as now*, e.g. **jiyà wàrhakà** = *yesterday at this time* ; **gòbe wàrhakà** = *tomorrow at this time* ; **wàrhakà sātī mài zuwà** = *at this time next week.*

3. Clock time is expressed by the use of the term **ƙarfè**, *o'clock* (lit. ' metal ' [5]) and several words borrowed from English :

---

[3] The differences between **rānā** and **kwānā** are :
rānā is used (i) for a specific single day
(ii) for the days of the week
kwānā is used (i) for a length of days (e.g. **kwānā nawà ka yi à Kanò ?** *How many days did you spend at Kano ?*)
(ii) for a vague time (e.g. **kwānan nàn**, *these days, recently*)
(iii) for dates of the month.
[4] Or, just as commonly, **yā kwāna biyu à gidāna.**
[5] From the former custom of beating a piece of iron hung in front of the police station to indicate the hours.

ƙarfè nawà (nē) ?	what time is it ?
ƙarfè ɗaya	one o'clock
ƙarfè ukù dà mintì gōmà	ten past three (mintì = minutes)
ƙarfè shidà dà kwatà	six fifteen
ƙarfè huɗu yā wucè dà mintì àshìrin	four twenty
ƙarfè (gōmà) shâ ɗaya dà rabì	eleven thirty
ƙarfè shâ biyu saurā mintì bìyar	five minutes to two
ƙarfè gōmà bâ mintì àshìrin dà bìyar	twenty-five to ten
ƙarfè bìyar na yâmmā	five p.m.
ƙarfè ukù na darē	three a.m.
ƙarfè tarà na sāfè	nine a.m.
ƙarfè ɗaya na rānā	one p.m.

4. Months of the year :

Jànairù	Yūlì
Fàbrairù	Àgustà
Mārìs	Sàtumbà
Afrìl/Àfrīlù	Òktōbà
Māyù	Nùwambà
Yūnì, Jun	Dìzambà

watà	month
watà mài zuwà	next month
watàn gòbe	next month
watàn jiyà	last month
watàn dà ya wucè	last month
watàn jībi	two months hence

5. Seasons of the year :

| dàmunā/ dàmanā/dàminā | rainy season (roughly May– September) |

kàkā	harvest season (October–November)
rānī	dry season (December–February) [6]
bazarā	hot, muggy season (March–April)

[6] The cold, harmattan part of the dry season occurring during some or all of the period between mid-December and February is also known as **ɗārī** (= *dry coldness*) or **hùntūrù** (= *harmattan*).

Lesson 34

Money and Marketing

1. The currency in Nigeria, until January 1973, followed the former English sterling system of pounds, shillings and pence, but had its own notes and coins. In January 1973, Nigeria converted to a decimal currency based on the *naira* (₦), which equals the former 10/- note. One *naira* is divided into 100 *kobos* (k). Currency notes are issued in denominations of ₦10, ₦5, ₦1 and 50k. Coins issued are 25k, 10k, 5k, 1k and ½k.

The recency of this change means that the names of previously issued units are still widely employed. For example, ₦2 is known as **fâm** (pound), 10k as **sulè** (shilling—though now only divided into 10 **kwabò** instead of 12)—5k as **sisì** (formerly 6 **kwabò**).

Up to 1960 a $\frac{1}{10}$ of a penny coin known as **ànínì** was minted. Though this coin has long been out of use the term is still heard in proverbial and other stylized expressions.[1]

2. The following chart summarizes the changes and their current (1973) British and American values:

New Nigerian Values	Former Nigerian Values	British Values (approx.)	American Values (approx.)
₦10	£5.0.0	£6·30	$15·20
₦5	£2.10.0	£3·15	$7·60
—	£1.0.0	£1·26	$3·04
₦1	10/- (= 120d)	63p	$1·52
50k	5/- (= 60d)	32p	76¢

[1] It is also used to mean *button* or *washer*.

New Nigerian Values	Former Nigerian Values	British Values (approx.)	American Values (approx.)
25k	2/6 (= 30d)	15p	38¢
10k	1/– (= 12d)	6p	15¢
5k	6d	3p	7½¢
—	3d	1½p	4¢
1k	1d	½p	1¢
½k	½d	—	½¢

3. The term for money, **kudī** is the plural of **wurì**, *cowry shell*. Though **kudī** (with its more modern reference) is now frequently regarded as singular it is still often used as a plural, e.g. **Kanà dà kudī ? Ā'à, bâ ni dà sū.** *Do you have (some) money ? No, I don't have (any of) them.*

4. Hausa currency terms (some terms refer to combinations of coins rather than to single coins) :

anīnī	$\frac{1}{10}$k	**nai**	7½k
darī,[2] **sīsin kwabò**	½k	**sulè**	10k
kwabò	1k	**fàtakà, dalà**	20k
āhù/àfù	1½k	**nairà**	₦1
tarō	2½k	**fâm**	₦2
sìsì	5k	**jàkā**	₦200

5. The following terms and expressions are important in **cìnikī** (= *market purchases, bargaining*). See also the vocabularies and dialogues of Lessons 13–16.

sâ sūnā	put a price on this (item)
kudinsà nawà (nē) ? *or*	
nawà nē (kudinsà) ?	how much does this cost ?
kudin dōzìn nawà (nē) ?	how much per dozen ?
(kudinsà) sulè nē	it costs 10k

[2] The same word as for *one hundred*. One hundred cowries used to equal ½d (roughly ½k).

(kuɗinsà) nairà biyu dà sulè takwàs (nē)	it costs ₦2·80
(kuɗinsà) sulè dà sīsì (nē)	it costs 15k
(kuɗinsà) sulè ukù bâ tarō (nè̱)	it costs 27½k
bà ni fàtakà	its price is (*lit.* give me) 20k
(kâi !) yā yi tsàdā *or* dà tsàdā	(oh !), that's expensive
dà àràhā	it is cheap
(kuɗinsà) yā yi yawà (ainùn)	it is (very) high priced
tàyā minì	make me an offer
nā tayà sulè	I offer (you) 10k
ràgē minì	reduce (the price) for me
nā ragè sīsì	I reduce (the price) by 5k
ƙàrā minì	increase (the price/the amount) for me
nā ƙārà sīsì	I increase (my offer) by 5k
àlbarkà !	I refuse your offer !
bàn sallàmā ba	I don't agree to sell
nā sallàmā	I agree to sell (at your price)
nā sallàmā à sulè ukù	I agree to sell at 30k
kàwō kuɗī !	pay (your) money ! (*i.e.* the deal is completed)
nawà ka kè sô ?	how many/much do you want ?
bà ni biyu	give me two (of them)
kàwō canjì	give (me my) change
ìnā gyārā ?	where's (my) extra ?[3]

---

[3] An *extra* is often thrown in by the seller (especially if a number of small items are bought) ostensibly to do away with any hard feelings aroused in the process of bargaining. It is not impolite to ask for a **gyārā**, especially if the bargaining has become heated or if the buyer has bought at a price quite close to the seller's original price. If the seller feels that the buyer has got the best of the bargain he will probably refuse to give a **gyārā**.

Lesson 35

Family and Kinship Terms

1. Hausa family and kinship terms do not necessarily correspond exactly with English family and kinship terms. The terms listed below are those employed to designate those persons and relationships considered important enough by the Hausa-speaking community to warrant specific designation. See Lesson 22, section 7 (*b*), for a listing of some of these terms in masculine, feminine and plural columns.

2. General terms :

mùtûm	man (= human being)
namijì	man (= male individual)
màcè	woman
yārò	boy
yārinyà	girl
namijì	male
ta màcè, tamàtā	female
dangì	relative(s)
zùriyà, zùrī'à	descendants, clan

3. Parental family :

Terms of reference :

iyàyē	parents (may also include other senior relatives)
ùbā	father
uwā	mother
ɗan'uwā	brother [1]
'yar'uwā	sister [1]
yàyā, wâ	elder brother [1]

---

[1] See footnote 2 on page 223.

yàyā, yâ	elder sister [2]
ƙanè	younger brother [2]
ƙanwà	younger sister [2]
àutā	youngest brother or sister
ɗan'ùbā	half-brother (= son of same father only)
'yar'ùbā	half-sister (= daughter of same father only)
'yan'uwā	brothers and sisters [2]
bappà	paternal uncle
kāwù, kàwū, rāfànī	maternal uncle
bābà	paternal aunt
iyà, innà, ìnnā	mother, maternal aunt
gwaggò, gwàggō	paternal aunt, father's wife (not one's mother), maternal uncle's wife

Terms of address (where different) :

bàba	father, paternal uncle
màmā, innà/ìnnā	mother, maternal aunt

4. Family of one's own marriage :

mijì	husband
màcè (*pl.* **mātā**)	wife
iyālì	family (man's wife or wives and children)
kīshìyā	co-wife
'yā'yā, ɗiyā [3]	children
ɗā *or* **ɗā namijì**	son
'yā, ɗìyā [3]	daughter
ɗan ƙārì	eldest son

---

[2] These terms are often extended to mean, for example, nephew, niece, cousin, etc. In fact, the words **ɗan'uwā, 'yar'uwā,** and **'yan'uwā** may be applied to *anyone* with whom one has any affinity of town, tribe, race, country, creed, trade, colour or common humanity.

[3] This word is used in Sokoto and the west.

'yar fārì	eldest daughter
àutā	youngest son or daughter
yārò	boy, son
yārinyà	girl, daughter
sauràyī (*pl.* sàmàrī)	young man (after puberty)
bùdurwā (*pl.* 'yam mātā)	young woman (after puberty)

5. Grandparents and grandchildren :

kàkā	grandfather, grandmother
kàkànī	grandparents
jīkà	grandson, granddaughter
jīkanyà	granddaughter
jīkōkī	grandchildren
tàɓà kunnē, ɗan jīkà	great-grandchild
tàttàɓà kunnē	great-great grandchild

6. In-laws :

sùrùkai	in-laws
sùrukī	male in-law
sùrukā, sùrùkuwā	female in-law

Lesson 36

Person-Aspect Pronouns and Pronoun Tables

1. Although the various sets of Hausa person-aspect pronouns are introduced in the grammar section of this course (see Lessons 7, 12, 16, 18, 20 and 26), it is helpful to be able to refer to the sets in chart form as well.

2. There are two basic sets of person-aspect pronouns :

Set I—the high-tone set, and *Set II—the low-tone set*. The completive, relative completive, continuative, relative continuative, habitual and future II aspects are built on the high-tone set—Set I. The subjunctive and future I aspects are built on the low-tone set—Set II.

(See charts on pages 226 and 227.)

3. Two constructions make use of direct object pronouns (plus the impersonal **a**) as person-aspect pronouns (see section 4 below for the direct object pronouns list) : the **zâ** construction (see Lesson 16) and the negative of the **yanà dà** possessive construction (see Lesson 18).

(See charts on pages 228 and 229.)

4. The non-p-a pronouns may also be conveniently charted. Discussions of these pronouns are found in the grammar as follows : independent, Lesson 6 ; inseparable and separable possessive, Lesson 9 ; direct and indirect object, Lesson 15.

(See chart on page 230.)

5. So-called *reflexive pronouns* are formed in Hausa with (usually) **dà** plus the word for *head, self*, **kâi,** and the inseparable possessive pronouns suffixed to it. These

Positive Forms :

	SET I—high tone					SET II—low tone		
Complet.	Rel. Complet.	Cont.	Rel. Cont.	Habitual	Fut. II	Subj.	Fut. I
nā	na	inà	na kè	na kàn	nâ	in	zân
kā	ka	kanà	ka kè	ka kàn	kâ	kà	zā kà
kin	kikà	kinà	ki kè	ki kàn	kyâ	kì	zā kì
yā	ya	yanà	ya kè	ya kàn	yâ	yà	zāi
tā	ta	tanà	ta kè	ta kàn	tâ	tà	zā tà
an	akà	anà	a kè	a kàn	â	à	zā à
mun	mukà	munà	mu kè	mu kàn	mâ	mù	zā mù
kun	kukà	kunà	ku kè	ku kàn	kwâ	kù	zā kù
sun	sukà	sunà	su kè	su kàn	sâ	sù	zā sù

Typical Translations (with go) :

I went	I am going	I go (regularly)	I shall go	let me go	I will go

Negative Forms :

Completive	Continuative	Habitual	Fut. II	Subj.	Fut. I
bà . . . ba (with Set II p-a pronouns) :	**bā . . .** (with fut. II[1] p-a pronouns but with low tone) :	**bà . . . ba** (with regular hab. aspect p-a pronouns, e.g. **bà na kàn tàfî ba**, *etc.*).	**bà . . . ba** (with regular fut. II p-a pronouns, e.g. **bà nā̀ tàfî ba**, *etc.*)	**kadà . . .** (with regular subj. p-a pronouns, e.g. **kadà in tàfî**, *etc.*)	**bà . . . ba** (with regular fut. I p-a pronouns, e.g. **bà zân tàfî ba, bà zā̀ kà tàfî ba,** *etc.*)
bàn tàfî ba **bà kà tàfî ba** **bà kì tàfî ba** **bài tàfî ba** **bà tà tàfî ba** **bà à tàfî ba** **bà mù tàfî ba** **bà kù tàfî ba** **bà sù tàfî ba**	**bā nà̀ tàfìyà** **bā kà̀ tàfìyà** **bā kyà̀ tàfìyà** **bā yà̀ tàfìyà** **bā tà̀ tàfìyà** **bā à̀ tàfìyà** **bā mà̀ tàfìyà** **bā kwà̀ tàfìyà** **bā sà̀ tàfìyà**				
Typical Translations : I did not go	I am not going	I do not go	I shall not go	lest I go	I will not go

[1] See Lesson 18, section 3 for alternate forms.

(a) The **zā̀** Construction (illustrated with **gidā̀**):

Positive Forms and Translations:

zā̀ ni gidā̀	I am going home
zā̀ ka gidā̀	you are going home
zā̀ ki gidā̀	you (*f.*) are going home
zā̀ shi gidā̀	he is going home
zā̀ ta gidā̀	she is going home
zā̀ a gidā̀	people are going home
zā̀ mu gidā̀	we are going home
zā̀ ku gidā̀	you are going home
zā̀ su gidā̀	they are going home

Negative Forms and Translations:

bà zā̀ ni gidā̀ ba	I am not going home
bà zā̀ ka gidā̀ ba	you are not going home

etc.

OR:

bà zā̀ ni gidā̀ ba
bà zā̀ ka gidā̀ ba, *etc.*

(b) The **yanà dà** Possessive Construction (illustrated with **aikì**) :

Positive Forms and Translations :		*Negative Forms and Translations :*	
inà dà aikì	I have work	**bā nà dà aikì**	I do not have work
kanà dà aikì	you have work	**bā kà dà aikì**	you do not have work
kinà dà aikì	you (*f.*) have work	*etc.* (using the p-a pronouns listed above for the	
yanà dà aikì	he has work	negative continuative aspect)	
tanà dà aikì	she has work		
anà dà aikì	someone has work	*OR :*	
munà dà aikì	we have work	**bā ni dà aikì**	
kunà dà aikì	you have work	**bā ka dà aikì,** *etc.* (using the p-a pronouns listed	
sunà dà aikì	they have work	above with **zā**)	

| INDEP. | POSSESSIVE | | OBJECT | |
	Inseparable	Separable	Direct	Indirect
nĭ	-na/-nā² -ta/-tā²	nàwa tàwa	ni/nĭ	minĭ/manĭ/mĭn
kai	-nkĭ -rkĭ	nākă tākă	ka/kă	makă/mā
kē	-nkĭ -rkĭ	nākĭ tākĭ	ki/kĭ	mikĭ/makĭ
shĭ	-nsă -rsă	nāsă tāsă	shi/shĭ	masă/mishĭ/mâr
ita	-ntă -rtă	nātă tātă	ta/tă	mată
mū	-mmŭ -rmŭ	nāmŭ tāmŭ	mu/mŭ	mană/mamŭ
kū	-nkŭ -rkŭ	nākŭ tākŭ	ku/kŭ	mukŭ/makŭ
sū	-nsŭ -rsŭ	nāsŭ tāsŭ	su/sŭ	musŭ/masŭ
Translations :				
I	my	mine, my	me	to *or* for me

² For the variable length of these pronouns see Lesson 9, section 3.

forms are ordinarily preceded by a nominal, often an independent pronoun, e.g. :

nī dà kâina	I myself	**mū dà kâmmù**	we ourselves
kai dà kânkà	you yourself	**kū dà kânkù**	you yourselves
kē dà kânkì	you (*f.*) yourself		
shī dà kânsà	he himself	**sū dà kânsù**	they themselves
ita dà kântà	she herself		

My own, his own, etc., are **na/ta kâina, na/ta kânsà**, etc. (lit. *that of myself, that of himself*, etc.).

The third person forms may be preceded by nouns, e.g. :

Audù dà kânsà	Audu himself
mutànemmù dà kânsù	our people themselves

Following are a few typical examples of the way these forms are used :

Nī kàm, bàn gan shì dà kâinā ba.	As for me, I didn't see it myself.
Yā yī shì dà kânsà.	He did it himself.
Kū dà kânkù, kun sanì.	You yourselves know (it).
Nī (dà) kâinā na ji àbîn dà ya fàɗā.	I myself heard what he said.
Sun kashè kânsù/ kāwunànsù.	They have committed suicide (*lit.* killed themselves).

A noun, **jūnā**, is used to mean *each other*, e.g. :

Kun san jūnā ?	Do you know each other ?
Sun ga jūnansù.	They saw each other.

Lesson 37

Verbals

1. The classification of verbals presented in these lessons divides the group into three categories : *verbs, specialized verbals* and *non-aspect verbals.*

2. The *specialized verbals* in Hausa are limited to a single aspect. They are divisible into two groups :

(*a*) Those which are preceded by their person-aspect pronoun (there are only two) :

> **nà** (see Lesson 18)
> **kè** (see Lesson 20)

(*b*) Those which are followed by their person-aspect pronoun. These are :

> **zâ** (see Lesson 16)
> **zā** (see Lesson 16)
> **bā** (see Lesson 18)
> **bâ** (see Lesson 18)
> **jè** (not previously introduced)
> **yā** (not previously introduced)

3. The *non-aspect verbals* are a group of four words which function in clauses as verbals but take no person-aspect pronouns. They may govern direct (but not indirect) objects (see Lesson 13). They are :

> **àkwai**
> **bābù/bâ**
> **dà** (= **àkwai** in meaning and function) [1]
> **gà**

---

[1] This **dà** is probably a shortening of **anà dà . . .**, *one has . . ..*

4. *Verbs* are by far the largest subcategory of verbals.[2]
For an introduction to this classification, see Lesson 25.
The student should also refer to the classification
provided by R. C. Abraham in the front of his dic-
tionary and the back of his grammar (both listed in the
Bibliography).

There follows a listing of the majority of the verbs
presented in these lessons arranged according to Parsons'
categories and with their method of deriving verbal
nouns indicated :

(a) Grade I verbs—a *basic grade* consisting of transitive
verbs (plus a few intransitives) which do not change
their final vowel (except for its length) before a
direct object. These verbs may govern direct and/or
indirect objects or, in most cases, be followed by no
object at all (although an object must frequently be
supplied in the English translation). Grade I verbs
ordinarily have high-low(-high) tone patterns and end
in -à.[3]

Grade I verbs form verbal nouns ending in **-wā**
(which are employed in the continuative aspect
when not followed by an object). When, in the
continuative aspect, an object follows the basic verb
itself is employed. Some Grade I verbs also have a
' secondary verbal noun ' of varying form which
operates like variable vowel verb irregular verbal
nouns [4] (see Lesson 19, section 6 (a)).

---

[2] Again (see also Lesson 25) we are summarizing material published
by F. W. Parsons in *The Verbal System in Hausa*. (See the Bibliography, page 299.)

[3] The **à** becomes **à** and the final high tone of a three-syllable verb
becomes low before a noun object.

[4] E.g. awō (from **aunà**), dūbā (from dūbà), ɗinki (from ɗinkà),
gyārā (from gyārà), kàràtū (from karàntā), rùbūtū (from rubūtā),
shiri (from shiryà), yankā (from yankà), zamā (from zaunà).

	Verbal Noun—
Verb	*Continuative*
yā kāmà	**yanà kāmàwā**
he caught (it)	he is catching (it)
yā kāmà shi	**yanà kāmà shi**
he caught it	he is catching it
yā kāmà dōkì	**yanà kāmà dōkì**
he caught the horse	he is catching the horse
yā kāmà minì dōkì	**yanà kāmà minì dōkì**
he caught me the horse	he is catching the horse for me

Transitive Verbs

amsà	gayà	kāmà	sallàmā
aunà	ginà	karàntā [5]	shâidā
bugà	gōgà	kasà	shiryà
cikà	gwadà	ƙārà	shūkà
daɗà	gyārà	matsà	taɓà
dafà	hanà	naɗà	tārà
dūbà	hūrà	nūnà	tayà
ɗinkà	jità	rērà	yankà
fārà	kafà	rubùtā [5]	zubà
gamà	kai	sâ	zūrà

Intransitive Verbs

gamà	kōmà	mântā [5]	zaunà
hūtà	kwântā [5]	tsayà	

(b) Grade II (or variable vowel) verbs—a *basic grade* consisting of transitive verbs which change their terminal vowel to **-ē** before a pronoun direct object and to **-i** before a noun direct object. These verbs may govern direct and/or indirect objects (see Lesson 15,

---

[5] When a **-wā** verbal noun is formed from a verb of more than two syllables (or a two-syllable verb with a falling tone on the first syllable) the syllable before **-wā** takes a falling tone, e.g. **karàntâwā, kwântâwā.**

section 8, for the forms they take before indirect objects) or, in most cases, be followed by no object at all. Grade II verbs ordinarily have low-high(-low) tone patterns and end in -ā [6] (see below).

The usual form of the verbal noun of Grade II verbs is the same shape as the verb when no object follows. Many Grade II verbs, however, have irregular verbal nouns of various types (but never of the -wā suffix type, except with **haifù** which has a special history). This verbal noun may be suffixed by the -n/-r genitival link, plus a noun or pronoun in the regular fashion for nouns to form a construction that corresponds to (and translates into English as) a verb plus direct object construction. If an indirect object occurs the verb form (which in this grade is a special form [7]) is employed. See Lesson 19. section 6.

Verb	Verbal Noun—Continuative
yā tàmbayà	yanà tàmbayà
he asked	he is asking
yā tàmbàyē shì	yanà tàmbayàrsà
he asked him	he is asking him
yā tàmbàyi mālàm	yanà tàmbayàr mālàm
he asked the teacher	he is asking the teacher
yā tambàyā/tambayam minì mālàm	yanà tambàyā/tambayam minì mālàm
he asked the teacher for me	he is asking the teacher for me

Verbs	Verbal Nouns	Verbs	Verbal Nouns
àikā	àikē, aikì	dòkā	dūkà
cìzā	cīzò	ɗaukà	ɗaukà

---

[6] Becoming (low-)low-high with final -i before a noun object; final -ē before a pronoun object.

[7] See Lesson 15, section 8.

Verbs	Verbal Nouns	Verbs	Verbal Nouns
fàɗā	fàɗā, faɗì	sāmù/sàmā	sāmù
fàhimtà	fàhimtà	sàyā	sàyē
gìrbā	gìrbā, girbì	tàimakà	tàimakà,
hàifā	haifùwā		tàimakō
hàrbā	hàrbā, harbì	tàmbayà	tàmbayà
kàrɓā	kàrɓā	zìyartà	zìyartà
nèmā	nēmā		

(c) Grade III verbs—a *basic grade* consisting mainly of low-high(-low) tone intransitive verbs with terminal **-a** plus certain irregular intransitives. The verbal noun commonly, though not invariably, may be formed by simply lengthening the final **-a** of the basic form. The **-wā** suffix is not used (except with the irregular **fàɗì**).

Grade III verbs usually employ high-toned forms in **-ar/-am** when followed by an indirect object, e.g. **kù fìtam minì gàrīna!**, *get out of my town!* Some also have forms in **-à** or **-è** (with Grade II-type tone change if the basic tone is low-high(-low)), e.g. **nā haƙùrā** (from **hàƙurà**) **masà**, *I waited patiently for him*; **yā zamè minì tīlàs**, *it was forced upon me*.

Low-High (-Low) Verbs	Verbal Nouns	High-Low Verbs	Verbal Nouns
fìta	fìtā	fàɗì	fàɗùwā
gàji	gàjiyà	tāshì	tāshì
hàƙurà	hàƙurà	wunì	wunì
màkarà	màkarà		
nùna	nùnā	*High(-High)*	*Verbal*
sàuka	sàukā	*Verbs*	*Nouns*
shìga	shìgā	hau	hawā
tàfasà	tàfasà	kwāna	kwānā
tàfì	tàfiyà	tsūfa	tsūfā
yàrda	yàrdā	zama	zamā

(d) Grade IV verbs—a *derived grade* of verbs with a basic high-low(-high) tone pattern and a terminal -è vowel.[8] The meaning of this form of the verb often indicates more complete, extensive or thorough action than the basic form of the verb. Grade IV verbs are usually transitive, though there are many common intransitives in this class as well.

The primary verbal noun is formed like that of Grade I (i.e. with -wā if no object follows). Some common Grade IV verbs have ' secondary verbal nouns ' as well.[9] When. in the continuative aspect. an object follows the verb itself is employed (as in Grade I).

Verb	*Verbal Noun—Continuative*
yā budè	**yanà budèwā**
he opened (it)	he is opening (it)
yā budè ta	**yanà budè ta**
he opened it	he is opening it
yā budè ƙōƒà	**yanà budè ƙōƒà**
he opened the door	he is opening the door
yā budè minì ƙōƒà	**yanà budè minì ƙōƒà**
he opened the door for me	he is opening the door for me

Transitive Verbs

ajìyē	**gānè**	**kwāshè**	**shārè**
budè	**gōdè**	**ƙyālè**	**tūrè**
ɗaurè	**kashè**	**riƙè**	**wankè**
fāyè	**kēwàyē** [10]	**rufè**	

---

[8] With the characteristic changes to short -e and (if the final syllable of the verb is high) to low final tone before a noun direct object.

[9] E.g. **àjìyà** (from **ajìyē**), **gòdiyā** (from **gōdè**), **kisà** (from **kashè**), **riƙò** (from **riƙè**), **rufì** (from **rufè**), **wankì** (from **wankè**).

[10] See footnote 5 on page 234.

Transitive or Intransitive Verbs
bushè   ƙètàrē [11]   sākè
ƙārè   ragè   wucè

Intransitive Verbs
dadè   shigè   warkè   zubè
jē

(e) Grade V verbs—a *derived grade* of verbs with high-high(-high) tone pattern and a terminal **-ar**. The meaning is usually causative, though other, less predictable, meanings frequently occur. Grade V verbs are transitive but require the relater **dà** to precede the direct object except in the **-shē** form (e.g. **yā sayar/sai dà shī** but **yā saishē shi,** *he sold it*).

The verbal noun is formed like that of Grade I. Note that, before the **-wā** suffix when no object follows, the **-ar-** syllable takes a falling tone. When an object follows in the continuative, the verb itself is employed as in Grade I.

Verb	*Verbal Noun—Continuative*
yā fitar	**yanà fitârwā**
he took (it) out	he is taking (it) out
yā fitar/fid dà shī	**yanà fitar/fid dà shī**
he took it out	he is taking it out
yā fisshē shì	**yanà fisshē shì**
he took it out	he is taking it out
yā fitar/fid dà kuɗī	**yanà fitar/fid dà kuɗī**
he took money out	he is taking money out
yā fitar minì dà kuɗī	**yanà fitar minì dà kuɗī**
he took money out for me	he is taking money out for me

[11] See footnote 5 on page 234.

Long Form	Short Form	-shē Form
bāyar	bā	bāshē
ciyar	cī	cīshē
fitar	fid	fisshē
gayar	gai	gaishē
kōmar	—	—
kawar	kau	kaushē
saukar	—	—
sayar	sai	saishē
shāyar	shā	shāshē
tsayar	tsai	tsaishē
zaunar	—	—
zubar	zub	zubshē

(*f*) Grade VI verbs—a *derived grade* of verbs with a high-high(-high) tone pattern and a terminal -ō.[12] The meaning typically indicates that the action had reference to or was completed in the vicinity of the scene of the conversation, though there are other meanings as well. Grade VI verbs derived from transitive verbs are ordinarily transitive, those derived from intransitive verbs are ordinarily intransitive.

The verbal noun is formed like that of Grade V (including the falling tone on the syllable preceding the -**wā** suffix). The pattern before objects in the continuative is likewise the same as Grade V (and I and IV, though without the change in final vowel length before a noun direct object).

Verb	*Verbal Noun—* *Continuative*
yā kāwō	**yanà kāwôwā**
he brought (it)	he brings (it)

---

[12] When the verb occurs utterance final the -ō usually shortens.

	Verbal Noun—
Verb	*Continuative*
yā kāwō shì	**yānà kāwō shì**
he brought it	he brings it
yā kāwō àbinci	**yanà kāwō àbinci**
he brought food	he brings food
yā kāwō minì àbinci	**yanà kāwō minì àbinci**
he brought me the food	he brings me food

Transitive Verbs		*Intransitive Verbs*	
aikō	**nēmō**	**dāwō**	**shigō**
ɗaukō	**sāmō**	**fìtō**	**tafō/tahō**
kāmō		**kōmō**	**tāsō**
		saukō	**zō**

Transitive or Intransitive
kāwō

(g) Grade VII verbs—a *derived grade* of verbs with (low-)low-high tone pattern and a terminal **-u**. Grade VII verbs are intransitive and usually passive in meaning, though an additional connotation of thoroughness or potentiality is often also present.

The verbal noun has the **-wā** suffix, but (unlike Grades V and VI) the preceding syllable remains high and the vowel short, e.g. :

sun tàru they assembled (themselves)	**sunà tàruwā** they are assembling

Verbs

àuku	**gàmu**	**kàfu**	**sàdu**
dàfu	**gògu**	**ƙàru**	**sàmu**
dàmu	**gyàru**	**màtsu**	**tàru**
fàru	**jìtu**	**nàɗu**	**yìwu**

Lesson 38

Nominals

1. The classification of nominals presented in these lessons divides the group into five categories : *independent, adjectival* and *adverbial nominals, specifiers* and *pronominals*.

2. The group termed *independent nominals* is the largest subcategory of nominals. It includes :

Nouns (most of the nouns employed in these lessons which are not listed in Lessons 10, 23 or 24 as belonging to one of the other subcategories),

Interrogatives and *indefinite nominals* such as those listed in Lesson 21, section 4.

Note that all the *relational nouns* illustrated in Lesson 17, section 5, except **zuwà** (which derives from a verb) are derived from independent nouns.

3. The group termed *adjectival nominals* includes :

Adjectival nouns (see Lesson 23 for a virtually complete listing of those employed in these lessons),

Quantifiers (see Lessons 11 and 32 and section 5 of Lesson 21).

4. The group termed *adverbial nominals* includes :

Adverbial nouns (see Lesson 24),

Interrogative and *indefinite nouns* such as those listed in Lesson 21, section 3.

5. The group termed *specifiers* includes :

Specifiers (see Lesson 10),

Interrogative and *indefinite specifiers* such as those listed in Lesson 21, section 6.

6. The group termed *pronominals* (Lesson 36, section 4)
includes :

   Independent pronouns (see Lesson 6),
   Inseparable possessive pronouns (see Lesson 9),
   Direct object pronouns (see Lesson 15).

7. Noun plurals are divisible into four major and
several minor categories (see Lesson 22). The majority of
the pluralizable nouns which occur in the vocabularies of
these lessons are listed below under the appropriate
plural class and subclassification. Some words occur
more than once since more than a single plural form is
common.[1]

8. Plural Class I— **-ōCī** ending, all high tones (**C** = final
consonant of singular form) :

àlāmà, alāmōmī	sign (see also IV (*a*) (i) and IV (*b*) (i))
asìbitì, asibitōcī	hospital
awà, awōwī	hour
bukkà, bukkōkī	grass hut, market stall
dabbà, dabbōbī	(domestic) animal
dūniyà, dūniyōyī	world
fartanyà, fartanyōyī	hoe (see also section 18)
fìtilà, fitilōlī	lamp, lantern (see also IV (*b*) (i))
hanyà, hanyōyī	path, road
kàsuwā, kāsuwōyī/ kāsuwōwī	market
kibiyà, kibiyōyī	arrow (see also IV (*d*))
kujèrā, kujērōrī	chair (see also IV (*b*) (i) and IV (*c*) (i))
kwal(a)bā, kwal(a)bōbī	bottle (see also III (*b*))

[1] This classification has been developed from an unpublished
paper by F. W. Parsons, though he is not responsible for certain
changes in the organization.

kwānò, kwānōnī	basin, iron roofing material (see also II (b) (ii))
kyânwā, kyanwōyī	cat
ƙōfà, ƙōfōfī	door(way)
lâifī, laifōfī	fault (see also II (b) (ii))
lēbùrà, lēburōrī	labourer
likità, likitōcī	doctor
makarantā, makarantōcī	school (see also IV (a) (i), IV (b) (i))
mìnistà, ministōcī	minister (of government)
mōtà, mōtōcī	automobile
muryà, muryōyī	voice
nāmà, nāmōmī	(wild) animal (see also IX)
ōfìs, ōfisōshī	office
sàna'à, sana'ō'ī	occupation, trade
tāgà, tāgōgī	window (hole)
tàmbayà, tambayōyī	question
tāsà, tāsōshī	bowl, dish
tashà, tashōshī	(railway) station
tàtsūnìyā, tātsūniyōyī	fable
tāyà, tāyōyī	tyre
tēbùr, tēburōrī	table
wāƙà, wāƙōƙī	song, poem
yātsà, yātsōtsī	finger (see also IX)
zūcìyā, zūciyōyī	heart (see also V (a))

9. Plural Class II— -uCà ending, all but final tones high (C = n, k or w) :

(a) -unà ending :

(i) Simple :

àddā, addunà	matchet
àgōgō, agōgunà	watch, clock (see also IV (a) (i))
àkàwū, akāwunà	clerk (see also X)
àkwàtì, akwātunà	box (see also IV (a) (i))

bàkī, bākunà	mouth (see also II (*a*) (ii))
cikì, cikkunà	stomach
ɗākì, dākunà	hut, room
gàrmā, garmunà	large hoe, plough (see also section 18)
jàkī, jākunà	donkey (see also IV (*a*) (i))
jìkī, jikunà	body (see also II (*a*) (ii), II (*c*) (ii))
kâi, kāwunà	head (see also II (*b*) (i), (*c*) (i))
kàntī, kantunà	canteen, shop
kèkē, kēkunà	bicycle, machine
kògī, kōgunà	river
rāmì, rāmunà	hole (see also II (*b*) (ii), IX)
rìgā, rīgunà	gown
sàndā, sandunà	stick, staff
sarkī, sarākunà	chief (see also IV (*a*) (i))
shāhò, shāhunà	hawk
wàndō, wandunà	trousers

(ii) Reduplicated :

bàkī, bākunkunà	mouth (see also II (*a*) (i))
jàkā, jakunkunà	bag, ₦200
jìkī, jikunkunà	body (see also II (*a*) (i), II (*c*) (ii))
māgànī, māgungunà	medicine

(*b*) **-ukà** ending :

(i) Simple :

aikì, ayyukà	work
kâi, kāyukà	head (see also II (*b*) (i), (*c*) (i))
kàrē, karnukà	dog (see also IV (*a*) (i), IV (*d*))
râi, rāyukà/rāwukà	life

(ii) Reduplicated

kwānò, kwānunnukà	basin, roofing material (see also I)

lâifī, laifuffukà	fault (see also I)
rāmì, rāmummukà	hole (see also II (a) (i), IX)
sulè, sulullukà	shilling

(c) -uwà ending :

  (i) Simple :

itàcē, itātuwà	tree, wood
hannū, hannuwà	arm, hand (see also III (a))
kâi, kāyuwà	head (see also II (b) (i))
kûnnē, kunnuwà	ear (see also III (a))
zanè, zannuwà	body cloth

  (ii) Reduplicated :

àbù, abūbuwà	thing
gàrī, garūruwà	town
jìkī, jikūkuwà	body (see also II (a) (i), II (a) (ii))

10. Plural Class III—-àCē ending, high-low-high tone pattern (C = y or final consonant of singular form) :

(a) -àyē ending :

bangō, bangàyē/	
bangwàyē	wall
ɓērā, ɓēràyē	mouse, rat
dōgō, dōgàyē/dōgwàyē	tall, long
gīwā, gīwàyē	elephant
gwànī, gwanàyē	expert
hannū, hannàyē	arm, hand (see also II (c))
jā, jājàyē	red (thing)
kûnnē, kunnàyē	ear (see also II (c) (i))
kūrā, kūràyē	hyena
mūgù, mūgàyē	evil (thing) (see also V (b) and VII (a))
sūnā, sūnàyē	name
tsuntsū, tsuntsàyē	bird

(b) -àCē ending (C = final consonant of singular form) :

bakī, bakàkē	black (thing)
farī, faràrē	white (thing)
gidā, gidàjē	compound, home
jirgī, jiràgē	boat
kwal(a)bā, kwalàbē	bottle (see also I)
kasā, kasàshē	land, country
mùtûm, mutànē	man
ruwā, ruwàyē ²	water
uwā, uwàyē/iyàyē ²	mother
wukā, wukàkē	knife
wurī, wuràrē	place

11. Plural Class IV—-ai, -ū, -ī, -au ending, all but final syllable low tone :

(a) -ai ending :

(i) Simple :

àbōkī, àbòkai	friend (see also IV (a) (ii))
àgōgō, àgògai	watch, clock (see also II (a) (i))
àkwàtì, àkwàtai	box (see also II (a) (i))
àlāmà, àlàmai	sign (see also I and IV (b) (i))
àllūrà, àllùrai	needle
àlmājìrī, àlmàjìrai	pupil, student
àlmakàshī, àlmàkàsai	scissors
àsīrī, àsìrai	secret (see also IV (b) (i))
bùkātà, bùkàtai	need (see also IV (b) (i))
dàlīlì, dàlìlai	reason
ìyālì, ìyàlai	family
jàkī, jàkai	donkey (see also II (a) (i))
kàrē, kàrnai	dog (see also II (b) (i), IV (d))

² Note that here as elsewhere (see kāsuwōyī) a -w- before a final -ē- or -ī- usually becomes -y-.

kuskurè, kùskùrai	mistake (see also IV (a) (ii))
kwabò, kwàbbai	kobo
làbārì, làbàrai	news (see also IV (b) (i), IV (b) (ii))
littāfì, littàfai	book (see also IV (a) (ii))
lōkàcī, lòkàtai	time
mabūdī, màbùɗai	key
macìjī, màcìzai	snake
màkānìkì, màkànìkai	mechanic
makarantā, màkàràntai	school (see also I, IV (b) (i))
mālàmī, màlàmai	teacher
sarkī, sàràkai	chief (see also II (a) (i))
wàkīlì, wàkìlai	representative

(ii) Reduplicated or extended :

àbōkī, àbòkànai	friend (see also IV (a) (i))
fiffikè, fìkàfìkai	wing
kuskurè, kùràkùrai	mistake (see also IV (a) (i))
littāfì, littàttàfai	book (see also IV (a) (i))

(b) **-ū** ending :

(i) Simple :

àlāmà, àlàmū	sign (see also I and IV (a) (i))
àsìrī, àsìrū	secret (see also IV (a) (i))
bùkātà, bùkàtū	need (see also IV (a) (i))
dàbārà, dàbàrū	plan, scheme
fìtilà, fìtilū	lamp (see also I)
gàjērē, gàjèrū	short (thing) (see also IV (b) (ii))
jēmāgè, jèmàgū	fruitbat
kujèrā, kùjèrū	stool, chair (see also I and IV (c) (i))

làbàrì, làbàrū   news (see also IV (a) (i),
                           IV (b) (ii))
makarantā,
  màkàràntū   school (see also I, IV (a) (i))
ràwayà, ràwàyū   yellow (thing)
shèkarà, shèkàrū   year

(ii) Reduplicated :
  gàjērē, gàjàjjèrū   short (thing) (see also IV
                           (b) (i))
  làbàrì, làbàrbàrū   news (see also IV (a) (i), IV
                           (b) (i))
  màganà, màgàngànū word

(c) -ī ending :
  (i) Simple :
    bàƙō, bàƙī   guest, stranger
    bāwà, bāyī   slave
    cìyāwà, cìyàyī   grass
    hànkākà, hànkàkī   crow
    kàzā, kàjī   chicken
    kujèrā, kùjèrī   chair, stool (see also I and IV
                           (b) (i))

  (ii) Reduplicated :
    sābō, sàbàbbī   new (thing)
    tsōhō/tsōfō, tsòfàffī old (thing)

  (iii) -kī ending :
    gōnā, gònàkī   farm
    kwānā, kwànàkī   day

  (iv) -nnī ending :
    ùbā, ùbànnī   father
    wàsā, wàsànnī   game
    watà, wàtànnī   month

(*d*) **-au** ending (with slight irregularities) :

kàrē, kàrnau	dog (see also II (*b*) (i), IV (*a*) (i))
kibiyà, kìbau	arrow (see also I)

12. Plural Class V—**-àCā/ū** ending (**C** = final consonant of singular form) :

(*a*) **-àCā** ending :

ƙarfè, ƙaràfā	metal
sirdì, siràdā	saddle
zūcìyā, zūkàtā	heart (see also I)

(*b*) **-àCū** ending :

dūtsè, duwàtsū	rock, mountain
idò, idànū	eye
ƙafà, ƙafàfū	leg, foot
mūgù, miyàgū	evil (thing) (see also III (*a*) and VII (*a*))

13. Plural Class VI—**-ā, -à** endings with singulars ending in **-ī** or **-ē** :

(*a*) **-ā** ending high-low-high tone pattern :

haƙōrī, haƙòrā	tooth
mad̃inkī, madĩnkā	tailor
mafàshī, mafàsā	highway robber
mahàrbī, mahàrbā	hunter
mahàucī, mahàutā	butcher
mahàukàci, mahàukàtā	insane person
makàdĩ, makàdā	drummer
makòyī, makòyā	learner, apprentice
maƙèrī, maƙèrā	blacksmith
maròƙī, maròƙā	beggar

(b) **-ǎ** ending, all but final syllable high tone (some also change their penultimate vowel) :

àlkalàmī, alkalumǎ	pen
cōkàlī, cōkulǎ	spoon
gàtarī, gāturǎ	axe, hatchet
ƙànƙanè, ƙanānǎ/	
ƙanƙanānǎ	small (thing)
tàkàlmī, tākalmǎ	shoe

(c) **-ā** ending, all tones high :

màcè, mātā	woman, wife
mijì, mazā	male, husband

14. Plural Class VII—other plurals ending in **ā** :

(a) **-V̂CCā/V̂Cā** ending (**V** = vowel of singular form ; **C** = consonant of singular form) :

bàbba, mânyā	big (thing)
gōrò, gwârrā	kola nut
kōrè, kwârrā	green (thing)
mūgù, mûggā	evil (thing) (see also V (b)
	and III (a))
shūdì, shûɗɗā	blue (thing)
yārò, yârā	boy
zōbè, zôbbā	ring

(b) **-āwā/-àwā** ending :

Bàhaushè, Hàusàwā	Hausa person
bàdūkù, dùkàwā	leather worker
bàfādà/bàfādè, fàdàwā	courtier, counsellor
Bàkanò/Bàkanè,	
Kanāwā	Kano person
Bàtūrè, Tùràwā	European
talàkà, talakāwā	common person, simple
	peasant, poor man

15. Plural Class VIII --aki̇̄/āki̇̄ ending, tones are usually all high :

àkwiyà, awākī	goat
dōkì, dawākī	horse
kāyā, kāyàyyakī	loads
tunkìyā, tumākī	sheep

16. Plural Class IX --ū ending, tones all high :

māshì, māsū	spear
nāmà, nāmū	(wild) animal (see also I)
rāmì, rāmū	hole (see also II (*a*) (i), II (*b*) (ii))
sānìyā/sâ, shānū	cow
yātsà, yātsū	finger (see also I)

17. Plural Class X—reduplicative plurals :

àkàwū, àkàwū-àkàwū	clerk (see also II (*a*) (i))
cìwò, cìwàce-cìwàcē	illness
ɗā, 'yā'yā	son
en'è, en'è-en'è	Native Administration
gudù, gùje-gùjē	running
irì, irì-irì	kind, sort
tsallē, tsàlle-tsàllē	jumping

18. There are other plural forms not classifiable in any of the above classes, e.g. :

wani, waɗansu	a certain one
wannàn, waɗànnân	this one
wancàn, waɗàncân	that one
fartanyà, farètanī	hoe (see also I)
gàrmā, garèmanī	large hoe, plough (see also II (*a*) (i))
ƙanè, ƙànnē	younger brother
ƙwaryā, ƙôrē	gourd bowl
yàyā, yâyyē	elder sibling

Part Four

Supplementary Materials

Lesson 39

Letter Writing

1. Letter writing in Hausa is traditionally done according to a rather prescribed outline. The main elements of this outline are each signalled by standard formulas.

2. The *salutation* is usually :

Takàrdan nàn tā fìtō dàgà hannun Mālàm Bellò zuwà gà Mālàm Ìsā This letter is from the hand of Malam Bello to Malam Isa.

Or simply :

Zuwà gà Mālàm Ìsā	To Malam Isa
Zuwà gà mài martabà Mālàm	To the respected
Sānī	Malam Sani

3. The *opening paragraph* is typically taken up with greetings such as :

Gaisuwā mài yawà dà   sô   dà   yàrdā   dà
Greetings very many and affection and approval and

amincì.   Inà   fātā   kanà   lāfiyà—dà   kū   dà
friendship. I   hope you're healthy—both you and

ìyālìnkà   dukà—kàmar yaddà mu kè   à nân. Inà
your family   all—just   as   we are here. I am

murnà kwarai dà gàskē   dà na sàmi   dāmā   ìn
happy   very much   that I   have opportunity to

rubùtā makà wannàn 'yar wàsīkà dòmin   ìn sàmi
 write you   this   short letter in order to receive

làbārìnkà (na) bāyan   ràbommù.
news of you (of) after   our separation.

If the writer is not well known to the reader he will use the next paragraph after the salutations to introduce himself.

4. The *body of the letter* is then introduced by some such formula as :

Bāyan gaisuwā . . . (often abbreviated **B/G**)	After greetings . . .
Nā sàdu dà wàsīk̃àrkà yâu . . .	I received your letter today . . . [1]
Inà sanad dà kai . . . *or* **Inà sanasshē kà** . . .	I am informing you . . .
Bāyan wannàn . . .	After this . . .

The body of the letter may come to several paragraphs and will contain whatever the writer is seeking to communicate. It may end with something like :

Sai mun gàmu/sàdu/hàɗu.	Until we meet.

5. The *final paragraph* will typically enjoin the receiver to greet mutual friends and ask God's blessing, e.g. :

Gai dà   mutànen gidā   dukà dà   su Audù dà Garbà
Greet (your) household   all   and   Audu   and Garba
dà   sauran   idòn sanì   dà   kè̃ wurinkù dukà.
and rest of   acquaintances who   are near you   all.
Allà   yà   bā   mù   lāfiyà.   Àmin.
God may he give   us   health.   Amen.

6. The traditional *ending* is the Arabic signing-off followed by the writer's signature :

Hāzā wasàlàm/wàsàlāmù.	That's that (*lit.* . . . and peace).

---

[1] Or **Wàsīk̃àrkà tā sàdu dà nī** . . ., *Your letter came into my hand* . . ..

This ending is, however, being displaced by its Hausa equivalent : **shī kè nan**, or by such formulas as :

Nī nè, . . .	I am, . . .
(Nī nè)nākà, . . .	(I am) yours, . . .
Nī nè àbōkinkà . . .	I am your friend . . .
Masòyinkà . . .	Your good friend . . .

Lesson 40

Proverbs and Riddles

1. The Hausa language is rich in proverbial and aphoristic expressions (known as **karin màganà**, literally *stylized word*) and these play a prominent role in Hausa speech. As in English (and probably every other language) the introduction of a proverb at the right moment can be much more effective in making a point than elaborate explanation. Also, as in English, the speaker will often merely allude to a proverb to make his point (rather than saying the whole proverb), depending upon the listener to know the reference.

2. While a complete listing of even the most important proverbs is impossible here, the following list includes many of the most common. The student is referred to Abraham's *Dictionary* and to several small collections of proverbs, such as *Karin Magana* (Gaskiya Corporation, 1961) and A. H. M. Kirk-Green *Ai, Hausa Ba Dabo Ba Ne* (1966). The most complete collection is that by C. J. Whitting (1940, reprinted 1967). That by G. Merrick, 1905, is, unfortunately, out of print and very difficult to obtain.

(*a*) Proverbs exhorting to proper conduct :

   (1) **À bar kàzā cikin gāshìntà.** Leave the chicken in its feathers. (*i.e.* Let sleeping dogs lie.)
   (2) **Bābù lâifī, bābù tùnànī.** (If one does) no wrong, there is no regret.
   (3) **Dà mugunyàr** [1] **rawā gwàmmà kîn tāshì.** Rather than (dancing) a bad dance (one would be better

---

[1] This is a variant feminine form of **mūgù** (see Lesson 23).

advised to) refuse to leave (his place). (*i.e.* Leave
well enough alone *or* Don't attempt what you're
incapable of performing.)

(4) ' Dà nā sanì ' k̃yēyà cē. ' If I had (only) known ' is
(like) the back of (one's) head. (*i.e.* No use crying
over spilt milk, what's done is done and cannot be
undone *or* You have to live with it.)

(5) **Don tuwon gòbe a kè wankè tukunyā.** For the sake
of tomorrow's food one washes the cooking-pot.
(*i.e.* Don't spoil your chances tomorrow by being
careless now.)

(6) **Gidā biyu māgànin gòbarā.** (Having) two homes
(provides) protection (against) an outbreak of fire.
(*i.e.* Don't put all your eggs in one basket.)

(7) **Hanà wani, hanà kâi.** (If one) refuses another,
(one) refuses oneself. (*i.e.* Niggardliness recoils on
the miser.)

(8) **Kàràmbànin àkwiyà, gai dà kūrā.** (It was pure)
meddlesomeness (on the part of) the goat (to think
he could) greet the hyena (without disaster.) (*i.e.*
Don't attempt the impossible.)

(9) **Kāyan sàmmakō, dà màràicē a kàn d̃aurè shi.**
Loads (prepared for) an early morning start, in the
(previous) evening they are tied together. (*i.e.*
Forewarned is forearmed.)

(10) **Kōmē ka yi, kà nèmi àbin kânkà.** Whatever you do,
look after your own needs. (*i.e.* Depend on yourself,
don't sponge off others.)

(11) **Kwàd̃àyī mabūd̃in wàhalà.** Greed is the key (*i.e.*
path) to trouble.

(12) **Rāmìn mùgùntā à ginà shi gàjērē.** Dig a pit of evil
shallow. (*i.e.* Be careful not to be caught in your
own trap.)

(13) **Tūsà bā tà hūrà wutā.** Breaking wind won't bring a
(dormant) fire to flame. (*i.e.* Don't depend on
someone/something that can't do the job.)

(b) Proverbs exhorting activity :

(14) **Allà yā cê, ' Tàshi ìn tàimàkē kà.'** God says, ' Get up, (and *then*) let me help you.' (*i.e.* God helps those who help themselves.)

(15) **Àmfànin hankàlī aikì dà shī.** The value of good sense (is in) making use of it.

(16) **Barìn kāshī à cikì bā yà māgànin yunwà.** Keeping (one's) excrement in (one's) stomach doesn't keep (one) from hunger. (*i.e.* Speak out when the time comes—remaining silent won't solve the problem.)

(17) **Dà yayyafī kògī kàn cìka.**[2] By means of drizzles a river fills up. (*i.e.* Persistence pays off.)

(18) **Rìgàkafì yā fi māgànī.** A preventative is better than a medicine. (*i.e.* An ounce of prevention is better than a pound of remedy.)

(19) **Zùmùntā à ƙafà ta kè.** Good relationships (depend upon) feet. (*i.e.* The maintenance of good relationships between people requires frequent visiting.)

(c) Proverbs exhorting patience :

(20) **Hàƙuri māgànin dūniyà.** Patience is the world's medicine.

(21) **Mahùƙùrcī mawàdàcī.** A patient person (is) a wealthy person.

(22) **Mài hàƙuri ya kàn dafà dūtsè yà shā rōmonsà.** A patient person will cook a stone and drink its broth. (*i.e.* Patience is a virtue.)

(23) **' Sànnu bā tà hanà zuwà ', ìn ji kùnkurū.** ' (Travelling) slowly doesn't keep (one) from arriving,' says the tortoise. (*i.e.* Slow but sure.)

(24) **Yâu dà gòbe kâ iyà.** Today and tomorrow (= little by little) you will be able. (*i.e.* Little by little one can accomplish a thing.)

---

[2] Note the omission of the pronoun. This is common with this aspect in the third person singular in proverbs.

(25) **Yâu dà gòbe shī ya sâ àllūrà ginin rījīyā.** (Doing a thing) little by little this made it possible for the needle to dig a well. (*i.e.* Perseverance wins out.)

(26) **Zuwà dà wurì yā fi zuwà dà wuri.** Coming with some money (*lit.* a cowrie) is better than coming in good time. (*i.e.* It is better to arrive late with even a small gift than to arrive early with nothing.)

(*d*) Proverbs stating facts of life :

(27) **Darē rìgar mūgù.** Night-time (is) the cloak of evil.

(28) **Don hannunkà yā yi ɗōyī, bā kà yankèwā kà yar.** Because your hand has become foul smelling, you wouldn't cut it off and discard it. (*i.e.* One cannot but pardon the faults of one's dependants.)

(29) **Gàba dà gàbantà.** (Everyone) in front has (someone) in front of him. (*i.e.* Even the greatest has someone greater than him.)

(30) **Jìkī magàyī.** The body (is) the informer. (*i.e.* Let your strength be your guide—don't overdo things.)

(31) **Kōmē nīsan darē gàrī yâ wāyè.** No matter how long the night, morning will come. (*i.e.* Every cloud has a silver lining.)

(32) **Kurùm mā màganà cē.** Even silence is speech. (*i.e.* Silence may be significant.)

(33) **Làbārìn zūcìyā à tàmbàyi fuskà.** (For) the news of the heart one should ask the face. (*i.e.* One's face shows what is in one's heart.)

(34) **Tsōhon dōkì mài sànē.** An old horse (is) a knowing one.

(35) **Wànzāmì bā yà sôn jàrfā.** The tatooer (*lit.* barber) doesn't like (to be) tatooed. (*i.e.* One who cheats/ hurts others doesn't like it when the tables are turned on him.)

(*e*) Proverbs dealing with cause and effect, remedy, result :

(36) **Àlbarkàcin kàzā ƙàdangarè ya shā ruwan kaskō.**
Thanks to the chicken the lizard drank water from a
bowl. (*i.e.* Some gain advantages through no virtue
of their own.)

(37) **Mài nāmà ya kàn nèmi wutā.** The one who (already)
has meat will look for fire. (*i.e.* A person doesn't
seek a thing unless he already has a reason for
needing it.)

(38) ' **Mù jē mù ganī** ' **māgànin maƙàryàcī.** ' Let's go see
(it) ' (is) the remedy for a liar.

(39) **Tsūtsàn nāmà, ita mā nāmà cē.** The maggot in the
meat is itself meat. (*i.e.* It's all the same.)

(40) **Ùngùlū bā tà sàukā banzā.** The vulture doesn't
descend without reason. (*i.e.* A (dire) effect does
not come about without a cause.)

(41) **Yārò bài san wutā ba sai tā ƙònà shi.** A child doesn't
know fire until it burns him.

(*f*) Miscellaneous proverbs involving comparison :

(42) **Àbōkin sarkī, sarkī nè.** A chief's friend (is) a chief.
(*i.e.* The friend of a person in high position shares the
advantages of that position.)

(43) **Àlhērì gadon barcī nè.** Kindness is a bed to sleep on.
(*i.e.* Doing a favour is a good investment.)

(44) **Allà shī nè sarkī.** God is the Chief (of chiefs). (*i.e.*
God is over all.)

(45) **Dà tsìrārà gāra baƙin bàntē.** Rather than nakedness
better a black loincloth. (*i.e.* Half a loaf is better
than none.)

(46) **Dūniyà màcè dà cikì cē.** The world is a pregnant
woman. (*i.e.* No one knows what will come of the
pregnancy—a boy, a girl, alive, dead, *etc.*)

(47) **Ganī yā fi** (*or* **yā kòri**) **jî.** Seeing is better than (or
chases away) hearing. (*i.e.* Seeing is believing.)

(48) **Gàskiyā tā fi kwabò.** Truth is better than money
(*lit.* a penny). (*i.e.* Honesty is the best policy.)

(49) **Gīwā à gàrin wani zōmō.** An elephant in another's town (is but) a rabbit. (*i.e.* A person who is important in his own town is just another ordinary person in another town.)

(50) **Harbì à wutsiyà yā fi kuskurè.** Shooting (something) in the tail is better than missing (completely). (*i.e.* Half a loaf is better than none.)

(51) **Jìkī yā fi kûnnē jî.** The body is better at sensing/ hearing than the ears. (*i.e.* If one refuses to listen to advice he will be taught by hard knocks.)

(52) **Kàmā dà Wānè bà Wānè ba.** Like So-and-so (is) not So-and-so. (*i.e.* The similarity of two things is far from saying that they are the same.)

(53) **Kō bà à gwadà ba lìnzāmì yā fi bàkin kàzā.** Even though no measurement is taken (one can see that) a bridle is too big for the mouth of a chicken. (*i.e.* Such-and-such is completely obvious.)

(54) **Lāfìyàr jìkī arzìkī nè.** Health is wealth.

(55) **Rashìn sanì yā fi darē duhù.** Lack of knowledge is darker than night time. (*i.e.* There is nothing worse than ignorance.)

(56) **Sāmù yā fi iyàwā.** Possessing (something) is better than expertise (in using it). (*i.e.* Possession is nine points of the law.)

(*g*) Proverbs for more specialized situations :

(57) **Aikìn banzā màkāhò dà wàiwàye.** (It is) worthless work (for) a blind man to turn his head to look. (*i.e.* An illustration of a supreme waste of effort.)

(58) **Â nèmi jinī gà fàrā ?** Would one seek blood from a locust ? (*i.e.* You can't get blood from a stone.)

(59) **Bâ dāmā tēshàn Kanò.** The Kano railway station is impossible. (*i.e.* Not a chance anywhere.)

(60) **Banzā tā kòri wòfī.** A worthless one has chased away a useless one. (*i.e.* Two villains queered each other's pitch.)

(61) **In nā yi makà rānā, kadà kà yi minì darē.** If I make
daylight for you, don't you make night for me. (*i.e.*
If I do good to you, don't you repay me with evil.)

3. *Riddles* are a common form of Hausa word game.
Riddles are typically presented as statements (rather
than as questions). If the answerer is stumped by the
riddle he will reply **Nā bā kà gàrī,** *I give up* (lit. *I give you
the town*). He is then told the answer.

4. The following short list of riddles is taken largely from
G. Merrick, *Hausa Proverbs*, London, 1905 :

(1) **Rìgātā gùdā ɗaya, àljīfuntà ɗàrī.** *Answer* : **Gidan
gàrā.** I have only one gown (but it has) 100 pockets.
Answer : An anthill.

(2) **Bàba nà ɗākì, gēmùnsà nà wàje.** *Answer* : **Wutā dà
hayāƙī.** Father is in the hut (but) his beard is outside. *Answer* : Fire and smoke. (*i.e.* Fires are built
inside of huts for warmth. As the smoke streams out
through a door, window or through a grass roof it
resembles a white beard.)

(3) **Hanyà ɗaya tā ràbu biyu.** *Answer* : **Wàndō.** A
single path divides into two. *Answer* : Trousers.

(4) **Shānuntà ɗàrī, maɗaurintà ɗaya.** *Answer* : **Tsintsiyā.** Its cattle number 100 (but) it only has one
rope/string (*lit.* tyer.) *Answer* : A broom. (*i.e.* A
single string ties 100 or more pieces of grass together
to form a broom.)

(5) **Kàsuwā tā ci tā wātsè, tā bar kàrē kālā.** *Answer* :
Harshè. The market was held and broke up, it left
a dog gleaning. *Answer* : The tongue. (*i.e.* After a
person finishes eating his tongue goes wandering
around in his mouth picking up the remaining food.)

(6) **Gōɗīyātā tanà dà cikì. Bā nà hawan gōɗìyâr, sai cikì
na kè hawā.** *Answer* : **Ɗākì dà gadō à cikī.** My mare

is pregnant. I don't ride the mare, (I) only ride the
unborn foal. *Answer* : A hut with a bed in it.

(7) **Rawànin sarkī yā fàskàri nadèwā.** *Answer* : **Hanyà.**
The chief's turban was impossible to wind around
(his head). *Answer* : A road.

(8) **Dākìn sauràyī bābù ƙōfà.** *Answer* : **Kwai.** The hut
of a young man has no doorway. *Answer* : An egg.

(9) **Nā wankè ƙwaryāta. Nā jē gabàs, nā jē yâmmā, nā
dāwō, bà tà būshè ba.** *Answer* : **Harshèn kàrē cikin
bàkinsà.** I washed my calabash. I went to the east,
I went to the west, I returned, it hadn't dried.
Answer : A dog's tongue in its mouth.

(10) **Ukù-ukù, gamà gàrī.** *Answer* : **Murfù.** Three each,
the town (is) complete. *Answer* : The three stones
on which pots are set over fire = a local kind of
stove. (*i.e.* No town is complete without cooking
places.)

Lesson 41

Additional Conversations

1. It has been possible to include only a limited number of typical dialogues in the regular lessons. A larger selection, arranged topically appears below. Full translations are not given. Where explanation is necessary an asterisk (*) appears referring the student to section 8, *Notes*, at the end of this lesson.

2. Additional greeting conversations:

(*a*) **Audù** meets **Mūsā** :

   Audù : Sànnu.
   Mūsā : Sànnu dai.
   Audù : Lāfiyà ?
   Mūsā : Lafiyà lau.
   Audù : Ìnā gàjiyà ?
   Mūsā : Bâ gàjiyà.
   Audù : Ìnā làbārì ?
   Mūsā : Làbārì sai àlhērì.
   Audù : Ìnā ìyālìnkà ?
   Mūsā : Lāfiyà dai.
   Audù : Tò mādàllā.
   Mūsā : Kanà lāfiyà ?
   Audù : Lāfiyà, bâ kōmē.
   Mūsā : Mutànenkà lāfiyà ?
   Audù : Lāfiyà ƙalau.
   Mūsā : Ìnā aikì ?
   Audù : Àlhamdùlìllāhì
   Mūsā : Mādàllā, sai an jimà.
   Audù : Yâuwā, mun jimà dà yawà.

(b) **Mammàn** meets **Sulè** resting in the heat of the day :

Mammàn : Sànnu dà hūtàwā.
Sulè : Yâuwā, maràbā dà zuwà.
Mammàn : Ìnā wunì ?
Sulè : Lāfiyà.
Mammàn : Ìnā gùmī ?
Sulè : Ai lōkàcinsà nē.
Mammàn : Gàskiyarkà.
Sulè : Kā zō lāfiyà ?
Mammàn : Lāfiyà dai.
Sulè : Gidankà lāfiyà ?
Mammàn : Kalau.
Sulè : Mādàllā, zō kà zaunà.
Mammàn : Ā'à, zâ ni kàntī.
Sulè : Tò bâ lâifī, sai kā dāwō kè nan.
Mammàn : Yâuwā, sai nā dāwō.

(c) **Bellò** visits **Jàtau** (who has been sick) at the latter's home :

Bellò : Sàlāmù àlaikùn.
Jàtau : Yâuwā, shìgō Bellò.
Bellò : Mādàllā, kanà lāfiyà ?
Jàtau : Lāfiyà dai.
Bellò : Ìnā gidā ?
Jàtau : Lāfiyà.
Bellò : Mutànenkà lāfiyà ?
Jàtau : Lāfiyà dukà.
Bellò : Tô, yàyà jìkī ? *
Jàtau : Kâi, jìkīnā yanà dàmuwā * sòsai !
Bellò : Kâi, sànnu ! Cīwòn cikì nē ?
Jàtau : Ā'à, ƙafà cē.
Bellò : Kâi, Allà yà bā dà sauƙī.
Jàtau : Àmin.

3. Conversations dealing with foodtime :

(*a*) **Bàtūrè** and his cook **Àlī** :

Bàtūrè : Àbinci yā yi ?
Àlī :   Yā yi.
Bàtūrè : Tò dà kyâu.
Àlī :   Kanà sô ìn kāwō shì ?
Bàtūrè : Ī, àmmā bàri ìn wankè hannū tùkùna.
Àlī :   Tô, zân dākàtā kàɗan.
Bàtūrè : Kâi, nā ji yunwà yâu.
Àlī :   Tò bâ lâifī, nā shiryà àbinci dà yawà.
Bàtūrè : Dà kyâu, mè ka shiryà ?
Àlī :   Nāmàn sānìyā dà wākē dà dànkalì.
Bàtūrè : Mādàllā, kàwō sù.
Àlī :   Tô, inà zuwà.*
Bàtūrè : Zā mù yi bàƙī * gòbe.
Àlī :   Tô, zân jē kàsuwā dà sāfē.
Bàtūrè : Dà kyâu, à sàyi ìsasshen * nāmà.
Àlī :   Tô, wànè irì nē ka kè sô ?
Bàtūrè : Na kàzā yanà dà àràhā yànzu ?
Àlī :   Ai dāma-dāma * yànzu.
Bàtūrè : Tô zā kà yi burōdì * kumā ?
Àlī :   Ā'à, nā yī shì yâu.
Bàtūrè : Dà kyâu. Kâi, nā ƙòshi ! *
Àlī :   Mādàllā, bàri ìn kāwō kòfī.*
Bàtūrè : Tò dà kyâu.

(*b*) **Àliyù** and **Hasàn** drinking tea :

Àliyù :   Bàri mù zaunà mù shā tî.*
Hasàn : Tô, bâ lâifī.
Àliyù :   Gà sukàr * dà madarā nân.
Hasàn : Tò ɗèbō * mini sukàr kàɗan kawài.
Àliyù :   Àshē, bā kà sônsà dà zāƙī * ?
Hasàn : Ī, bâ dāɗī hakà.
Àliyù :   Ai bàn yàrda ba.
Hasàn : Kanà sôn sukàr dà yawà ?

Àliyù :   Sôsai !
Hasàn :   Tò bâ lâifī.
Àliyù :   Gà biskitì * kumā.
Hasàn :   Tô, nā gōdè.

4. Conversations on the road :

(a) Ìsā meets Garbà on the way to market :

Ìsā :   Sànnu Garbà, ìnā zuwà ? *
Garbà :   Ai, zâ ni kàsuwā.
Ìsā :   Tô, bàri mù jē tàre.
Garbà :   Mādàllā, mè zā kà yi à kàsuwā ?
Ìsā :   Zâ ni ìn gai dà ɗan'uwāna.
Garbà :   Tò dà kyâu. Dàgà gàrī ya kè ?
Ìsā :   Ā'à, dàgà ƙauyè * nē, àmmā yanà zuwà kàsuwā kullum.
Garbà :   Dà kyâu.
Ìsā :   Sàyē zā kà yi ?
Garbà :   Wàtàkīlà. Zân nèmi ƙōtàr * fartanyà.
Ìsā :   Tākà tā tsūfa nè ?
Garbà :   Ì, tanà sô tà karyè.*
Ìsā :   Lallē, yā kàmātà à sàmi sābuwâr.

(b) Daudà takes a trip in a lorry * :

(i) Bargaining for the price with the driver :

Daudà :   Dirēbà, inà sô ìn tàfi Kanò.
Dirēbà * :   Tô, kàwō sulè bakwài.
Daudà :   Habà !, Dâ mā kuɗinsà sulè shidà nē.
Dirēbà :   Bà cikin kyàkkyāwar mōtà kàmar wannàn ba.
Daudà :   Òhō. Zân nèmi wani dirēbà.
Dirēbà :   Zā kà biyā shidà dà sīsì nē ?
Daudà :   Bābù ! In bà shidà ba, zâ ni nēman wani.
Dirēbà :   Tô, kàwō kudī. Shìga dà saurī, zân bugà * yànzu.

(ii) On the road, chatting with the motor boy :

    Daudà :   Kâi, wannàn mōtà tā iyà gudù !
    Kàren Mōtà * : Sòsai ! Wannàn dirēbà tsōfon
                      hannū * nè.
    Daudà :   Yā dadè yanà aikìn dirēbà nē ?
    Kàren Mōtà : Hakà nē—wajen shèkarà
                      àshìrin.
    Daudà :   Kâi ! Wannàn mōtà tāsà cē ?
    Kàren Mōtà : Ì mànà ! Yanà dà mōtà ukù.
    Daudà :   Àshē ? Àmmā yā arzùtā ! *
    Kàren Mōtà : Gàskiyarkà. Ai, yā yi hajì *
                      bàra.
    Daudà :   Tabdì ! Dà mōtàrsà ?
    Kàren Mōtà : Ā'à, dà jirgin samà.
    Daudà :   Àshē ?
    Kàren Mōtà : Ì, anà cê dà shī, ' Àlhajì Jirgin
                      Samà.' *

(iii) Stopping for a ' rest stop ', talking with fellow
passenger **Bàlā** :

    Daudà : Bàri mù sàuka mù hūtà.
    Bàlā :   Tô, zâ ni dājì ìn yi fitsārī * tùkùna.
    Daudà : Tô, zân nèmi ràkē.*
    Bàla :   Dà kyâu, à sayō minì na tarō.

(iv) Starting again, the driver and the motor boy :

    Dirēbà :   Tô, à kirāwō * fasanjōjī.*
    Kàren Mōtà : Tô, sunà nan.
    Dirēbà :   Dukànsù ?
    Kàren Mōtà : Sai daya. Kai ! Zō maza !
    Dirēbà :   Yàyà yànzu ?
    Kàren Mōtà : Shī kè nan, bùgà mâi ! *

(v) Back on the road, **Daudà** and **Bàlā** :

    Daudà : Kâi, hanyàn nan tā 6àcì ! *
    Bàlā :   Lallē. Àkwai gàngarà * dà yawà.

Daudà :   Ĩ, dà santsī * kumā.

Bàlā :   Hakà nē, ruwan samà nē ya 6àtà * ta.

Daudà :   Har, wai, wani kògī yā cìka yā kwāshè gadà.*

Bàlā :   Ĩ, àmmā an gyârtā.*

Daudà :   A'a, mõtà ta tsayà !

(vi) Stuck on a slippery hill, the driver and motor boy giving orders :

Dirēbà :   Kàren mõtà ! Sã wejì ! *

Kàren Mõtà :   Tô, nā sã.

Dirēbà :   Kõwā yà sàuka yà tūrà.*

Kàren Mõtà :   (to passengers) Sàuka ! Sàuka !

Dirēbà :   Tô, tùra !

Kàren Mõtà :   Tô, bùga !

                   Shĩ kè nan, tā fìta.

                   (to passengers) Kù hau ! Kù hau !

                   (to driver) Tô, bùga !

5. Conversations at work :

(a) On the farm—when to plant :

Sà'īdù :   Kâi, ruwā * yā fārà zuwà sòsai !

Nūhù :   Gàskiyarkà, zân fārà shūkà gòbe.

Sà'īdù :   Àshē, bà kà sõmà * ba tùkùn ?

Nūhù :   Ĩ, nā yi ɗan lattì * bana.

Sà'īdù :   Ĩnā dàlīlì ?

Nūhù :   Ai uwātā tā ràsu * sātin nàn.

Sà'īdù :   Kâi, sànnu ! Mātankà fà ?   Sun màkarà kumā ?

Nūhù :   Ã'à, sun sõmà tun dà wuri.

Sà'īdù :   Dà kyâu, bà zā kù ji yunwà * ba.

Nūhù :   Hakà nē.

(b) On the farm—Nigerian versus Western hoes :

Bàtūrè :   Nī, bàn ta6à aikì dà irìn tākù fartanyà ba.

Hārūnà : Àshē ? Bābù irìntà à kasarkù ?

Bàtūrè : Ì, irìn tāmù tanà dà dōguwar kōtà * nē.

Hārūnà : Hakà nē. Don mè bà à kāwō sù nân ba ?

Bàtūrè : Ai, an kāwō, àmmā bâ su dà àmfànī.

Hārūnà : Àshē ?

Bàtūrè : Ì. Dōguwar kōtàrsù ta kàn karyè * dà saurī.

Hārūnà : Sabò dà taurin * kasā kè nan ?

Bàtūrè : Hakà nē.

Hārūnà : Ai, wàtàkīlà à kasarmù irìn tāmù tā fi kyâu.

Bàtūrè : Sòsai.

Hārūnà : Àmmā aikì dà irìn tāmù dà wùyā.

Bàtūrè : Gàskiyā nè—sai à sùnkwìye.*

Hārūnà : Hakà nē—har wani sā'ì mùtûm zâi ji cīwòn bāyā.

Bàtūrè : Kâi, mutànenkù sunà shân wàhalà !

Hārūnà : Ai dōlè nē. In bābù nōmā, bābù àbinci.

Bàtūrè : Gàskiyarkà—kō à kasarmù hakà ya kè.

(c) On the farm—anticipating harvest :

Yàkubù : Dà yàrdar Allà * hatsimmù * zâi yi kyâu bana.

Bàtūrè : Gàskiyarkà, ya tsìra sòsai.

Yàkubù : Har jân * yā fārà nùnā * yànzu.

Bàtūrè : Zā à yi girbìnsà à watàn Sàtumbà kō ?

Yàkubù : Ā'à, sai ruwā yā ɗaukē * tùkùn.

Bàtūrè : Tô, sai Òktōbà kè nan.

Yàkubù : Hakà nē. Anà girbìnsà sā'ì ɗaya dà gērō.*

Bàtūrè : Tô, farar dāwà fà ?

Yàkubù : Ai farâr, sai Nùwambà.

Bàtūrè : Àmmā ita cè mài kyânsù kō ?

Yàkubù : Sòsai ! Farâr tā fi dukà dāɗī.

Bàtūrè : Ràwayà * fà—an fi sôntà * dà jā ?

Yàkubù : Ì, àmmā bà tà kai farâr ba.

Bàtūrè : Yàushè a kàn gìrbē tà ?

Yàƙubù : Wajen farkon Nùwambà nē.
Bàtūrè : Kâi, kunà shân aikì dà kàkā.*
Yàƙubù : Gàskiyā nè. Àmmā munà sāmùn hūtū
     kàɗan dà rānī.*
Bàtūrè : Bābù aikì dà rānī ?
Yàƙubù : Ā'à, àkwai dà yawà, àmmā sai na gidā.*
Bàtūrè : Tò bâ lâifī.

(d) At the office—Gàmbo is a clerk (àkàwū), Sulè and
Yūsufù are messengers (māsinjà).

 (i) Gàmbo : Sulè !
    Sulè : Nà'am.
    Gàmbo : Zō kà kai wannàn wàsīƙà fâs ōfîs *
    Sulè : Rânkà yà daɗè !
    Gàmbo : Gà sulè biyu. Kà sayō kân sarkī * na
       āhù-āhù kà sâ biyu à kân wàsīƙàr.*
    Sulè : Tò shī kè nan ?
    Gàmbo : Shī kè nan.

 (ii) Gàmbo : Yūsufù, kàwō littāfîn ràsît.*
    Yūsufù : Tô, ngō.*
    Gàmbo : Tô, yànzu kà jē kàntin littàttàfai,* kà
       sayō sābon irìnsà.
    Yūsufù : Tô, nawà nē kuɗinsà ?
    Gàmbo : Yanà tsàkānin sulè ukù dà sulè huɗu.
       Gà sulè huɗu.
    Yūsufù : Tô, shī kè nan ?
    Gàmbo : Shī kè nan.

 (iii) Sulè : Nā dāwō. Gà kân sarkī.
    Gàmbo : Tô. Yànzu kà kai wannàn takàrdā *
       zuwà bàbban àkàwū à Jànhôl *—
       sūnansà Àlī.
    Sulè : Tô.
    Gàmbo : In kā kai tà cân sai kà biyō ta kàntin
       littàttàfai kà sayō minì kwalbar jar
       tàwadà.* Gà sulè.

Sulè :   Tô.
Gàmbo :   In kā ga Yūsufù cân kà cê masà yà
              dāwō dà wuri. Inà bùkātàrsà.
Sulè :   Tò nâ yi.
Gàmbo :   Shī kè nan.

6. Conversations dealing with health :

(a) Sùlèmānù meets Būbà on the path :

Sùlèmānù :   Inā zâ ka àbōkī ?
Būbà :   Ai, zâ ni asìbitì ìn shā māgànī.
Sùlèmānù :   Àshē ? Bā kà dà lāfiyà nē ?
Būbà :   Ī, bàn yi barcī ba yâu * kō kàɗan.
Sùlèmānù :   Zàzzàɓī nè ?
Būbà :   Ī, dà cīwòn kâi.
Sùlèmānù :   Kâi, bâ kyâu !
Būbà :   Hakà nē. Dâ yanà zuwà lōtò-lotò kawài
              àmmā yànzu nā yi kwānā ukù bàn
              ràbu * dà shī ba.
Sùlèmānù :   Likità zâi bā kà àllūrà nē ?
Būbà :   Wàtàkīlà. Hakà na kè sô.
Sùlèmānù :   Allà yà sawwàkē ! *
Būbà :   Àmin.

(b) Lawàl is chatting with Dōgo :

Lawàl :   Uwargidankà tā yi cikì * nē ?
Dōgo :   Hakà nē. Tanà dà na * watà bìyar.
Lawàl :   Mādàllā. Na farkō nè ?
Dōgo :   Ā'à, ta yi wani bàra àmmā yā zubè.*
Lawàl :   Tô, àmmā lāfiyà ta kè yànzu ?
Dōgo :   Ai dāma-dāma.* In Allà yā yàrda zā tà haifù
          lāfiyà.
Lawàl :   Tò Allà yà sâ.
Dōgo :   Àmin.

(c) Àbūbakàr has come to the doctor with a complaint :

Àbūbakàr :	Kâi, likità, cikìnā yanà dāmùnā * ƙwarai !
Likità :	Kâi, sànnu ! Yàushè nē ya sōmà ? *
Àbūbakàr :	Ai yā daɗè—kàmar sātī biyu.
Likità :	Tô. Kwàntā * à tēbùr nân mù dūbà.
Àbūbakàr :	Tô.
Likità :	Kanà zāwò * nē ?
Àbūbakàr :	Ā'à. Ai cikì yā ɗaurè.*
Likità :	Tô. In nā taɓà nân, dà zāfī * nè ?
Àbūbakàr :	Ā'à, bài fi na * sauran cikì ba.
Likità :	Tô, kā iyà tāshì yànzu. Kà jē kà cikà wannàn kwalbā dà fitsārī,* kà cikà wannàn dà bāyan gidā, kà bar sù nân, kà dāwō gòbe.
Àbūbakàr :	Tô.
Likità :	Shī kè nan, sai gòbe wàrhakà.*
Àbūbakàr :	Yâuwā, sai gòbe.

7. Conversations dealing with weather :

(a) Ìmâm and Sambò sitting outside the latter's home :

Ìmâm :	Kâi, gìzàgìzai * sun yi yawà.
Sambò :	Ai, dàmunā tā kusa.*
Ìmâm :	Gàskiyarkà, watàn Afrìl nē.
Sambò :	Inà bègē * dàmunā zā tà yi kyâu bana.
Ìmâm :	Nī mā hakà. Bàra ruwā bài yi sòsai ba.
Sambò :	Har hatsin * wasu yā ƙōnè.*
Ìmâm :	Hakà nē. Sabò dà wannàn waɗansu sunà jîn yunwà yànzu.
Sambò :	Waɗansu mā sun ci bāshì dòmin hātsinsù yā kāsà.*
Ìmâm :	Gàskiyarkà. Àmmā in Allà yā yàrda àbîn zâi gyàru * bana.
Sambò :	Allà yà sâ.

(b) **Àdàmu** explains Nigerian seasons to a European :

Bàtūrè : À ƙasarmù ruwā yanà zuwà kōwànè lōkàcī.

Àdàmu : Àshē ? Bà hakà ya kè à wurimmù ba.

Bàtūrè : Yàyà ?

Àdàmu : Sai dà dàmunā nè mu kè sāmùn ruwā.

Bàtūrè : Bābù ruwā dà rānī ?

Àdàmu : Kō kàɗan.

Bàtūrè : Dà bazarā * fà ?

Àdàmu : Ai wani sā'ì àkwai ruwā kàɗan dà bazarā.

Bàtūrè : Tô, àmmā bâ yawà kō ?

Àdàmu : Wani lōkàcī zâi zō dà ɗan yawà.

Bàtūrè : Àshē ?

Àdàmu : Ī, àmmā an jimà sai yà ɗâukē.*

Bàtūrè : Tô, ìdan an shūkà dà bazarā zâi yi * nè ?

Àdàmu : Wàtàkīlà, àmmā yawancin lōkàcī bā yà yî.

Bàtūrè : Mài shūkà zâi shā wàhalà kō ?

Àdàmu : Hakà nē. Àbinsà sai yà lālàcē.*

Bàtūrè : Kâi, wannàn bâ kyâu !

Àdàmu : Gàskiyarkà, àmmā lâifin kânsà * nē.

8. Notes on asterisked items from the conversations presented in sections 2–7 of this lesson :

2 (c)	**yàyà jìkī ?**	how's (your) illness (lit. body) ? (see Lesson 31, section 5)
	dàmuwā	the verbal noun from **dàmu**
3 (a)	**inà zuwà**	I'm coming (i.e. just a minute and I'll have it done)
	yi bàƙī	have guests
	ìsasshē	enough (from **isa,** be enough)
	dāma-dāma	a bit better (than formerly)
	burōdì/brōdì	bread, rolls
	ƙòshi	have become full (of food)
	kòfī	coffee
3 (b)	**tî**	tea

	sukàr	sugar
	ɗēbō	dip out (into my cup) (from ɗībà, *extract, draw out*)
	zāƙī	sweetness
	bìskitì	biscuit (British English), cookie (American English)
4 (*a*)	ìnā zuwà = ìnā zâ ka	
	ƙauyè	village, suburb
	ƙōtà	handle (of hoe, axe, *etc.*)
	karyè	snap, break (as a stick breaks)
4 (*b*)	in a lorry	lorries are the ordinary means of transportation for people as well as goods over large areas of Nigeria. There are buses and other passenger vehicles in and between certain large urban centres as well.
4 (*b*) (i)	dirēbà	driver
	bugà	start (the engine), start (driving)
4 (*b*) (ii)	kàren mōtà	motor boy (*lit.* motor dog). He is the person responsible to see that loads, people, etc., are all in place before the lorry starts, to inform the driver if anything goes wrong, to put wedges behind the wheels when the lorry stops, (sometimes) to collect the fares, etc.
	tsōfon hannū	' old hand ', experienced person
	arzùtā	has become wealthy
	hajì	pilgrimage to Mecca
	Àlhajì Jirgin Samà	an Alhaji who has made the pilgrimage by aeroplane. (The title is used humorously.) Alhaji is the title given to anyone who has made the pilgrimage.

4 (b) (iii)	**fìtsārī**	urinate. It is not considered indelicate for a person to state that the reason for his going off is to urinate.
	ràkē	sugarcane
4 (b) (iv)	**kirāwō**	call here (the **-ō** form of **kirā**)
	fasanjōjī	the plural of **fasànjà** = passenger
	bùgà mâi	start going ! (*lit.* hit the petrol. 'step on the gas')
4 (b) (v)	**ɓācì**	is ruined, spoiled
	gàngarà	bumpiness
	santsī	slipperiness
	ɓātà	ruin, spoil
	gadà	bridge (from English 'girder')
	gyârtā	= **gyārà**, fix, repair
4 (b) (vi)	**wejì/wajì**	wedge. Each lorry carries two or more wooden blocks (usually approximately four inches square with one end whittled down to form a handle) which the motor boy puts behind (or in front of) the rear wheels whenever the lorry is stopped, to keep it from rolling.
	turà	push
5 (a)	**ruwā**	in a context such as this it means *rain*
	sōmà	= **fārà**, begin, start
	lattì	late
	ràsu	died (the **-u** form of **rasà**, lack)
	ji yunwà	here it means *go hungry, starve*
5 (b)	**ƙōtà**	handle (of hoe, axe, *etc.*—see also under 4 (a) above)
	karyè	snap, break (as a stick—see also under 4 (a) above)

	taurī	hardness, toughness
	à sùnkwìye	stooped over
5 (c)	dà yàrdar	
	Allà	by God's grace
	hatsī	grain
	jân	red variety of guinea corn—the earliest maturing and lowest prestige type of guinea corn
	nùnā	ripening
	ɗâukē	(rain) stops
	gērō	early maturing variety of millet
	ràwayà	yellow variety of guinea corn
	fi sô	prefer
	kàkā	harvest season
	rānī	dry season
	na gidā	work at home (e.g. repairing the huts, re-roofing, making new mats, etc.)
5 (d) (i)	fâs ōfis	post office (also called gidan wayà = home of the tele-phone/telegraph)
	kân sarkī	postage stamp (lit. head of the king)
	wàsīk̃à	letter
5 (d) (ii)	ràsît	(littāfin ràsît = receipt book)
	ngō/ungō	here, take it !
	kàntin	
	littàttàfai	bookstore, bookshop
5 (d) (iii)	takàrdā	letter (lit. paper)
	Jànhôl/Jàn hwâl	John Holt canteen (name of a prominent commercial firm)
	jar tàwadà	red ink
6 (a)	yâu	the Hausa day begins at 6 p.m. Thus, I didn't sleep today in Hausa is I didn't sleep last night in English.

	ràbu	be separated (**-u** form of **rabà,** *separate, divide*)
	Allà yà sawwàḳē	may God lighten (your) trouble (see Lesson 31, section 5)
6 (*b*)	**yi cikì**	become pregnant
	na	(*i.e.* pregnancy of)
	zubè	(pregnancy) aborted
	dāma-dāma	better than before (at least)
6 (*c*)	**yanà dāmùnā**	it is bothering me
	sōmà	= **fārà** (see also under 5 (*a*) above)
	kwàntā	(from **kwàntā,** *lie down*) lie down !
	zāwò	diarrhoea
	cikì yā ɗaurè	I'm constipated (*lit.* stomach has tied up)
	dà zāfī	is there pain ? (**zāfī** = heat, pain)
	na	*i.e.* pain of
	fitsārī	urine (see also under 4 (b) (iii) above)
	(gòbe) wàrhakà	at this time (tomorrow) (see Lesson 33, section 2)
7 (*a*)	**gìzàgìzai**	(plural of **girgijè,** *raincloud*) clouds
	kusa	is close (verb form of the noun **kusa,** *close*)
	bègē	a noun meaning *hope*
	hatsī	grain (see also under 5 (*c*) above)
	ḳōnè	burn (*i.e.* from the heat of the sun and lack of moisture)
	kāsà	run short, fall short
	gyàru	be repaired, corrected (**-u** form from **gyārà,** *fix, repair*)
7 (*b*)	**bazarā**	hot, muggy season (March–April) just before the rains come

ɗâukē	(rain) stops (see also under 5 (*c*) above)
zâi yi ?	will it mature ?
lālàcē	spoil (= **ɓācì** under 4 (*b*) (v) above)
lâifin kânsà	his own fault

Lesson 42

Additional Texts

1. Several fables have already been introduced as conversational materials in the foregoing lessons (see Lessons 20, 23, 26, 27, 30). Several more are introduced below. Since some version of each of these has already appeared in print (usually minus any indication of tone and vowel length) a reference to these is given for each text.

2. Màkāhò̀ Mài Fìtìlà

Wani sauràyī yanà̀ yāwò̀ dà dàddarē sai ya hàngi wani mùtûm dà fìtìlà à hannunsà. Dà sukà̀ gàmu ya ga—àshē, màkāhò̀ nē!

Sai ya cề, ' Kai, màkāhò̀, kanà̀ hàukā nề ? Mề ya kai kà yāwò̀ dà fìtìlà ? Darē dà rānā bà̀ duk ɗaya su kề gàrē kà ba ? '

Màkāhò̀ ya cê, ' Ai, duk ɗaya nề mànà ! Har, in dà darē nề nà̀ fī kà ganī. Fìtìlàn nan, nā riƙề ta bà̀ don kâinā ba nề, àmmā don irìnkù nē—màsu idò̀ àmmā maràsā hankàlī—don kù gan nì dà dàddarē, kadà̀ kù tūrề ni ! '

Notes :

See *Ka Kara Karatu*, NORLA (now Gaskiya Corporation), 1954, page 4. See also Abraham, R. C., *Hausa Literature*, 1959, page 37.

màkāhò̀	blind man
sauràyī (*pl.* sàmàrī)	young man
dà dàddarē = dà darē	at night

hàngā (i/ē)	see from a distance
hàukā	going mad
duk ɗaya	it's all the same
irìnkù	the likes of you
màsu idò	able to see (*lit.* possessing eyes)
tūrè	knock over

3. Dilā da Zalɓè

Wata rānā dilā yanà cîn kàzā, sai wani ƙàshī mài tsìnī ya kākàrē masà à màƙōgwàrō. Ya bi nân, ya bi cân, yanà nēman wandà zâi cirè masà ƙàshîn. Ya cê duk wandà ya cirè masà, zâi bā shì lādā.

Tô, sai zalɓè ya zō, ya cè shī zâi yi. Dilā ya būɗè bàkī, zalɓè ya sâ kânsà, ya cirō ƙàshîn.

Dilā ya jūyà, zâi yi tàfiyàrsà, sai zalɓè ya cê, ' Ìnā lādāna ? '

Dilā ya amsà, ya cè, ' Ai, lādankà kè nan : kā sâ kânkà cikin bàkin dilā, kā fìta lāfiyà ! '

Notes :

See *Ka Kara Karatu*, NORLA (now Gaskiya Corporation), 1954, page 7. See also Abraham, R. C., *Hausa Literature*, 1959, page 37.

zalɓè	common grey heron
ƙàshī	bone
tsìnī	sharp point
kākàrē	become jammed
màƙōgwàrō	throat
ya bi nân, ya bi cân	he went hither and thither
cirè	pull out
duk wandà	whoever
lādā	reward
cirō	pull out (-ō form of cirè)
jūyà	turn (*i.e.* turned to go)
lādankà kè nan	this is your reward

4. Kwàɗī Biyu

Waɗansu kwàɗī gùdā biyu sukà �fàɗà cikin ƙwaryar madarā, sukà kāsà fìtā. Sunà ta iyò, sunà ta iyò, bâ dāmā. Anà nan, sai ɗayansù ya gàji, ya cê, ' Yâu kwānānā ya ƙārè.' Ya bar ƙòƙarī, ya nutsè, ya mutù. Dayân, mā, ya yi ta yî. Mòtsinsà kumā, ya sâ mâi ya tàru, ya yi cūrì. Sā'àn nan ya hau bisà cūrìn mân, ya yi tsallē, ya fìta. Allà ya cê, ' Tàshi ìn tàimàkē kà.'

Notes :

See *Ka Kara Karatu*, NORLA (now Gaskiya Corporation), 1954, page 4. See also Abraham, R. C., *Hausa Literature*, 1959, page 37.

kwàɗī (*sing.* kwàɗō)	frogs
kāsà	run short, fall short
ta	in the process of
iyò	swimming
bâ dāmā	it is/was impossible (dāmā = chance, opportunity)
anà nan	after awhile
nutsè	vanish (under water)
yi ta yî	keep on trying
mòtsī	movement, motion, activity
mâi	= mân shānū
tàru	gather together, collect (-u form of tārà, *gather, collect*)
cūrì	a ball
sā'àn nan	then . . .
tsallē	a jump

5. Mūgùn Àlƙālī

Akà kai wani ƙārā wurin àlƙālī, akà yi shàrī'à. Àlƙālī ya ga wandà akà yi ƙārarsà bâ shi dà gàskiyā, ya cê masà, ' Kanà dà màganà ? '

Mùtumìn ya cê bā yà dà màganà àmmā à ɓòye yā kwatàntà ukù dà hannunsà. Dà àlƙālī ya ga mùtumìn ya kwatàntā dà hannunsà hakà ya yi tsàmmānì zâi bā shì awākī ukù nē. Sai ya yankè shàrī'à, sukà tāshì.

Dà mùtumìn ya kōmà gidā, ya aikō wà àlƙālī dà kàbēwà gùdā ukù. Dà ganin hakà àlƙālîn ya kirāwō mùtûm, ya cê masà, ' Kai, dai, munāfùkī nè, kā cùcē nì ! Allà wadankà ! Tàshi, tàfi ! '

Dà mùtumìn ya fìta wàjē, ya cê, ' M̂, wànzāmì bā yà sôn jàrfā.'

Notes :

See *Ka Kara Karatu*, NORLA (now Gaskiya Corporation), 1954, page 6. See also Abraham, R. C., *Hausa Literature*, 1959, page 37.

àlƙālī	judge
shàrī'à	administration of justice
wandà akà yi ƙārarsà	the accused
à ɓòye	hidden (from ɓòyè, *hide*)
kwatàntā	indicate, compare (here, the man held up three fingers)
yankè shàrī'à	pass sentence, give the verdict
aikō . . . dà	send to (-ō form of aikà, *send*)
kàbēwà	pumpkin
dà ganin hakà	when he saw this
kirāwō	call (here) (the -ō form of kirā, *call*)
munāfùkī	hypocrite, traitor
cùtā (i/ē)	cheat
Allà wadankà	may God curse you !
m̂	(exclamation of slight surprise)
wànzāmì	barber (who shaves people's heads, performs scarification, tattoos, *etc.*)
jàrfā	tattoo marks
wànzāmì . . .	for the meaning of this proverb see Lesson 40, proverb 35

6. Kwàɗī dà Shānū

Waɗansu kwàɗī sunà̀ kīwò à fàdamà̀, sai sukà̀ hàngi bìjìmai gùdā biyu sunà̀ faɗà̀. Sai ɗayansù ya cê, ' Kâi ! Faɗà̀ ɗìn nan fa, dà ban tsòrō ! Mū, waɗàndà bā mù dà ƙarfī, yà̀yà̀ zā mù yi dà kâmmù ? '

Wàncan, kumā, ya cê, ' Kâi, ìnā ruwansù dà mū ? Sunà̀ yī tsàkāninsù kawài, don duk wandà̀ ya fi ƙarfī tsàkāninsù yà̀ gājè̀ mātan shānūn dà kè̀ cikin garkèn nân. Ai, bā sà̀ kùlā dà irìmmù ƙanānà̀.'

Na farkō, mā, ya amsà̀ cêwā, ' Hakà̀ nē. Nā sanì, kōmē nāsù dàban ya kè̀ dà nāmù. À̀l'àdun zamansù bà̀ ɗaya su kè̀ dà nāmù ba. Àmmā fa, duk dà hakà̀, kō dà su kè̀ dà nīsa yànzu, wandà̀ ya kāsà̀ cikinsù zâi shēƙà̀ dà gudù̀, bà̀ zâi kùlā dà kōmē ba sai kânsà̀. Wàtàkīlà̀ zâi zō yà̀ tattàkē mu cikin gudù̀. Lallē, faɗànsù yā shà̀fē mù ! '

Àshē gàskiyā nè̀ akà̀ cê, ' Ìdan mânya-mânyā sunà̀ faɗà̀ kō talakāwā su kàn shā wàhalà̀.'

Notes :

See *Al'mara*, Oxford University Press and Gaskiya Corporation, 1952, page 4.

kīwò	grazing, searching for food; tending animals
fàdamà̀	marshy ground
bìjimī/bàjimī	
(*pl.* **bìjìmai/bàjìmai**)	big bull
faɗà̀	fighting, arguing
fa	(emphasis particle or insert) indeed
ban tsòrō	frightening, terrifying (*lit.* giving fear)
wàncan	the other one, the one in question
ìnā ruwansù ?	what do they care ? (**bā̀ ruwansà̀** it is none of his concern ; **ìnā ruwankà̀ ?** what business is it of yours ?)

gājè	inherit (-è form of gàdā, *inherit*)
garkè	herd, flock
kùlā dà	pay attention to
kōmē nāsù	everything about them
àl'ādà (*pl.* àl'àdū)	custom
àl'àdun zamansù	their way of life
ɗaya	here it means *same*
kō dà	even though
shēƙà dà gudù	take to (his) heels
tattàkē	trample under foot (from tākà, *tread on, walk along*)
mu	a direct object pronoun is high after a high-low-high tone verb
shàfā (i/ē)	affect, wipe
mânya-mânyā	the influential/wealthy of the world

7. Farkē dà Birai

An yi wani farkē, àttājìrī. Wata rānā ya ɗàuki hūlunàn dàrā gùdā gōmà zâi kai kàsuwā. Yanà kân hanyà sai ya rātsè gìndin wani itàcē don yà hūtà. Dà ya ji barcī yanà nēman kāmà shi, sai ya sâ duk hūlunàn à bisà kânsà— ɗaya bisà ɗaya—māgànin ɓàràyī kè nan. Shī kè nan, barcī ya kwāshè shi har dà minshārī.

Cân sai waɗansu birai sukà biyō ta wurîn dà farkên nan kè barcī, sukà gan shì. Tô, kun san halin birai dà sôn wàsā. Sai birì gùdā ya laɓàɓā, ya zārè hùlâd dà kè bisà, ya sâ à kânsà. Sauran birai, kumā, dà ɗai-ɗai sukà yi hakà. Sukà bar farkē dà tsōhuwar hùlarsà kawài. Sukà hayè kân itàcē, sukà zaunà, sunà kallonsà.

Farkē ya farkà bai ga hūlunànsà ba. Ya ɗagà kâi samà, sai ya yi arbà dà ɓàràyinsà à kân itàcē! Haushī ya kāmà shi. Ya cirè hùlâd dà kè kânsà, ya wurgar! Nan dà nan birai, kumā, sukà kwàikwàyē shi, sukà yi ta wurgō tāsù ƙasà. M̀hm̂! Mādàllā! Farkē ya tsincè kāyansà, ya tàfi yanà farin cikì.

Notes :

See *Mu Koyi Hausa,* Gaskiya Corporation, 1960.

farkē/falkē	itinerant trader
birì (*pl.* birai)	monkey
àttājìrī	wealthy trader
hŭlā (*pl.* hūlunà)	hat, cap
dàrā	fez (hŭlad dàrā = *fez*)
rātsè	turn aside, swerve (*e.g.* from a road)
daya bisà daya	one on top of the other
ɓàrāwò (*pl.* ɓàràyī)	thief
minshārī	snoring
cân	used this way cân = *later*
biyō ta wurîn . . .	came by the place . . .
halī	character, temperament
sôn wàsā	playfulness (*lit.* liking playing)
laɓàɓà	sneak up on
zarè	grab
dà dai-dai	one by one
hayè	climb (hayè kân itàcē = *climb up into the tree*)
dagà	lift up
yi arbà	come upon unexpectedly
haushī	vexation, anger
cirè	pull (thing) off, pull (thing) out
wurgar	throw (violently) (-ar form of wurgà, *throw*)
kwàikwayà(i/ē)	imitate
wurgō	throw down (-ō form of wurgà, *throw*)
m̀hm̂	exclamation of approval of an action
tsincè	pick up, find by chance (*e.g.* along the road) (-è form of tsìntā, *pick up*)
farin cikì	happiness (*lit.* white stomach)

Lesson 43

Bibliography

1. Publication of materials in and on Hausa started well before the beginning of the twentieth century. The first important grammar of the language was published by J. F. Schön in 1862, followed by his Hausa dictionary in 1876,[1] and by 1911 it was possible for Struck to produce a bibliography of Hausa which lists 227 items.[2] An excellent survey of early writings in Hausa is P. E. H. Hair, *The Early Study of Nigerian Languages* (Cambridge University Press, 1967).

In addition to a substantial number of books and articles by Europeans, Hausa students are fortunate to have at their disposal a large number of publications *in* Hausa. The contents of these publications include fables, history, biography, proverbs, poetry, geography, nature study, religious materials and much more. The abundance of such material is due largely to the efforts of the Gaskiya Corporation in Zaria, which has also published a weekly newspaper for over twenty-five years.[3] Since 1969, much of this initiative has passed to the Northern Nigerian Publishing Company, Zaria.

There follows a selection of the publications in English or Hausa which are of value to students beginning the study of Hausa.

2. *Grammars* of a language are of two types : reference grammars and pedagogical (teaching) grammars. In

---

[1] Schön, J. F., *Grammar of the Hausa Language*. London : Church Missionary House, 1862. *Dictionary* (same publisher), 1876.

[2] ' Linguistic Bibliography of Northern Nigeria ', *Journal of the African Society*, XI, 1911–12, pp. 47–61, 213–230.

[3] First issued January, 1939, editor Abubakar Imam.

spite of certain modifications made in the present grammar to make it usable as a pedagogical grammar, it is basically an introductory reference grammar. It is recommended that this book be used whenever possible in conjunction with a good pedagogical grammar, plus a native speaker of Hausa, for maximum effectiveness.

(a) *Pedagogical Grammars.* Two pedagogical grammars can be recommended. The first will be most easily usable with this book because of the similarity of approach. Tape recordings are available for use with each of these books.

Kraft, Charles H. and Marguerite G., *Spoken Hausa: Introductory Course.* Los Angeles, University of California Press, 1973.

Hodge, Carleton T., and Ibrahim Umaru, *Hausa Basic Course.* Washington, D.C. : U.S. Government Printing Office (for the Foreign Service Institute), 1963.

An earlier pedagogical approach which, though brief, is useful (if obtainable) is H. L. Ogilvie, *Helps to the Study of Hausa.* Jos : Sudan Interior Mission, 1942–1951.

(b) *Reference Grammars.* The majority of the grammars of Hausa which have been published must be classified as reference grammars (although many, like the present volume, provide vocabularies and exercises to assist the beginning student).

(i) Only one of these grammars provides any accurate and thoroughgoing representation of tone and vowel length. It also provides a more accurate treatment of Hausa grammar than any of its competitors and thus, in spite of grave defects in the way the book is organized must, be regarded as the best available :

Abraham, R. C., *The Language of the Hausa People*. London : University of London Press, 1959. This edition is a rearrangement of *A Modern Grammar of Spoken Hausa*, 1941.

(ii) Other reference grammars with which the student may come into contact are listed and briefly evaluated below.

Maxwell, J. Lowry, and Eleanor M. Forshey, *Yau da Gobe*. Jos : Niger Press, n.d.
A valuable, though traditional, outline presentation of Haùsa grammar. It ignores tone and vowel length but is generally reliable and more convenient to use than most of the other reference grammars listed here.

Robinson, Charles H., *Hausa Grammar*. London : Routledge and Kegan Paul, 1925 (reprinted 1959).
Once the standard grammar of Hausa. Produced between 1897–1925 by one of the greatest of Hausa scholars. A brief treatment of Hausa grammar with no attention to tone or vowel length but containing some valuable cultural materials.

Taylor, F. W., *A Practical Hausa Grammar*, London : Oxford University Press, 1923 (reprinted 1959).
A more complete grammar than Robinson's. Among the more useful of the older grammars but not always accurate.

Migeod, F. W. H., *A Grammar of the Hausa Language*. London : Kegan Paul, 1914.
The most extensive of the older grammars.

(iii) Passing mention may also be made of the following grammars which because of age, incompleteness or unreliability are of less value than those already listed :

Miller, W. R., *Hausa Notes*. London : Church Missionary Society, 1901.

Miller, E. P., *Wata Biyu (A Guide to Hausa)*. Jos : S. I. M. Bookshop, revised edition 1939.

Howeidy, A., *Concise Hausa Grammar*. Oxford : George Ronald, 1953 and 1959.

Skinner, A. N., *Hausa for Beginners*. London : University of London Press, 1958. 2nd edition, 1968.

Brauner, S., and M. Ashiwaju, *Lehrbuch der Hausa-Sprache*. Leipzig : VEB Verlag Enzyklopadie, 1966.

3. *Dictionaries*.   There are two good dictionaries of Hausa : [4]

Abraham, R. C., *Dictionary of the Hausa Language*. London : University of London Press, 1949 (reprinted 1962).

Bargery, G. P., *A Hausa–English Dictionary and English–Hausa Vocabulary*. London : Oxford University Press, 1934 (reprinted 1951).

Abraham's dictionary provides a more accurate tonal analysis and marks tone and vowel length throughout. It contains, however, no English to Hausa section. Both dictionaries cover virtually the same ground.

A. N. Skinner's, *Hausa–English Pocket Dictionary : Kamus na Hausa da Turanci* (London : Longmans, Green and Company, 1959, revised 1968) and *An*

[4] The earlier dictionaries by Schön (1876) and Robinson (1900), ' good ' in their day, do not compare with Abraham or Bargery.

English–Hausa Dictionary (Zaria ; Gaskiya Corporation, 1966) are very much ' for the pocket '. Unfortunately, they either ignore or are untrustworthy in their representation of tone and vowel length.

A more useful book (although it does not represent tone or vowel length) is *Hanyar Tadi da Turanci*, published by Longmans, Green and Company in 1957 (by A. N. Skinner though no author is indicated). This book is subtitled *A Dictionary of English Conversation for Hausa Students* but is very useful as an English to Hausa guide, containing over 300 pages of ordinary and idiomatic Hausa expressions.

4. *Reading Materials in Hausa.* As mentioned above there is an abundance of such materials and more are being produced all the time. Of the hundreds of items that could be listed, the following is a small sampling.

Abraham, R. C., *Hausa Literature and the Hausa Sound System.* London : University of London Press. 1959.

The first two thirds of this volume is an unorganized collection of Hausa literature with English translations of varying quality. This and Kraft's, *Hausa Readings* are, however, the only published collections of Hausa literature which are marked for tone and vowel length.

Ainslie, Marian D., *Nijeriya.* London : Longmans, Green and Company and Zaria : Gaskiya Corporation, 1960.

A 90-page elementary school geography book.

Baker, R. L. and L. O. Musawa, *Oxford Hausa Reader*, series 1, 2, 3. London : Oxford University Press, 1957–58.

Three well illustrated primary school reading primers.

Bello, Alhaji, *Gandoki*, Zaria : Gaskiya Corporation, 1934. 4th edition 1968.

A 73-page historical novel.

Bamalli, Nuhu, *Mungo Park Mabudin Kwara*. Zaria : Gaskiya Corporation, 1948 (reprinted 1955).
A 153-page account of Mungo Park's first and his last journeys seeking the mouth of the Niger River.

Bamalli, Nuhu, *Bala da Babiya*. Zaria : Gaskiya Corporation, 1950.
An 82-page elementary health book.

Court, J. W., ed., *Kungurus Kan Kusu*. London : Longmans, Green and Co., 1958.
A short selection of fables in Hausa.

East, Rupert, and Abubakar Imam, *Ikon Allah*. Zaria : Gaskiya Corporation, 1949 (reprinted 1952).
A nature study book of nearly 400 pages.

Edgar, Frank (vols I and II), and Malam Mamman Kano (vols III, IV, V), *Dare Dubu da Daya* (five volumes). Lagos : CMS Bookshop and Zaria : Gaskiya Corporation, 1924–64.
The Arabian Nights in Hausa.

Johnston, H. A. S., ed., *A Selection of Hausa Stories*. London : Oxford University Press (Oxford Library of African Literature Series), 1966.

Kirk-Greene, A. H. M., and Yahaya Aliyu, *A Modern Hausa Reader*, London : University of London Press, 1966.
A collection of speeches and newspaper reports illustrating contemporary Hausa.

Kraft, C. H., *Hausa Reader*. Berkeley and Los Angeles: University of California Press, 1973.
Cultural, geographical and historical texts in Hausa (all marked for tone and vowel length).

Imam, Alhaji Abubakar, *Magana Jari Ce* (three volumes). Zaria : Gaskiya Corporation, 1937–39. 5th edition 1960.

A good, full-length (over 650 pages) novel. A bit advanced for a beginner but excellent reading at a later stage. A classic of Hausa literature.

Maƙarfi, Abdullahi, *Namun Daji da Tsuntsaye*. Zaria : Gaskiya Corporation, 1958.
A 71-page description of several wild animals and birds of West Africa.

Mani, Abdulmalik, *Zuwan Turawa Nijeriya Ta Arewa*. London : Longmans, Green and Company, and Zaria : Gaskiya Corporation, 1957.
A 218 page history of the arrival of the British in Northern Nigeria.

Rimmer, E. M., *et al.*, *Zaman Mutum da Sana'arsa*. Zaria : Gaskiya Corporation, 1955.
A 200-page treatment of various customs and crafts of certain of the world's peoples.

Skinner, A. N., *Hausa Tales and Traditions*, vol. I. London : Frank Cass, 1969.
This is the first of three volumes giving for the first time an English translation of F. Edgar's classic three-volume collection of Hausa folktales published in 1911–13 as *Litafi na Tatsuniyoyi na Hausa*.

Skinner, A. N., *Hausa Readings*. Wisconsin University Press, 1968.
A collection of readings from Edgar in Hausa with notes. Some are in *ajami* (Arabic) as well as romanized script.

Tafawa Balewa, Alhaji Sir Abubakar, *Shehu Umar*. Zaria : Gaskiya Corporation, 1946 (reprinted 1955).
The first novel of the late Prime Minister of Nigeria (49 pages), dealing with the travels of Shehu Umar from Bornu to Arabia. An English translation by M. Hiskett was published by Longmans in 1967.

Miscellaneous story booklets published by Gaskiya Corporation and Northern Nigerian Publishing Company :

Ka Kara Karatu (47 pages of fables).

Ka Yi Ta Karatu (77 pages of fables).

Al'mara (29 pages of fables).

Karamin Sani (two booklets, 56 and 62 pages of helpful information for elementary school children).

Jiki Magayi (a 51-page novelette).

Littafi Na Karantawa (48 pages of fables).

Ka Koyi Karatu (a 30-page elementary reader)

Ruwan Bagaja (a major novel).

Idon Matambayi (elementary reader).

Labaru Na Dā Da Na Yanzu (a schools' favourite).

5. *Specialized Studies.* These include general historical and cultural background materials both in English and Hausa.

Ames, David, and King, Anthony, *Glossary of Hausa Music . . . in Social Contexts.* Northwestern University Press, 1971.

Dalziel, J. M., *A Hausa Botanical Vocabulary.* London, 1916.

The standard work on this topic.

Hassan, A., and S. Naibi, *Chronicle of Abuja.* Lagos : African Universities Press, 1962.

An excellently illustrated account of Hausa society in Abuja.

Hill, Polly, *Rural Hausa : A Village and a Setting·* Cambridge University Press, 1972.

Hogben, S. J., and A. H. M. Kirk-Greene, *The Emirates of Northern Nigeria.* London : Oxford University Press, 1966.

Detailed history of the Hausa kingdoms.

Kirk-Greene, A. H. M., ' Neologisms in Hausa : A Sociological Approach,' *Africa*, vol. XXXIII, 1963, pp. 25–44.

A treatment of many of the fascinating borrowings coming into Hausa recently through contact with European languages (primarily English).

—— A Preliminary Inquiry into Hausa Onomatology. Zaria : Ahmadu Bello University, 1964.

Three studies in the origins of personal, title and place names.

——, *Ai, Hausa Ba Dabo Ba Ne*, Ibadan : Oxford University Press, 1966.

A collection of 500 Hausa proverbs with translations and notes.

Madauci, Ibrahim, Yahaya Isa and Bello Daura, *Hausa Customs*. Zaria, N.N.P.C., 1968.

A useful exposition of Hausa customs, crafts, pastimes, etc. Published in English.

Rattray, R. S., *Hausa Folk-Lore, Customs, Proverbs*. Oxford : Clarendon Press, 1913 (reprinted 1968).

An important collection, mostly gathered in Northern Ghana.

Smith, Mary F., *Baba of Karo*. London : Faber and Faber, 1954 (reprinted 1964).

A valuable biography of a Hausa woman in English with an introduction to Hausa society by M. G. Smith.

Smith, M. G., *The Economy of a Hausa Community of Zaria*, London : Her Majesty's Stationery Office, 1955.

A detailed study of the economics of a Hausa village.

—— *Government in Zazzau*. London : Oxford University Press, 1960.

An excellent political analysis of a Hausa state, 1800–1950.

Taylor, F. W., and A. G. Webb, *The Customs of the Hausa People*. London : Oxford University Press, 1932.
A useful collection of cultural texts in Hausa and English.

Tremearne, A. J. N., *Hausa Superstitions and Customs*. London : J. Bale, Sons, 1913 (reprinted Frank Cass 1970).
A large collection in English of cultural materials.

Whitting, C. E. J., *Hausa and Fulani Proverbs*. Lagos : Government Printer, 1940 (reprinted by Gregg International, Farnborough, Hants, England, 1967).
A major collection of 2000 Hausa and 600 Fulani proverbs with English translations.

6. *Technical Studies*. A few of the many technical studies in English are noted here for those who wish to go more deeply into Hausa study. The titles indicate the content.

Other important technical articles in English will be found in such journals as *African Language Studies, Journal of African Languages, Journal of West African Languages, Bulletin of the School of Oriental and African Studies, Studies in African Linguistics, Afrika und Übersee*, etc. There are, in addition, several prominent Hausa scholars who customarily write in languages other than English. Among these are D. Olderogge of Russia, C. Gouffé of France, J. Lukas of Germany, P. Zima of Czechoslovakia and N. Pilszczikowa of Poland. In 1972 the Nigerian Languages Centre of Abdullahi Bayero College, Kano, produced the first issue of an African languages review written in Hausa, *Harsunan Nijeriya*. The most complete recent listing of writings on Hausa is that compiled by D. W. Arnott for the revised edition (1970) of D. Westermann and M. A. Bryan, *The Languages of West Africa* (International African Institute).

Carnochan, J., ' Glottalization in Hausa,' *Transactions of the Philological Society*, 1952, pp. 78–109.

Carnochan, J., ' A Study of Quantity in Hausa,' *Bulletin of the School of Oriental and African Studies*, 1951, pp. 1032–1044

Greenberg, Joseph H., ' Arabic Loan-Words in Hausa,' *Word*, 1947, pp. 85–97.

—— ' Some Problems in Hausa Phonology,' *Language*, 1941, pp. 316–323.

Hodge, Carleton T., *An Outline of Hausa Grammar*, supplement to *Language*, 1947.

Kraft, Charles H., ' The Morpheme nà in Relation to a Broader Classification of Hausa Verbals,' *Journal of African Languages*, 1964, pp. 231–240.

—— *A Study of Hausa Syntax* (3 volumes). Hartford, Connecticut : Hartford Seminary Foundation Bookstore, 1963.

Newman, Paul, ' Ideophones From a Syntactic Point of View ', *Journal of West African Languages*, V, 1968, pp. 107–17.

Parsons, F. W., ' An Introduction to Gender in Hausa,' *African Language Studies I*, 1960, pp. 117–136.

—— ' The Operation of Gender in Hausa : The Personal Pronouns and Genitive Copula,' *African Language Studies II*, 1961, pp. 100–124.

—— ' The Operation of Gender in Hausa : Stabilizer, Dependent Nominals and Qualifiers, *African Language Studies IV*, 1963, pp. 166–207.

—— ' Suppletion and Neutralization in the Verbal System of Hausa ', *Afrika und Übersee*, LV, 1971, pp. 49–97.

——, ' The Verbal System in Hausa,' *Afrika und Übersee*, XLIV, 1960, pp. 1–36.

Schachter, Paul, ' A Generative Account of Hausa ne and ce ', *Journal of African Languages*, V, 1966, pp. 34–53.

PART FIVE

APPENDICES

Key to Exercises

Hausa to English Exercises : [1]

Lesson 5 :

1. It's water.
2. They are donkeys.
3. It's an elephant.
4. She's an old woman.
5. He's a European.
6. It's a bird.
7. He's (my) grandfather.
8. It's a rat.
9. He's a student.
10. He's a man.

Lesson 6 :

1. Who is it ?
2. It's a town.
3. He's not the chief.
4. It is a school.
5. It's a bucket.
6. It's not a compound.
7. They are not children.
8. It's me.
9. It is her.
10. It is us.

---

[1] It should be noted that there is often more than one possible translation for a given sentence. Only one translation (usually the most probable) is given here. The translations are designed to provide the most natural English equivalent of the Hausa rather than to be word for word literal renderings.

Lesson 7 :

1. They didn't go away.
2. I haven't eaten yet.
3. They didn't bring the book.
4. The girl didn't return.
5. Audu didn't come to school.

Lesson 8 :

1. Where is the chief's home ?
2. He's the chief's boy.
3. I brought Garba's lamp.
4. It is cat food.
5. The girl went to the schoolteacher's farm.

Lesson 9 :

1. The boy went to Kano with his mother.
2. Your teacher went to his farm this morning.
3. Why did you put your book on my chair ?
4. My horse entered your friend's town.
5. He brought my bicycle. He didn't bring yours.

Lesson 10 :

1. A (certain) boy fell into the water.
2. This river is the Niger.
3. You (have) put this spoon in this box.
4. Where is the chair ? There's the chair.
5. These people went to a certain town.

Lesson 11 :

1. There are two mangoes on the table.
2. Arithmetic is difficult. But I understand.
3. He put the banana in his mouth, he ate (it).
4. Where is the large box ? Bello has gone to his home
   with it.

5. How many guavas did you bring ? Ten.
6. Good heavens ! Audu has forgotten my name. This is not good.

Lesson 12 :

1. Don't do this work.
2. Don't let the girl eat this food.
3. Come and sit down (to a female).
4. Don't do thus.
5. Go out and close the door.

Lesson 13 :

1. I am hungry. Is there food ?
2. Did you bring that man ? Yes, here he is.
3. Isn't there a spoon here ? Yes (there is not).
4. Have the children gone to school ? Not yet.
5. Haven't you got ready ? No (on the contrary, we have got ready).
6. Here is Malam Garba's book. Where is mine ?

Lesson 14 :

1. What happened at Yakubu's house ?
2. The storm has passed now. Let's play.
3. Stop and tie up your loads.
4. His horse ran swiftly to the town.
5. He went to his friend's.

Lesson 15 :

1. Bello brought us meat.
2. Take them this book and return quickly.
3. Who gave you the eggs ? The trader at the side of the road.
4. She went to market, she bought an expensive yam.
5. You (*f.*) picked them up. You (*f.*) took them to your husband's home.

Lesson 16 :

1. I am very hungry. Because of this I will eat now.
2. We won't eat here.
3. What will you (*f.*) do ? I shall return to town after a while.
4. Will you tell me the news of your trip ?
5. Are you going to market today ? No, we're going to my friend's home.

Lesson 17 :

1. He fell into the water.
2. After the dance we will go to the chief's.
3. If he returns then I shall go.
4. He did his work like a boy.
5. Before I go he will come.
6. The guest put his shoes under my chair.

Lesson 18 :

1. I don't have (any) farming implements.
2. His father is coming now.
3. My wife is working very well on the farm.
4. The chief wants to come and talk to us tomorrow.
5. (My) wife has our food in her hut.
6. The people of that town don't dance.

Lesson 19 :

1. She is drinking water.
2. Does he open the door ? Yes, he opens (it).
3. Do they sell motor cars ? Yes, they sell (them).
4. This box is heavy.
5. This work is not difficult.

Lesson 20 :

1. The people who are coming will stay here a long time.
2. The one who came today left early.

3. There is no one whom they fear.
4. What was done at Kano the day before yesterday ?
5. I didn't see those that you want there.

Lesson 21 :

1. Where is the money I gave you yesterday ?
2. Which lorry will you go in ?
3. I saw a kind of dance that I hadn't seen before.
4. Whenever he comes I don't want to see him.
5. I won't buy anything at market today.

Lesson 22 :

1. Lorries killed many people last year.
2. People want doctors to do their work well.
3. Men are stronger than women.
4. Where are the compounds in which we left our loads yesterday ?
5. He sent me to the leading men of the town because they want(ed) me to talk to them.

Lesson 23 :

1. Some large aeroplanes landed at Kano.
2. Those looking for food obtained a little.
3. This little book is better reading than that big one.
4. Little children are playing in the old man's home.
5. He put on (his) big gown but didn't dance.

Lesson 24 :

1. During the rainy season this river filled to the brim with water.
2. All of us got up at the same time, we threw him outside.
3. When I saw him all of a sudden he mounted his horse (and) ran off.

4. Long ago there was an old man who prepared his farm at the edge of this road.
5. It is imperative that they get work right away. Will you give it to them ?

Lesson 25 :

1. They dismissed her from (her) work.
2. Sell it to me please.
3. Don't you (*pl.*) worry, nothing has happened yet.
4. Pour it in the basin. After that water the horse.
5. Why won't you reveal your secret from within your heart ?

Lesson 26 :

1. May God permit us to be successful in our trading. If this does not happen we'll have to borrow.
2. Let me increase my efforts in this work. Why, haven't you got tired ? Won't you leave (it) yet ?
3. I've never seen this type of dance. Let me try to do it. God forbid! Good gracious, you won't be able to do it!
4. I talked to him last week but he hasn't returned this week.
5. In the past they rode horses but now they prefer cars. Is that so ? It's true.

Lesson 27 :

1. I had planned to go to his home (anyway) to greet him, then I heard the news and decided it would be best for me to tell him.
2. Before he (first) came I had worked here a long time.
3. When I came upon him immediately he broke into a run.
4. Is our food all gone ? No, there is a little left. Do you want me to cook some more ?
5. Will the Minister of Education give a speech at Gusau ? Yes, let's get ready and go.

Lesson 28 :

1. Why, I forgot to bring the food cooked. I brought it uncooked.
2. It will be best for you to wait here for now. Before you return again it will be foodtime.
3. We kept asking everywhere in town but we got no news of him.
4. Heavens ! An amazing thing happened yesterday— the noise of an aeroplane frightened me so that I almost ran away !
5. I'm going to the canteen to buy tinned food, bottled beer and (some) other things that I need.

Lesson 29 :

1. I need to cut this cloth. Pick up the scissors and help me.
2. He's not a person of good character. He is trying to keep my friend from (obtaining) work.
3. When he had entered his market stall he sat down and started sewing.
4. I'll wait for him. That is, I shall wait here until he returns.
5. There are indications that you will have trouble here if you don't relocate your things right away.

Lesson 30 :

1. A snake bit the messenger but the doctor gave him medicine so that he got well.
2. He's not a Hausa, he's a Fulani. But in spite of this he speaks the Kano dialect (of Hausa) well.
3. Zaria is south-west of Kano. Katsina is to the north-west of it.
4. We had planned to work together but he was late. Because of this I lack anything to sell at market.
5. Moses is an expert. There is no one who can do this work except him alone. We should engage him instead of Audu.

English to Hausa Exercises : [2]

Lesson 5 :

1. Sūnā nè.
2. Sâ nē.
3. 'Bèràyē nè.
4. Bàhaushè nē.
5. Mātā nè.
6. Màcè cē.
7. Wàsā nè.
8. Zàkarà nē.
9. Gidā nè.
10. Watà nē.

Lesson 6 :

1. Makarantā cè.
2. Mùtûm nē.
3. Yârā nè.
4. Sarkī nè.
5. Shī kè nan.
6. Bà sâ ba nè, sānìyā cè.
7. Bà yârā ba nè.
8. Kuɗī nè.
9. Bà idò ba nè.
10. Bà kàsuwā ba cè.

Lesson 7 :

1. Mùtûm bài yi gōnā ba.
2. Bài zō dà sāfē ba.
3. Yārinyà bà tà tàfi gōnā ba.
4. Bàn yi aikì ba tùkùna.
5. Bà à kāwō kujèrā ba.

---

[2] It should be noted that there is often more than one possible translation for a given sentence. Only one translation (usually the most probable) is given here. The translations are designed to provide the most natural Hausa equivalent of the English rather than to be word for word literal renderings.

Lesson 8 :

1. Wannàn gidan sarkī nè ?
2. Ùban yārò yā tàfi Kanò.
3. Mālàmin makarantā bài ci àbinci ba.
4. Ìnā àbincin dōkì ?
5. Gà sānìyar Audù.

Lesson 9 :

1. Uwātā dà ùbānā sun tàfi gidankà jiyà.
2. Ìnā sàbulùna ? Nā sâ shi cikin ɗākìna. Gà nākà.
3. Gidammù à Kanò nē. Ìnā nākà ?
4. Ùbantà yā fìta gàrī à kân hanyàr Kanò.
5. Yàushè àbōkīnā ya ci àbincinsà. Dà sāfē.

Lesson 10 :

1. Wannàn yārò àbōkīnā nè.
2. Kin sâ wancàn kujèrā nân.
3. Waɗànnân yârā. Waɗàncân yârā.
4. Bàn sanì ba tùkùna.
5. Nā tàfi gàrin càn.

Lesson 11 :

1. Yārinyà tā zaunà à kujèrā.
2. Nā yi kuskurè cikin lìssāfìna.
3. Yā kai kèkē zuwà gidansà.
4. Mun bi hanyà à bàkin kògī.
5. Kâi !, àkwai mùtûm takwàs cikin wancàn mōtà.

Lesson 12 :

1. Kadà kà buɗè tāgà !
2. Tsàya ! Shìga ! Zàuna !
3. Kì kāwō àbinci nân.
4. Bàri yà yi aikìnsà.
5. Kù zō kù ci àbincinkù à gidammù.

Lesson 13 :

1. Uwātā tā dāwō (nè) ? Ā'à, bà tà dāwō ba.
2. Bellò bài tàfi Kanò jiyà ba ? Ā'à, yā tàfi.
3. Àkwai aikì ? Ī, àkwai aikì dà yawà àmmā bābù kuɗī.
4. Àkwai ƙwai dà madarā nân ? Àkwai madarā, àmmā
   bābù ƙwai.
5. Nā ji yunwà. Kai fà ?

Lesson 14 :

1. Tā wucè ƙōfà.
2. Sun tàfi sù zaunà cikin inuwàr itàcē.
3. Yā fàru nân jiyà.
4. Audù yā kōmà gidā shēkaranjiyà.
5. Tā tàfi kàsuwā dà wuri.

Lesson 15 :

1. Yā gan nì ? Ī, àmmā bài san kà ba.
2. Yā sàmi nāmà. Tā dafà shi. Sun cī shi dà saurī.
3. Mun bar mangwàrò (gùdā) ukù cikin mōtàrsà. (Kà)
   tàfi kà sàmē sù.
4. Tā shiryà manà àbinci cikin inuwàr bàbban itàcē.
5. Yā sàyi kāyan aikì. Bàn san dàlīlì ba.

Lesson 16 :

1. Zā mù tàfi rawā à kàsuwā gòbe.
2. Bà zā kà tàfi makarantā ba.
3. Zā sù tàmbàyē kà kà bā sù kuɗī.
4. Ìnā zâ ka ? Zâ ni yāwò.
5. Gòbe Mālàm Bellò zâi tàfi Kanò. Zâi kāwō dōkìn
   ùbansà.

Lesson 17 :

1. Nā ga Yūsufù dà ùbansà à gidansù.
2. Kō nī kō ita zâi zō makarantā gòbe dà sāfē.

3. Nā nềmi àkwiyầ ƙàrƙashin tēbừr àmmā bần gan tầ ba.
4. Ìdan nā dāwō watầ mầi zuwầ sai ìn sàyē shì.
5. Ìdan kầ yi minì aikì zā kầ sầmi kuɗī dầgầ gầrē nì (*or* dầgầ wurīna).

Lesson 18 :

1. Sunầ màganầ tầre.
2. Yā yìwu yanầ Ìkkō yànzu.
3. Yanầ dầ bầbban itầcē gầban gidansầ.
4. Yanầ dầ 'yan'uwā (gùdā) ukừ à gidā.
5. Bâ ni dầ shī. Don Allầ kadầ kầ yi fushì!
6. Ìdan yanầ nan bầ zân tầfi cikin jirgin ƙasā ba.

Lesson 19 :

1. Ƙōfầ tanầ bừɗe. Rùfē shì.
2. Tanầ kāwō ƙwaryā.
3. Yanầ sàyen àbinci? Ì, yanầ sàyē.
4. Bầ tầ hūrầ wutā ba? Ā'ầ, tā hūrầ.
5. Yanầ tsàye dầ kāyā mầi nauyī à kânsầ.

Lesson 20 :

1. Tīcầ nē mukầ ganī.
2. Wancàn màcè tanầ aikì nân.
3. Yầushè kikầ zō?
4. Gầ yârā waɗầndầ zā sừ tầfi cikin mōtầ.
5. Zā mừ sầmē sừ à wurîn dầ mukầ gan sừ jiyầ.

Lesson 21 :

1. Kā san shì nē? Yanầ dầ zằzzằɓī.
2. Ìnā ka tàfi dầ mōtầrmừ?
3. Wàcè irìn rìgā nề ka kāwō dầgầ kàntī?
4. Inầ dầ aikì dầ yawầ kō'ìnā cikin gàrin nàn.
5. Cân nā ga sarkîn dầ ya zō gàrī jiyầ.

Lesson 22 :
1. Àkwai màkàràntū dà yawà à ƙasàshen Afirkà.
2. Hàusàwā sunà dà kùjèrū dà yawà cikin gidàjensù.
3. Waɗansu lìttàttàfai sunà dà tātsūniyōyī à cikī.
4. Bābù mōtōcī dà yawà à waɗansu ƙasàshē.
5. Marōƙā waɗàndà su kè nan jiyà bā sà nan yâu.

Lesson 23 :
1. Kanò bà tà kai Ìkkō girmā ba.
2. Rìgarsà ja-ja cè.
3. Dōkìnsà yā kai nàwa gudù.
4. Gàjèrū dà yawà sunà zàune à ɗākì.
5. Faràrē sun fi baƙàƙē kyâu.

Lesson 24 :
1. Tāyà waddà na ganī sābuwā ful cè.
2. Gùdu maza-maza kà kāwō ruwā.
3. Zā tà shiryà àbinci yâu yâu.
4. Inà sô ìn tàfi gidānā tùkùn.
5. An jimà kàɗan zā mù kōmà gidàjemmù.

Lesson 25 :
1. Kâr kà zub dà shī ! Kàmā shì kà shìga.
2. Sun sayō itàcē.
3. Kā tabbàtā tā shā shì dukà ? Ì, tā shā.
4. Sàukar dà shī nân. Yànzu kwàntar dà shī.
5. Mun fisshē shì, mun tsayar dà shī.

Lesson 26 :
1. Nā zìyàrci gidan sarkī àmmā yā rigā yā tàfi.
2. Kâi, wancàn mùtûm yā cikà ƙaryā ! Sabò dà wannàn bā nà sônsà.
3. Anà ruwā dà yawà dà dàmunā. Hakà nē.

4. Bài daɗè à Nījēriyà ba àmmā yā iyà Hausā kàmar jàkin Kanò.
5. Inà sô ìn ci bāshì dòmin ìn sàyi sābuwar mōtà.

Lesson 27 :

1. Waɗansu mafàsā sunà sô ìn gayà masù làbārìn gàrī.
2. Nā sàmē shì yanà aikì. Shī màkānīkì nē. Yā daɗè yanà gyāran mōtōcī.
3. Dâ mā yā yàrda yà dākàtā nân har ìn zō, àmmā yànzu bàn san àbîn dà zâi yi ba.
4. Sarkī yā cê, kadà kà sākè zuwà gidansà. Yā fi kyâu kà sàmē shì à ōfìshinsà.
5. Yā iyà Hausā àmmā tanà masà wùyā ainù.

Lesson 28 :

1. Nawà-nawà nē gwēbà ? Kwabò-kwabò (nē), bâ ragì.
2. Câ na kè zā kà zō gòbe àmmā kā zō jiyà.
3. Àkwai abūbuwà màsu bā dà màmākì dà yawà à dūniyà yâu.
4. Yā fi kyâu à ci dàfaffen àbinci dà tàfàsasshen ruwā kadà à ji cīwò.
5. Ìdan bàn yi jarràbâwā ba bà zân cī tà ba.

Lesson 29 :

1. Kà ɗinkà minì kyàkkyāwar rìgā. Zâ ni rawā gòbe.
2. Inà sô kà tàimàkē nì ìn kau dà kèken ɗinkìnā zuwà wata bukkà.
3. Nī, kàm, zân jirā shì nân—wàtàkīlà zâi zō an jimà.
4. Bàn nūnà masà àgōgonkà ba. Wai, yā gan shì à hannunkà.
5. Bài ci ba tùkùna. Dom mè ? Dòmin nā hanà masà àbinci har kà dāwō.

Lesson 30 :

1. Shī màntau nè. Kadà kà gayà masà yà yi makà wani àbù.

2. Jìm kàɗan ma'àikàtā dukà sukà tàfi. Bàn san àbîn
   dà zân yi ba.
3. Kàwō mabūɗī nân. Bàri ìn būɗè ƙōfà.
4. Nā dākàtā kàɗan har makàɗā sukà fārà kasà kûnnē.
5. Inà tsàmmānì ìdan màtarsà tā rērà wāƙà sarkī zâi yi
   màmākì.

Translations of Dialogues and Fables

Lesson 4 :

B. Greetings at (your) coming, Isa.
I. Greetings.
B. How's (your) tiredness ?
I. There's no tiredness.
B. How's (your) work ?
I. (I'm) thankful for work.
B. What's the news ?
I. The news (is) only good.
B. Good.
I. Did (you) sleep well ?
B. Fine.
I. How's (your) family ?
B. Very well.
I. Good. (See you) tomorrow.
B. Good, may God take us (to tomorrow).
I. Amen.

Lesson 5 :

M. Greetings student.
A. Greetings teacher.
M. What's this ?
A. This is a donkey.
M. Okay, what's this ?
A. It's a bird.
M. What's this ?
A. It's a goat.
M. Okay, what's this ?
A. This is a sheep.
M. Good, until tomorrow.
A. Okay, may God take us (to tomorrow).

Lesson 6 :

Y. Greetings at your coming David.
D. Greetings.
Y. Did you sleep well ?
D. Very well.
Y. Who went to town ?
D. Audu.
Y. Has he returned ?
D. No, not until tomorrow.
Y. Good.

Lesson 7 :

B. How's (your) day (going) ?
G. Fine.
B. How's (your) tiredness ?
G. There's no tiredness.
B. Good.
G. Have you come well ?
B. Fine, nothing's wrong.
G. Is your family well ?
B. Very well.
G. Where's Bello ?
B. He went to Kano.
G. Good. Did he go to market ?
B. No, he didn't go to market.
G. Okay. (See you) later.
B. Okay. (See you) later.

Lesson 8 :

U. What is this called ?
A. It's a bicycle.
U. Whose is it ?
A. This is the bicycle of the chief's son.
U. Okay, where's Audu's bicycle ?
A. There it is in the hut.

U. Good, thank (you).

A. Okay.

Lesson 9 :

Ad. Is this compound yours ?

Ab. Yes, it's mine.

Ad. Where is your farm ?

Ab. There's my farm over there.

Ad. Good.

Ab. I finished planting yesterday.

Ad. Fine, when did you start ?

Ab. At the beginning of this month.

Ad. As for me, I haven't finished mine yet.

Ab. That's okay. I (have to) go now.

Ad. Okay, until another time.

Ab. Fine, may God take us (to another time).

Ad. Amen.

Lesson 10 :

K. Some people have come to our compound.

M. Good, I've brought food from market today.

K. Good. There's plenty of drinking water too.

M. The chief of the town has come.

K. (You're) right. He has come with an important man.

M. Is that man a chief also ?

K. Yes, his boy has brought a large box.

M. Good, what's in the box ?

K. I don't know.

Lesson 11 :

M. Two and three are how many ?

D. They are five.

M. That's right. How about six and seven ?

D. Thirteen.

M. Good. Four times two is how many ?

Ɗ. It's nine.
M. No ! You made a mistake.
Ɗ. (You're) right. It's only eight.
M. Okay. How many is six times three ?
Ɗ. Eighteen.
M. Good. Is this arithmetic difficult ?
Ɗ. No, it's not difficult.
M. Good.

Lesson 12 :

H. Jacob, greetings.
Y. Greetings.
H. Is your family well ?
Y. Very well. Have you come well ?
H. Fine. Nothing's wrong.
Y. Good. Enter, let's sit down.
H. Good. Gosh, the sun is hot today.
Y. (You're) right. Boy, bring drinking water !
H. I've come to greet you.
Y. Good. Thank (you). Have you come from market ?
H. No, I've come from home just now.
Y. Fine. Here's water to drink.
H. Good, thanks. I (have to) go now.
Y. Okay. Until another time.
H. Fine, until another time.

Lesson 13 :

M. Are there potatoes at market today ?
G. No, but there are a lot of yams.
M. Good. How much do yams cost ?
G. 1 shilling and 5 kobos to 2 shillings.
M. Wow they are expensive !
G. Not so ! They are all large.
M. That's all right. Are there also bananas ?
G. Yes there are, but not many.
M. Fine, how about guavas ?

G. A lot. There are also plenty of mangoes and citrus.

M. Good. Let's go and get (some).

G. Good, let's go.

Lesson 14 :

B. How much does a bicycle tyre cost ?

M. Well, there are three kinds. There are white, black and red.

B. Fine, how much does each cost ?

M. A white one is 1 naira, 6 shillings.

B. Wow, that's expensive !

M. But that's the best one.

B. How about a black one ?

M. 1 naira, 4 shillings.

B. What about a red one ?

M. The red ones are the least expensive at 1 naira, 2 shillings.

B. Good.

Lesson 15 :

B. Okay, I'll buy the white one for 1 naira, 4 shillings.

M. No sale. That's the price of a black one.

B. All right, how much is the real price ?

M. I reduce (the price) 3 kobos.

B. I increase (my price) by 5 kobos.

M. Come, come now sir !

B. Speak the truth.

M. Pay ₦1·55.

B. Okay, I offer (you) ₦1·50.

M. I'll agree to ₦1·52½.

B. Good, here's the money.

Lesson 16 :

A. Where are you going Kande ?

K. I'm going to the canteen to buy a new body cloth.

A. Why ?

K. To put on to go to the dance the day after tomorrow.
A. Good. Boy, your present body cloth is no good !
K. You're right. It has really got old.
A. Did your husband give you the money ?
K. No ! I sold (some) peanuts.
A. Okay.

Lesson 17 :

M. Greetings in (your) work Dogo.
D. Greetings at (your) coming.
M. How's (your) day (going) ?
D. Fine, nothing wrong.
M. Good.
D. Are you heading for town ?
M. No, I'm just out for a stroll.
D. Okay. Let's sit down and chat.
M. Okay. Here's (some) good shade.
D. Goodness, it's (really) hot today !
M. You're right, it's the time for it.
D. Right.
M. I hear you will go to Kano tomorrow.
D. Yes. I'll go by lorry in the morning.
M. Good, what will you do there ?
D. I'm going to sell my guinea corn in the market.
M. Good. Will you stay long in Kano ?
D. Yes, I'm going to look for work there.
M. Fine. When will you return (here) ?
D. Not until next month.
M. Good. I have to go now.
D. Okay. (See you) when I return from Kano.
M. Right, may you return safely.
D. Amen.

Lesson 18 :

J. I want to talk to the head of the house.
G. The head of the house isn't here today.

J. Okay, when will he return ?

G. Why, I don't know. He went to Lagos.

J. Did he go by aeroplane ?

G. No, by train.

J. How many days will he stay there ?

G. Oh it won't be more than a week.

J. Is he going to buy supplies there ?

G. Probably. But he went because his brother has died.

J. Will he most probably return next week ?

G. Yes.

J. When he returns tell him I need his help.

G. Okay, I'll tell him.

J. Good. (See you) later.

G. Okay, (see you) later.

Lesson 19 :

T. In schoolwork what is the most difficult for you ?

A. Well, only arithmetic gives me trouble.

T. Is that right ? What about English ?

A. Well, English is very difficult but arithmetic is more so.

T. Reading isn't difficult ?

A. No. It's easy. Reading is also (very) enjoyable.

T. Good. Do you read a lot ?

A. Yes indeed ! All the time.

T. But you can't do arithmetic ?

A. No, I can do (it) all right. But it is difficult.

T. Okay. Continue with your efforts.

Lesson 20 :

The Hyena, the Lizard and the Dog

In olden times there was a hyena. One day she was very hungry. So she arose and went out. She was looking for food when there was a lizard stealing beans. When she saw the lizard she caught him. She was about to eat him when she saw a dog.

So she said (to herself), ' Let me take the lizard home before I return to catch the dog.'

So she took the lizard home.

When she returned she didn't see the dog. While she was taking the lizard home the dog ran off into the bush.

When the hyena returned home she didn't see the lizard. While she was looking for the dog the lizard left the hyena's hole and went into the bush.

The hyena was amazed, she said, ' Why, whatever you seek in the world, if it is not your lot, you won't get (it) ! '

Lesson 21 :

S. (My) wife told me you are not well.

B. That's right.

S. What's bothering you ?

B. It's a headache.

S. Oh, (I'm) sorry ! Have you taken (some) medicine ?

B. Yes. The doctor gave me a shot.

S. Good. Is there also a fever ?

B. Formerly there was but it is better now.

S. Good. When did it hit you ?

B. Why it was yesterday, while I was (working on my) farm.

S. Well, I hope that God will make (you) better.

B. Amen.

Lesson 22 :

S. What are they doing in town ?

I. Why they're dancing—the market day dancing.

S. Good. What kind of dancing do they do ?

I. Every kind. There's no kind that they will not do.

S. Are there a lot of people there ?

I. There certainly are ! There are men and women, children and old folks.

S. Will they allow me to go and watch ?

I. Why certainly they'll agree ! Let's go together.
S. Good. Are you going to dance ?
I. Good heavens, I don't dance anymore. I'm too old !
S. That's okay.
I. How about you ? Do you want to try (this type of) dancing ?
S. No. *I* can't do your kind of dancing.
I. Okay, let's just stand and watch.
S. Fine.

Lesson 23 :

Everyone Has One Who Is Stronger Than He Is

One day a small bird caught a worm. He was about to eat it when the worm cried out saying, ' Please let me go ! '

The bird said, ' No. Why, I'm going to eat you, because I'm stronger than you are.'

So he picked up the little worm and ate it.

When he finished eating it a hawk saw him. So the hawk caught the little bird. As he was about to eat him the bird cried out saying, ' Be patient with me, let me go ! '

The hawk refused saying, ' Why, you are my food for today, because I'm stronger than you are.'

So the hawk ate the bird that had eaten the little worm.

Before the hawk had finished eating the bird a griffon fell upon him. So the hawk began to cry out, but the griffon didn't release him because she was stronger than he was.

After a little while the griffon flew up into the air. She didn't get very far (*lit.* stay long) before she felt an arrow in her body. Why, a certain hunter had seen her and killed her.

The griffon had come up against the one who was the strongest of all.

Lesson 24 :

L. Gosh, the rainy season is really upon us!

H. You're right. I went to the river this morning. I couldn't get across.

L. Is it full ?

H. It is completely full ! To the extent that the strength of the current made me fearful.

L. That's certainly something to fear. It is very swift.

H. (You're) right ! Why, sometimes it carries a person off.

L. That's so. If someone falls in he will die.

H. (You're) right ! This kind of a river is an evil thing.

L. Well, what shall we do ?

H. Why, we'll have to follow a different road.

L. But another road will be (very) long. Won't it ?

H. Yes. But there's no other way.

L. You're right. We have to go the long way.

H. Okay, let's go.

Lesson 25 :

U. You've returned from the city, have you ?

B. Yes, I returned the day before yesterday morning.

U. Fine. But I heard that there was trouble there.

B. That's for certain ! Wow ! Some compounds caught fire, it burned them up completely !

U. Gosh ! (Those) people are certainly unfortunate ! How about you ?

B. Why, I'm okay. It didn't come near where I was living.

U. Good ! Previously I had thought that perhaps it had come near where you were.

B. No. It didn't bother us at all. But some had a lot of trouble.

U. That's for certain.

B. Why, one day I met a friend of mine and asked him about the fire. He said their compound had burned completely.

U. Good heavens ! What did you do ?

B. Why, I had to fix him a place in my room.

U. Fine, but what happened to his family ?

B. Oh they stayed at another person's home.

U. Good ! When will they (be able to) start a new compound ?

B. They won't wait long. They'll gather the materials and start right away.

U. Good. May God help them.

B. Amen !

Lesson 26 :

Audu and Ali

Audu and Ali were travelling. They were on their way to market with (some) goods. All at once there was something at the side of the path. Ali picked it up and looked at it. Why it was a bag of money !

So Audu said, ' Gosh, we have fallen into luck today ! '

Ali said, ' What ? *We* have fallen into luck ? Or is it *I* who have fallen into luck ? '

Audu said, ' Okay, (have it your way), may God grant us safety.'

They continued on their way until they came to a forest. Then some highway robbers fell on them. Audu and Ali took off on the run. The robbers followed after them.

After awhile Ali got tired because of his heavy load. He said, ' Alas. Today we have fallen into misfortune.'

Audu said, ' What ? *We* have fallen into misfortune. Or is it *you* who has fallen into misfortune ? '

Lesson 27 :

The Fruitbat Doesn't Pay Taxes

One day the king of the animals called his representative (*wakili*) and said to him, ' Go everywhere in my country to the homes of all the animals and collect taxes from each of them.'

The *wakili* said, ' May you live long, I'll do it right away.'

So the *wakili* went all over the land and collected the tax from every home. But when he came to the home of the fruitbat (the latter) refused to pay the money.

' Why, I'm not an animal,' said the fruitbat. ' Well, is there any one of the subjects of the king of the animals who has wings like I have ? Is there any who can fly in the air like me ? Well, I'm not going to pay taxes to the king of the animals.'

That was that. The *wakili* of the king of the animals left him and returned to the palace and told the king. The king, for his part, thought a bit and said, ' Well, he's right. The fruitbat is not our kind, leave him alone.'

The next day the king of the birds called *his* representative (*wakili*) and sent him to collect taxes from every bird. When the *wakili* came to the fruitbat's home and asked him for the tax money, the fruitbat laughed at him saying, ' As for me, I won't pay him taxes.'

' Have you ever seen a bird with teeth,' he said. ' Or one who gives birth to its young alive and breast-feeds them ? Come, come ! I'm not a subject of the king of the birds ! '

When the *wakili* returned to the palace and told the king of the birds, they (all) agreed : the fruitbat is not a bird.

For this reason the fruitbat is betwixt and between : he isn't an animal, he isn't a bird.

Lesson 28 :

T. David !

D. Yes ?

T. Where are you going ?

D. I'm headed home. I've just now left work (and arrived here).

T. Fine. Where do you work ?

D. Well, I'm a clerk at a canteen.

T. Is that so ? I thought you were in school.

D. No. Last year I left (*i.e.* having completed) Primary School. I couldn't get into Secondary School.

T. Didn't you pass the examination ?

D. No, it was very difficult for me. But that's okay, since I've (been able to) get work.

T. Good. What kind of work do you do ?

D. Well, I have various jobs : sometimes I arrange goods, sometimes I sell goods, sometimes even the head clerk gives me paperwork to do.

T. Hm. Are most of your goods brought from European countries ?

D. Yes. But now they have started to make certain things in this country—like shoes, cloth, cement and bottled drinks.

T. Good ! Is it true that bottled drinks are only made from boiled water ?

D. Of course ! It's not like our own beer !

T. How about tinned food—is it all cooked ?

D Yes. They say that they cook it when they prepare it.

T. Gracious ! It really is amazing how it is possible to cook a lot of food, put it in tins, and set it aside for even as much as five years !

D. You're right. Well, that's the way the world is now — it is full of amazing things.

T. Indeed it is.

Lesson 29 :

H. Greetings, tailor !

G. Why, Aaron ! Greetings in the (late) afternoon.

H. Greetings. How's (your) work today ?

G. Well, work never runs out.

H. Good. That's the way one wants it.

G. You're right. Are you (just) wandering in the market ?

H. No. I've been looking for your stall.

G. Oh. The other day I moved my things to this place.

H. Good. Before you were in a grass (mat) stall but this one is (made) of corrugated roofing (pan).

G. Right. I've been fortunate.

H. Good. Could you sew me some clothing ?

G. Well, it's my occupation ! What kind do you want ?

H. I need two (pair of) shorts and a big gown.

G. Fine. Did you bring (*lit.* come with) the material ?

H. Yes. Here's the khaki cloth for making the shorts and white cloth for making the gown. How much is the cost of sewing (it) ?

G. The whole job will be 45/----that is, 4 naira and 5 shillings.

H. Heavens ! that's too much ! If you don't agree (to do it) for 4 naira I'll (have to) look for someone else (to do it).

G. Okay, I agree. Leave the cloth there.

H. Good. When shall I come and get (it) ?

G. Not till tomorrow. I can't finish sewing them all today.

H. Okay, see you tomorrow.

G. Okay, until tomorrow.

Lesson 30 :

The Jackal Is The Chief of Schemers

One day a crow was wandering about. He was looking for something to eat. Then he saw a little piece of meat on the ground near a rock. He descended and picked it up in his mouth. He rose into the air with the meat in his mouth and landed in a tree.

Well, a jackal was watching him—he saw everything that the crow did. The jackal, for his part, was hungry.

He wanted to get the meat. So he worked out a scheme to get (it).

So the jackal went to the base of the tree, he greeted the crow. He said to him, ' Gosh, the other day I heard you singing a song. Your voice was very pleasant indeed. How long (will I have to wait until) I can hear your song again ? '

The crow listened (attentively). What the jackal said pleased him (very much). When he heard it he forgot about the thing in his mouth. He opened his mouth. He was about to (oblige by) singing a song.

That was that ! The meat fell down. The jackal picked (it) up and said, ' Thanks.' He went off with it. That's the end !

Hausa–English Vocabulary

This vocabulary includes all the words and most of the idiomatic expressions found anywhere in these lessons (with the exception of some of the less common forms listed in Lesson 39, section 7). Note that the alphabetical order in which the words are arranged is Hausa (that is with separate sections for **ɓ, ɗ, ƙ, sh, ts** and **'y**) rather than combining these letters with the most similar letter of the English alphabet as most Hausa dictionaries do.

Note : *the student is cautioned against assuming that he can learn the meaning of a word or construction by simply referring to the over-brief glosses provided in these short vocabularies. He should at least cross-check with one of the large dictionaries before attempting to make use of these items on his own.*

a, (impersonal p-a pronoun employed with **zâ**)

à, (impersonal subjunctive p-a pronoun)

à, at, in

à kân, atop, on top of

à, (impersonal p-a pronoun employed after **bā**)

â, (impersonal future II p-a pronoun)

a'a, (exclamation of amazement)

ā'à, no

a'àhā, (exclamation of concern over misfortune)

àbin, (see **àbù**)

àbinci, food

àbōkī (*f.* **àbōkìyā** ; *pl.* **àbòkai**), friend

àbù (*pl.* **abūbuwà**), thing

— **àbîn dà,** what, the thing which

— **àbin màmākì,** a marvellous thing

— **àbinsà,** (about) his own business

— **àbin shâ,** something to drink

Àbūbakàr, (man's name)

ādalcì, justice, fairness, acting honestly

ādàlī (*pl.* **àdàlai**), just, honest, righteous (person)

Adàm, (man's name)

Ādàmū, (man's name)

àddā (*f.*) (*pl.* adduna̱), matchet

af/ap, (exclamation of surprised recognition)

Afrìl/Àfrīlù, April

āfù, (see āhù)

àgōgō (*pl.* agōguna̱), watch, clock

Àgustà, August

āhù/āfù, 1½ kobos

ai, why, well (introductory exclamation)

aibu̱ (*pl.* aibōbī), fault, blemish

àikā (i/ē), *v.* send (on errand)

aikì (*pl.* ayyuka̱), work

aikō, *v.* send here

ainù(n), very much, too

àjìyayyē (*f.* àjìyayyiyā; *pl.* àjìya̱yyū), (something) set aside

ajìyē, *v.* set aside, put, place

aka̱, (impersonal relative completive p-a construction)

a ka̱n, (impersonal habitual p-a construction)

à kân, (see à)

àka̱wū (*pl.* akāwuna̱), clerk

— ba̱bban àka̱wū, head clerk

a ke̱, (impersonal relative continuative p-a construction)

àkwai, *v.* there is/are

àkwa̱tì (*pl.* akwātuna̱), box

àkwiya̱ (*f.*) (*pl.* awākī), goat

àl'āda̱ (*f.*) (*pl.* àl'a̱dū), custom, tradition

àladē (*pl.* àla̱dai), pig

àlaika̱ sàlāmù/sàlâm, greetings (in reply to sàlāmù/sàlâm àlaikùn)

àlāma̱/hàlāma̱ (*f.*) (*pl.* àla̱mai), sign, indication

àlbarka̱, no sale !

àlbarka̱cī, kindness at the hands of, benefits received from

àlbishìrī, good news

Àlhajì, (title of one who has made the pilgrimage—hajì—to Mecca)

àlhamdù lillāhì, praise God !, fine ! (an exclamation of gratefulness)

Àlha̱mîs (*f.*), Thursday

àlhērì, kindness, liberality, favourable attitude

— sai àlhērì, (reply to inā là bārì ?), only good (news)

Àlī, (man's name)

alìf, 1000

Àliyù, (man's name)

àljīfū/àljīhū (*pl.* aljīfuna̱), pocket

àlkala̱mī (*pl.* alkaluma̱), pen

àlƙālī (*pl.* àlƙàlai), judge
Allà, God
— allà ?, is that so ?
— allà !, it is true
àllō (*pl.* allunà) school-
slate, blackboard
àllurà (*f.*) (*pl.* àllùrai),
needle, inoculation
àlmājìrī (*f.* àlmājìrā ; *pl.*
àlmàjìrai), pupil, student
disciple
àmfànī, usefulness
àmin, amen, may it be so
Amìnā, (woman's name)
amincì, reliability, friendship
Amirkà (*f.*), America
àmmā, but
amsà, *v.* or *n.* (*f.*) answer
an, (impersonal completive
aspect p-a pronoun)
— an jimà, after a while
(*lit.* one has waited
awhile)
anà, (impersonal continuative p-a construction)
— anà nan, after a while
angò, bridegroom
angwancì, being a bride-
groom, marriage-feast
ànīnī (*pl.* ànìnai), 1/10 of a
kobo, button
àrā (i/ē), *v.* borrow (other
than money)
arō, a loan, borrowing

àràhā, cheapness, inexpensiveness
— yā yi àràhā, it is in-
expensive
arbà, 4000
— yi arbà, *v.* happen on
unexpectedly
àrbà'in, 40
àrbàminyà, 400
arèwā, north
— arèwā masò gabàs,
north-east
— arèwā masò yâmma,
north-west
— arèwā sak, due north
arèwa, northward, to the
north
arzìkī/azzìkī, prosperity,
wealth
arzùtā, *v.* become pros-
perous
Àsabàr (*f.*), Saturday
asìbitì (*pl.* asibitōcī),
hospital
àsīrī (*pl.* àsìrai), secret
àshē, well !, oh !, really ?
àshìrin, 20
àttājìrī (*pl.* àttàjìrai),
wealthy trader,
merchant
Audù, (man's name)
aukà, *v.* fall on
àuku, *v.* happen
aunà, *v.* weigh, measure
àurā(i/ē), *v.* marry
aurē, marriage

àutā, youngest of several children

awà (f.) (pl. awōwī), hour

àyàbà (f.), banana(s)

bā, v. not be in the process of

bā/bâ, v. give

— bā dà, v. give

— bā dà màmākì, be amazing (lit. give amazement)

— ban tsòrō, causing (lit. giving) fear

bâ/bābù, v. there is no/not

— bâ kōmē, there's nothing (wrong), it doesn't matter

— bâ kyâu, it is not good

bà ... ba, (negative particles employed with most p-a pronouns)

— bài ... ba, (third person masculine singular negative particles)

— bàn ... ba, (first person singular negative particles)

bà ... ba, (negative particles employed with nouns, noun phrases, etc.)

bābà, paternal aunt

bàba, father, paternal uncle

bàbba (pl. mânyā), big

(thing), important

(thing), adult person

bābù, (see bâ/bābù)

bàdūkù (pl. dùkàwā), leather worker

bàɗi, next year

bàfādà/bàfādè (pl. fàdàwā), chief's servant, courtier

Bàfàransì (f. Bàfàransìyā ; pl. Fàrànsâi), Frenchman

Bàfìlācè (f. Bàfìlātà ; pl. Filànī), Fulani person

Bàhaushè (f. Bàhaushìyā ; pl. Hàusàwā), Hausa person

bài, (see bà ... ba)

bàjimī, (see bìjimī)

Bàkanè/Bàkanò (f. Bàkanùwā ; pl. Kanāwā), Kano person

bàkī (pl. bākunà), mouth, edge

— bàkin hanyà, edge of the road

bakwài, seven

baƙī (f. baƙā ; pl. baƙàƙē), black (thing)

— baƙi-baƙi, blackish

— baƙī ƙirin/sidiƙ/sil, pitch-black, jet-black

— baƙin dājì, forest (lit. black bush)

Bàƙo, (man's name)

bàƙō (f. bàƙwā ; pl. bàƙī), guest, stranger

— **yi bàƙō,** have a guest

Bàlā, (man's name)

Bàlārabè (*f.* **Bàlārabìyā ;** *pl.* **Lārabāwā),** Arab person

bàlle, much more/less ...

bàn, (see **bà ... ba)**

bana, this year

bangō, wall, book cover

bàntē, loincloth

ban tsòrō, causing (*lit.* giving) fear, frightening

banzā, worthless (thing), uselessness

bappà, paternal uncle

barcī, sleep

bàra, last year

barì/bar, *v.* let, allow

barkà (*f.*), greetings

bàsarākè (*pl.* **sarākunà),** office-holder under a chief

bàtū, conversation, matter, affair

— **bàtun,** concerning, regarding

Bàtūrè (*f.* **Bàtūrìyā ;** *pl.* **Tùràwā),** European person

bāshì, debt, loan

— **ci bāshì,** *v.* incur a debt

Baucī (*f.*), the town of Bauchi

bàutā, slavery

bāwà (*f.* **bâiwā ;** *pl.* **bāyì),** slave

bāyā, the back

— **bāyan,** behind

— **bāyân dà,** after

— **bāyan gidā,** lavatory, toilet, faeces

bāya, backwards, to/towards the rear

bāyar, *v.* give

bazarā (*f.*), hot, muggy season just before the rains come

bèbàntakà (*f.*), being deaf and dumb

bēbē (*f.* **bēbìyā ;** *pl.* **bèbàyē),** deaf-mute

bègē, longing, hope

Bellò, (man's name)

bi, *v.* follow

bî, following (*v.n.* from **bi)**

bìjimī/bàjimī (*pl.* **bìjìmai/ bàjìmai),** big bull

Bīnuwài (*f.*), Benue River

birì (*pl.* **birai),** monkey

birnī (*pl.* **birànē),** (walled) city

— **birnin Arèwā,** capital/ most important city of the Northern Region

bìskitì (*pl.* **biskitōcī),** biscuit, cookie

bìsmillà, go ahead and start (whatever is to be done) !

bismillāhì, (formula said on standing up, sitting down, starting work, beginning a meal, *etc.*)

biyā, *v.* pay

biyằ, paying (verbal noun from biyā)

biyar, five

biyō, v. follow (here)

biyu, two

brōdì, (see burōdì)

bubbùgā, v. keep on beating (from bugà)

Būbà, (man's name)

bùdurwā (pl. 'yam mātā), unmarried girl of marriageable age

būɗà, v. clear away, prepare, open

bùɗe, open

— à bùɗe, open

būɗè, v. open

bugà, v. beat

— bugà mâi, step on the gas, start a lorry/car

bùgā (i/ē), v. beat, thrash

bugè, v. beat and knock over/out

bugù, thrashing, beating

bùkātà (f.) (pl. bùkàtū), a need/requirement

bukkà (f.) (pl. bukkōkì), hut of grass (mats) or stalks, market stall

burōdì/brōdì bread, roll

būsà, v. blow

būshè, v. get dry

but, sudden action (an ideophone)

— yā yi but, he made a sudden leap

ɓācì, v. become spoiled

ɓàrāwò (pl. ɓàràyī), thief

ɓātà, v. spoil

ɓērā (pl. ɓèràyē), rat, mouse

ɓòye, hidden

— à ɓòye, hidden, in secret

ɓōyè, v. hide (something)

ɓutuk, stark naked (an ideophone)

— yā fitō ɓutuk, he came out naked

câ, thinking

—câ ni/na kè, I thought (that) . . .

can/cân/càn, there, that

cân, later

canjì, change

càsà'in, ninety

cē/cè, (see nē)

cê/cè, v. say

cêwā, saying, quote, that

ci, v. eat, win (a contest)

— ci bāshì, incur a debt

— ci jarràɓâwā, pass a test

cî, eating

cī dà, (see ciyar)

cif, exactly (an ideophone)

— ƙarfè ukù cif, exactly three o'clock

cigàba, v. continue

cikà, v. fill

cika, v. become full

— yā cika fal, it is full to the brim

cìkakkē (*f.* cìkakkiyā ; *pl.*
  cìkàkkū), full
cikè, *v.* fill completely
cikì, stomach, pregnancy
— bakin cikì, sadness (*lit.*
  black stomach)
— cikì yā daurè, I am
  constipated (*lit.* stomach
  has become tied up)
— farin cikì, happiness
— yi cikì, become pregnant
cikī, inside
— (à) cikin, inside
cînyē, *v.* eat completely
cirè, *v.* pull out of
cirō, *v.* pull out of
cīshē, *v.* (form of ciyar)
città, four days hence
cīwò, illness, pain
— cīwòn cikì, stomach-
  ache
— cīwòn kâi, headache
ciyar/cī (dà), *v.* cause to
  eat, feed
cìyāwà (*f.*) (*pl.* cìyàyī),
  grass
cìzā (i/ē), *v.* bite
cōkàlī (*pl.* cōkulà), spoon
cūrì, ball (of something)
cùtā (*f.*), illness, disease,
  wound
cùtā (i/ē), *v.* injure, cheat

dà, with, and ; that
  (= wandà)
— kō dà, even though

dà, *v.* there is/are
  (= àkwai)
dà, if, when
dâ, in the past, formerly,
  previously
— dâ-dâ, long in the past
— dâ mā, it has been
  planned that, it is well
  known that, already
— tun dâ, from earliest
  times
dàban, different
dàbārà (*f.*) (*pl.* dàbàrū),
  plan, scheme
dabbà (*f.*) (*pl.* dabbōbī),
  (domestic) animal
daddàfā, *v.* keep on cooking
  (from dafà)
dàddarē, at night
dadà, *v.* increase
dadè, *v.* spend a long
  time
dadèwā, spending a long
  time
— tun dà dadèwā, from a
  long time ago
dādī, pleasantness
dafà, *v.* cook
dàfaffē (*f.* dàfaffiyā ; *pl.*
  dàfàffū), cooked
dàfu, *v.* be cooked
dàgà, from
dai, indeed, however, on
  the other hand (an
  insert)
daidai, correct, exactly

dājì, ' bush ' country, un-
inhabited land
— **baƙin dājì,** forest
dākàtā, *v.* wait for
dalà (*f.*) (*pl.* **dalōlī**), florin,
two shillings (= **fàtakà**)
dàlīlì (*pl.* **dàlìlai**), reason,
cause
dāmā (*f.*), chance, opportunity
— **bâ dāmā,** there's no
chance
dāma (*f.*), to the right
— **dāma-dāma,** so-so,
slightly (better)
— **hannun dāma,** right
hand/arm
dàmā, *v.* worry
dāmà, *v.* wet-mix
dàmu, *v.* be worried
dāmù, worrying
dàmunā/dàmanā/dàminā
(*f.*), rainy season
dàmuwā (*f.*), being wor-
ried/concerned
dangì, relatives
dànkalì, (sweet) potato(es)
dàrā (*f.*), fez
— **hùlad dàrā,** fez
darē, night
— **dà (dàd) darē,** at night
dàriyā (*f.*), laughter
Daudà, (man's name
= David)
dāwà (*f.*), guinea corn

dawà, ' bush ' country
(= **dājì**)
dāwō, *v.* return here
dāwôwā, returning here
dilā, jackal
dingà, *v.* keep on (doing)
dirēbà, driver
Dìzambà (*f.*), December
Dōgo, (man's name)
dōgō (*f.* **dōguwā** ; *pl.*
dōgàyē), tall, long
dòkā (i/ē), *v.* thrash, beat
dòkā (*f.*) (*pl.* **dōkōkī**),
order, rule
— **ɗan dòkā** (*pl.* **'yan dòkā**),
N.A. policeman
dōkì (*pl.* **dawākī**), horse
dōlè, perforce, of necessity,
' must '
don, (see **dòmin**)
— **don Allà,** please, for
God's sake
— **dom mè,** why ?
dòmin/don, because of, in
order to
dōyà (*f.*), yam(s)
dōzìn, dozen
dūbà, *v.* look (at), inspect
dubū, 1000
duddūbā, look everywhere,
keep on looking (from
dūbà)
duhù/dufù, darkness
dukà/duk, every, all
— **duk dà (hakà),** in spite
of (this), nevertheless

— **duk ɗaya,** all the same

— **duk wandà,** anyone who

dūkà, *v.* beat, thrash

dūniyà (*f.*), world

dūtsè (*pl.* **duwàtsū**), stone, rock, mountain

ɗā (*pl.* **'yā'yā**), son

— **ɗan Adàm** (*pl.* **'yan Adàm**), person, human being (*lit.* son of Adam)

— **ɗan dòkā** (*pl.* **'yan dòkā**), N.A. policeman (*lit.* son of the orders/rules)

— **ɗan fārì,** firstborn son

— **ɗan jīkà,** great-grandchild

— **ɗan Kanò** (*pl.* **'yan Kanò**), native of Kano

— **ɗan sàndā** (*pl.* **'yan sàndā**), Government policeman (*lit.* son of a stick)

— **ɗan'ùbā** (*pl.* **'yan'ùbā**), half brother (*lit.* son of one's father)

— **ɗan'uwā** (*pl.* **'yan'uwā**), brother (*lit.* son of one's mother)

ɗagà, *v.* lift up, raise

ɗai-ɗai, one by one, singly

ɗākì (*pl.* **ɗākunà**), hut, room

ɗālìbī (*pl.* **ɗàlìbai**), student

ɗan, (see **ɗā**)

ɗanyē (*f.* **ɗanyā** ;   *pl.*

ɗanyū), raw/uncooked (thing)

ɗārī, coldness due to wind (usually *dry-cold* as opposed to **sanyī** = *damp-cold*)

ɗàrī, 100 ; ½k (= **sīsìn kwabò**)

ɗaukà (**i/ē**), *v.* take/pick up, carry

ɗaukè, *v.* pick up all of

ɗâukē, *v.* (rain) stop, remove

ɗaukō, *v.* carry here

ɗaurà, *v.* tie on to

ɗaurè, *v.* tie (completely/well) on to, tie up

ɗàure, tied up

— **à ɗàure,** tied up

ɗaya, one

— **ɗaya tak,** one only (*i.e.* no more, no less than one)

ɗàzu, just a little while ago

ɗēbō, *v.* dip out and bring (-ō form of **ɗībà**)

ɗēbè, *v.* remove, subtract

ɗībà, *v.* dip out, extract

ɗìn, the one in question

ɗin, particle used with numbers (see Lesson 11, section 5)

ɗinkà, *v.* make by sewing

ɗinkè, *v.* sew (up) completely)

ɗinkì, sewing

ɗiyā (*f.*), daughter (= **'yā**)

d̓òyī, stench, unpleasant odour

en'è (*pl.* **en'è-en'è**), Native Administration (abbreviated N.A.)

fa, indeed, on the other hand (an insert)

fà ?, what about ?

Fàbrairù, February

fādà (*f.*), chief's residence/ audience chamber

fàdamà (*f.*) (*pl.* **fadamōmī**), marshy, swamp

fàdàwā, (see **bàfādà**)

fad̓à, quarrel, fighting, argument

fād̓à, *v.* fall into

fàd̓ā (i/ē), *v.* say

fàd̓ā (*f.*), thing said, spoken words, conversation

fād̓ì, *v.* fall (down/on)

fād̓ō, *v.* fall down to some-one

fàhimtà (i/ē), *v.* understand

fàhìmtaccē (*f.* **fàhìmtac-ciyā** ; *pl.* **fàhìmtàttū**), understood, intelligent

fal, completely (see **c̓ika**)

fâm, 2 naira

fànsā (i/ē), *v.* redeem, ransom

fārà, *v.* start, begin

fàrā (*f.*) (*pl.* **fàrī**), locust, grasshopper

Fàransà (*f.*), France

Fàrànsâi, (see **Bàfàransì**)

fàrarrē (*f.* **fàrarriyā** ; *pl.* **fàràrrū**), having been begun

fārì, beginning, start (= **farkō**)

— **na/ta fārì,** the first (= **na/ta farkō**)

farī (*f.* **farā** ; *pl.* **faràrē**), white (thing), whiteness

— **fari-fari,** white-ish

— **farī fat,** snow-white

— **farin cikì,** happiness (*lit.* white stomach)

farkē/falkē (*pl.* **fatàkē**), itinerant trader

farkō, beginning, start (= **fārì**)

— **na/ta farkō,** the first (= **na/ta fārì**)

fartanyà (*f.*) (*pl.* **fartan-yōyī**), hoe

fàru, *v.* happen

fasànjà (*pl.* **fasanjōjī**), passenger

fàskarà (i/ē), *v.* be beyond doing, be impossible

fâs ōfìs, post office

fat, (see **farī**)

fātā, hoping (for)

fātà (*f.*) (*pl.* **fātū**), skin, hide

fàtakà, florin, two shillings (= **dalà**)

fâutā, *v.* cut up meat for sale

fayè, v. be characterized by

fensìr(ī) (pl. **fensirōrī),** pencil

fi, v. surpass, exceed

— **nā fi sô . . .,** I prefer . . .

— **yā fi dukà . . .,** it is the best in . . .

yā fi . . . kyâu, it is better than . . .

--- **yā fi kyâu,** it is better (that we do . . .)

ficè, v. (see **wucè)**

fiffikè (pl. **fikàfikai),** wing

fiffìtà, v. keep going out (from **fita)**

Filànī, (see **Bàfilācè)**

fīlī (pl. **fīlàyè),** open country, space

firamàrè, primary school

fisshē, v. (form of **fitar)**

fìta, v. go out

fìtā, going out

fitar/fīd (dà), v. take out, remove, depose, expel

fìtilà (f.) (pl. **fìtilū),** lantern, lamp

fìtō, v. come out

fìtò, ferrying

fìtō, guinea-corn beer

fìtôwā, coming out (from **fìtō)**

fìtsārī, urine

ful, (see **sābō)**

furā (f.), a food made of cooked flour mixed with milk

fuskà (f.) (pl. **fuskōkī),** face

fushī, anger

— **yi fushī,** get angry

ga, (see **ganī)**

gà, v. here/there is . . .

— **gà shi . . .,** seeing that, indeed, for

— **sai gà . . .,** then behold . . .

gà/gàrē, in the presence of, regarding, in the possession of

gàbā, front

— **gàban,** in front of

gàba, in front

— **gàba ɗaya,** all together, at once

gabàs, east

— **gabàs sak,** due east

gadà (f.), (permanent) bridge

gadō (pl. **gadàjē),** bed

gāfarà (f.), pardoning, forgiving ; excuse me !

gai dà, v. (see **gayar)**

gaishē, v. (form of **gayar)**

gaisuwā (f.), greetings

gājè, v. inherit

gàjērē (f. **gàjērìyā ;** pl. **gàjèrū),** short

Gàjere, (man's name)

gajertà (f.), shortness

gàji, v. be tired

gàjiyà (f.), tiredness, fatigue

gamà, *v.* finish ; join together

Gàmbo, (man's name)

gàmu (dà), *v.* meet (with)

gānà, *v.* chat (confidentially)

gànannē (*f.* **gànanniyā ;** *pl.* **gànànnū),** seen

gānè, *v.* understand

ganī/gan/ga, *v.* see

ganī, seeing

gāra, it would be better that

gàrā (*f.*), white ant(s), termite(s)

Garbà, (man's name)

gàrī (*pl.* **garūruwà),** town

— **garī yā wāyè,** it has dawned

gàrī, flour

garkè, herd of cattle

gàrmā (*f.*) (*pl.* **garèmanī),** large type of hoe, plough

gāshì, hair, feathers

gàskē, real

— **dà gàskē,** extremely (see also **ƙwarai)**

gàskiyā (*f.*), truth

gātà, three days hence

gàtarī (*pl.* **gāturà),** axe, hatchet

gayà, *v.* tell (requires an indirect object)

gayar/gai (dà), *v.* greet

— **gayar minì dà,** greet for me . . .

gēmù, beard

gērō, millet

gidā (*pl.* **gidàjē),** home, compound

— **gidan saurō,** mosquito net

— **mài gidā,** head of the house, husband

— **uwar gidā,** woman of the house, (first) wife

giginyà (*f.*), deleb-palm

ginà, *v.* build (usually with clay, brick or cement)

gindī, base, bottom, buttocks

gìrbā (i/ē), *v.* reap, harvest

girbì, harvesting

girgijè (*pl.* **gìzàgìzai),** raincloud

girmā, bigness, honour, importance

gishirī, salt

gīwā (*f.*) (*pl.* **gīwàyē),** elephant

giyà (*f.*), (native) beer

gòbarā (*f.*), catching fire

gòbe (*f.*), tomorrow

gōdè, *v.* thank

gòdiyā (*f.*), thanks, gratitude

— **dà gòdiyā,** with thankfulness

gōdìyā (*f.*), mare

gōgà, *v.* rub, polish

gōgè, *v.* rub (completely)

gògu, *v.* be experienced, has been rubbed

gōmà, ten

— **gōmà-gōmà,** ten apiece/
each

-- **gōmà shâ ɗaya,** eleven

gōnā (*f.*) (*pl.* **gònàkī**), farm

gōrò, kolanut

gùdā, a unit

gudù, *v.* run

gudŭ (*pl.* **gùje-gùjē**), running (see also **gùje-gùjē**
below)

gùgā (*pl.* **gūgunà**), bucket
(of skin, gourd or metal)
for dipping from a well

gùje, speedily, on the run

— **à gùje,** on the run,
running

gùje-gùjē, running in track
and field competition

gùmī, perspiration

guntū (*pl.* **guntàyē**), short
(thing), fragment (of
something)

Gùsau (*f.*), (town in N.
Nigeria)

gwadà, *v.* measure, test

gwaggò, gwàggō, paternal
aunt, father's wife (not
one's mother), maternal
uncle's wife

gwàmmà, rather, it would
be better that . . .

gwangwan (*pl.* **gwangwàyē**), tin (of food)

gwànī (*f.* **gwànā** ; *pl.*
gwanàyē), expert

gwànintà (*f.*), skill

gwàuràntakà (*f.*), being
wifeless

gwaurō/gwamrō (*pl.*
gwauràyē), wifeless man,
bachelor

gwēbà, guava

gyàɗā (*f.*), groundnut(s).
peanut(s)

gyārà, *v.* repair

gyārā, a ' makeweight '
given by seller ; re-
pairing

gyârtā, *v.* repair

gyàru, *v.* be repaired

habà, come now !, don't be
a fool !, nonsense !

haɓà (*f.*), chin

hadarì/hadirì, storm

hàɗu, *v.* meet, be joined

hagu/hagun, left-hand side

haifù (**i/ē**), *v.* give birth

hajì, the pilgrimage to
Mecca

hakà, thus, so

hakùntà, *v.* administer,
possess jurisdiction over,
give verdict

haƙōrī (*pl.* **haƙòrā**), tooth

hàƙurà, *v.* be patient

hàƙurī, patience, resigna-
tion

hàlakà, *v.* perish, die

hàlāmà, (see **àlāmà**)

halī, character, tempera-
ment

hàmsàminyà, 500

hàmsin, fifty

hanà, *v.* prevent, forbid, refuse

hàngā (i/ē), *v.* see afar off

hànkākà (*pl.* **hànkàkī**), crow

hankàlī, intelligence, sense ; careful

— **à hankàlī,** carefully

hannū (*pl.* **hannàyē**), arm (including hand), hand

hanyà (*f.*) (*pl.* **hanyōyī**), path, road, way

har, until, to the extent that

hàrājì, tax

hàrbā (i/ē), *v.* shoot

harbì, act of shooting

harshè (*pl.* **harsunà**), tongue, language

Hārūnà, (man's name = Aaron)

hàsārà, loss due to some unlucky incident, misfortune

Hasàn, (man's name)

hatsī, grain staple (*i.e.* guinea-corn or millet)

hau, *v.* mount, climb

hàukā, madness, insanity

Hausā (*f.*), the Hausa language, the Hausa people ; language

haushī, vexation, anger

hawā, mounting, riding on

hayākī, smoke

hayè, *v.* mount, climb, cross over (*e.g.* a river)

hāzā wasàlàm(mù), (formula used at end of a letter = yours faithfully)

hudu, four

hùlā (*f.*) (*pl.* **hūlunà**), cap, hat

hūrà, *v.* blow on, light (fire)

hūtà, *v.* rest

hūtàwā (*f.*), resting

hūtū, resting, holiday, vacation

ī, yes

— **ī mànà,** yes indeed !

ì/yì ta yâu, today week

ìdan/in, if, when

idò (*pl.* **idànū**), eye, sight

— **idòn sanì,** acquaintance

igiyà (*f.*) (*pl.* **igiyōyī**), rope, string

Ìkko, Lagos

ilmì/ilìmī, knowledge, education

Ìmâm, (man's name, from **lìmân,** *Muslim priest*)

in, (see **ìdan**)

— **in shā Àllā(hù),** if God wills

ìn, (first person singular subjunctive p-a pronoun)

— **ìn ji . . .,** according to, quote . . ., says . . .

inà, (first person singular continuative p-a construction)

inā, where ?

îndà, (place) where (= wurîn dà)

Ingilà (f.), England

innà/innā/iyà, mother, maternal aunt

inuwà (f.), shade

in shā Àllā(hù), (see in)

irì, kind, sort, seed

— irì-irì, various kinds, all kinds

Isā, (man's name = Jesus)

isa, v. be sufficient, reach (a place)

isasshē (f. isasshiyā; pl. isàssū), enough, sufficient

iskà (f. or m.), wind, air

isō, v. arrive (here)

Ishāƙù, (man's name = Isaac)

ita, she (third feminine singular independent pronoun)

itàcē (pl. itātuwà), tree, piece of wood, twig, wood

iyà, v. be able to . . .

— yā iyà Hausā, he can speak Hausa well

iyà, (see innà)

iyā/iyàkā (f.), boundary, limit

— iyā gindī, (one's) waist

iyālì, man's wife/wives and children, one's household

iyàwā (f.), ability

iyàyē, parents

iyò, swimming

jā (pl. jājàyē), red (thing)

— ja-ja, reddish

— jà wur/jir/zur, bright red, scarlet

jā, v. pull, drag, draw

jàkā (f.) (pl. jakunkunà), bag, ₦200

jàkī (f. jàkā ; pl. jākunà), donkey

Jànairù, January

Jànhôl/Jàn hwâl, John Holt canteen

jàrfā (f.), tattoo marks

jarràbâwā (f.), school examination

— ci jarràbâwā, pass an examination

— yi jarràbâwā, take an examination

jārùmī (f. jārùmā ; pl. jàrùmai), brave person

Jàtau, (man's name— usually given to light-skinned person)

jāwō, v. pull (here), drag (toward speaker)

jàyayyà (f.), controversy, dispute

jē, v. go to

— jè ka, go away !

jēfà, *v.* throw

jèfā (i/ē), *v.* throw at

ji, *v.* hear, sense, feel

— **ji ƙai,** *v.* have mercy, be sympathetic

— **ji yunwà,** *v.* be hungry

jî, hearing, feeling

— **jîn ƙai,** mercy, sympathy

jìbi, day after tomorrow

jìbì, meal, feast

jīfà, throwing at

jīkà (*pl.* **jīkōkī**), grandchild

jīkanyà, granddaughter

jìkī (*pl.* **jikunà**), body

jimà, *v.* spend quite a time at

— **an jimà,** (see **an**)

— **jìm kàɗan,** after a little while

sai an jimà, see you later

jinī, blood

jir, (see **jā**)

jirā, *v.* wait for

jirà, waiting for

jirgī (*pl.* **jiràgē**), boat, canoe, ship

— **jirgin ƙasā,** railway train

— **jirgin samà,** aeroplane

jirif, kerplunk ! (an ideophone)

— **ùngùlū tā sàuka jirif,** the vulture landed kerplunk

jità, *v.* wear, put on (clothing)

jìtu, *v.* be on good terms, get along well

jiyà (*f*), yesterday

jìyayyà (*f.*), being on good terms

Jumma'à (*f.*) Friday

Jun, June

jūnā, each other

jùrum, be despondent (an ideophone)

— **sun yi jùrum,** they stood despondently

jūyà, *v.* turn

ka, (second singular masculine relative completive p-a pronoun and the form employed after **zâ, bâ, jè**)

— **ka kàn,** (second singular masculine habitual p-a construction)

— **ka kè,** (second singular masculine relative continuative p-a construction)

ka/kà, (second singular masculine object pronoun)

kā, (second singular masculine completive p-a pronoun)

kâ, (second singular masculine future II p-a pronoun)

kà, (second singular masculine p-a pronoun used
with **bā**)

kà, (second singular masculine subjunctive p-a pro-
noun)

-kà, (second singular masculine possessive pro-
noun)

kàbēwà (*f.*) (*pl.* **kàbēyī**),
pumpkin

kadà/kâr, do not, lest (followed by subjunctive)

kàdai, (used with **sànnu**
and **barkà** as below)

— **sànnu/barkà kàdai**
(reply to **sànnu/barkà**),
hello (in reply)

Kadunà, Kaduna

kaɗà, *v.* beat a drum

kaɗai, only

kàɗan, a few, a little,
slightly

— **kàɗan-kàɗan,** very
slightly

kafà, *v.* establish, build,
erect, set up

kàfìn/kàfin, (= **kàmin**)

kàfu, *v.* be established

kai, you (masculine singular independent pro-
noun)

kai, *v.* carry, take to, reach,
be enough, be equal to

kâi (*pl.* **kāwunà**), head, top

— **à kân,** on top of

— **kân,** atop

— **kân sarkī,** postage
stamp

kâi, self

— **nī dà kâina,** I myself

kàkā (*f.*), harvest season

kàkā (*pl.* **kàkànī**), grandfather, grandmother

ka kàn, (see **ka**)

ka kè̀, (see **ka**)

kākàrē, *v.* become jammed

kàkī, khaki cloth

kakkaràntā, *v.* read in
succession

kakkāwō, *v.* keep on
bringing

kal, (see **farī**)

kālā, gleaning

kallō, looking at

kàm, indeed, on the other
hand (an insert)

kam (see **kullè**)

kāmà, *v.* catch, seize

— **cīwò yā kāmà ni,** I've
become ill (*lit.* illness has
caught me)

— **yā kāmà hanyà,** he went
on his way

kàmā, similarity

— **kàmar,** like . . .,
about . . ., as if . . .

kāmàwā, catching

kàmìn/kàmin, before (followed by subjunctive)

kāmō, *v.* catch and bring
here

kàn, (particle employed with habitual aspect— see **ka kàn,** etc.)

kân, (see **kâi**)

kanà, (second singular masculine continuative p-a construction)

Kanancī, the Kano dialect of Hausa

Kanāwā, (see **Bàkanè**)

Kànde, (woman's name)

Kanò, Kano

kàntī (pl. **kantunà**), shop selling (primarily) imported goods

kâr, (see **kadà**)

kàràmbànī, meddlesomeness, nuisance

karàntā, v. read, study

kàràtū, reading, studying, education

kàrɓā (i/ē), v. receive

kàrē (pl. **karnukà**), dog

— **kàren mōtà,** motor boy (lit. motor dog)

karyè, v. (stick) snap, break

kasà, v. arrange in heaps, pile

— **kasà kûnnē,** prick up (one's) ears, pay attention

kāsà, v. fall short (in amount, ability, etc.)

kashè, v. kill

kàshègàrī, on the next day

kāshī, excrement, faeces

kaskō, small, earthenware, bowl-shaped vessel

kàsuwā (f.) (pl. **kāsuwōyī**), market

kau/kawad (dà), v. remove to another place

kawài, only, merely

kāwō, v. bring

kāwôwā (f.), bringing

kāwù/kàwū (pl. **kàwùnai**), maternal uncle (see **rāfànī**)

kāyā (pl. **kāyàyyakī**), load, outfit, belongings

— **kāyan aikì,** tools, implements of one's work

kàzā (f.) (pl. **kàjī**), hen

kē, you (f.) (second singular feminine independent pronoun)

kè, v. be in process of, be at (specialized verbal employed in relative continuative aspect)

— **kè nan,** it is (emphasizes the phrase or clause which precedes it)

kèkē (pl. **kēkunà**), bicycle, machine

— **kèken dinkī,** sewing machine

kēwàyā, v. go around place

kēwàyē, v. go roundabout way, go around place, encircle

ki, (second singular feminine p-a pronoun em-
ployed after **zā, bā, jè**)
— **ki kàn,** (second singular
feminine habitual p-a
construction)
— **ki kè,** (second singular
feminine relative con-
tinuative p-a construc-
tion)
ki/kì, (second singular
feminine object pro-
noun)
kì/kyà, (second singular
feminine p-a pronoun
employed after **bā**)
-kì, (second singular feminine possessive pronoun)
kibiyà (*f.*) (*pl.* **kibiyōyī**),
arrow
kikà, (second feminine relative completive p-a pro-
noun)
ki kàn, (see **ki**)
ki kè, (see **ki**)
kikkirā, *v.* keep calling
kin, (second singular feminine completive p-a pro-
noun)
kinà, (second singular feminine continuative aspect
construction)
kirā, *v.* call
kirāwō, *v.* call (here)
kirkì, excellence, good
character, honesty

kīshìyā (*f.*) (*pl.* **kīshiyōyī**),
co-wife
kīwò, (animal) seeking
food, grazing ; (person)
tending animal
kō, or, whether, perhaps,
(question particle), (prefix converting an interrogative nominal into an
indefinite nominal)
— **kō dà,** even, even
though, even if
kòfī, coffee
kògī (*pl.* **kōgunà**), river
kō'ìnā/kōìnā, wherever
kōmà, *v.* return (there)
kōmar (dà), *v.* return,
restore
kōmē, everything,
anything, whatever
— **kōmē dà kōmē,** everything
kōmō, *v.* return here
kōnawà, however many
kōrè (*f.* **kōrìyā** ; *pl.*
kwârrā), grass-green,
emerald-green
— **kōrè shar,** bright green
kōwā, everyone
— **kōwā dà kōwā,** everyone
kōwàccē, (see **kōwànnē**)
kōwàcè, (see **kōwànè**)
kōwàɗànnē, (see **kōwànnē**)
kōwàɗànnè, (see **kōwànè**)
kōwànè (*f.* **kōwàcè** ; *pl.*
kōwàɗànnè), every, any

kōwǎnēnè/kōwǎnē nè (f.
kōwǎcēcè/kōwǎcē cè),
everyone, whoever
kōwǎnnē (f. kōwǎccē ; pl.
kōwǎɗànnē), everyone
kōyàushè/kōyàushe, when-
ever
kōyàyà, however
kū, (second plural inde-
pendent pronoun)
ku, (second plural p-a pronoun employed with zâ,
bâ, jè)
— ku kàn, (second plural
habitual p-a construc-
tion)
— ku kè, (second plural
relative continuative
p-a construction)
ku/kù, (second plural
object pronoun)
kù, (second plural subjunctive p-a pronoun)
kù, (second plural p-a pronoun employed with bā)
-kù, (second plural possessive pronoun)
kudù, south, southwards
— kudù sak, due south
kuɗī, money
— kuɗin ƙasā, tax
(= hàrājì)
kujèrā (f.) (pl. kùjèrū),
stool, chair
kūkā, weeping, crying
kūkà (f.) (pl. kūkōkī),

baobab tree, pods or
leaves
kukà, (second plural relative completive p-a pro-
noun)
ku kàn, (see ku)
ku kè, (see ku)
kùlā (dà), v. pay attention
(to), take notice (of)
kullè, v. lock
— nā kullè ƙōfà kam, I
locked the door tightly
kullum/kullun, always
kumā, also
kun, (second plural com-
pletive p-a pronoun)
kunà, (second plural con-
tinuative p-a construc-
tion)
kùnkurū (pl. kunkurà),
turtle, tortoise
kûnnē (pl. kunnuwà), ear
kūrā (f.) (pl. kūràyē),
hyena
kurùm (f.), silence ; only
(= kawài)
kusa, nearness, closeness
— kurkusa/kusa-kusa,
very close, ever closer
kusa, v. approach, get near
kuskurè, mistake, error,
missing the mark in
shooting
kùwā, indeed, as for . . .,
however, on the other
hand (an insert)

kwâ, (second plural future
II p-a pronoun)

kwà, (second plural p-a
pronoun employed with
bā)

kwabò (*pl.* kwàbbai), kobo

kwàɗàyī, keen desire, greed

kwàɗō (*pl.* kwàɗī), frog,
padlock

kwàikwayà (i/ē), *v.* imitate

kwal, (the form of kwāna
employed before lāfiyà)

kwalabā/kwalbā (*f.*) (*pl.*
kwalàbē), glass bottle,
crowbar

kwānā (*pl.* kwànàkī),
night-time, a twenty-
four hour day (when
counting days)

— kwānā biyu, a long time
(*lit.* two days)

— kwānā gōmà, ten days

kwāna/kwal, *v.* spend the
night

— nā kwāna biyu à wurîn,
I spent a long time there

kwānò (*pl.* kwānōnī), any
metal bowl or basin,
headpan, roofing pan

kwântā, *v.* lie down, (wind,
dispute, *etc.*), subside,
(mind) be at rest

kwantar (dà), *v.* cause to lie
down

Kwârà (*f.*), Niger River

kwāsà, *v.* dip out

kwāshè, *v.* collect and remove (all of)

kwatà (*f.*), quarter

kwatàntā, *v.* compare, give
a rough idea, imitate

kyà, (second singular feminine future II p-a pro-
noun)

kyà, (second singular feminine p-a pronoun em-
ployed with bā)

kyàkkyāwā (*m.* or *f.*) (*pl.*
kyāwàwā) good, hand-
some, beautiful, (often
= mài kyâu)

kyar, difficulty (used only
with dà as below)

— dà kyar, with difficulty

kyâu, goodness (usually to
the sight), handsome-
ness, beauty

— dà kyâu, good, handsome
beautiful (*lit.* possessing
goodness)

ƙàdangarè (*pl.* ƙàdàngàrū),
lizard

ƙàhō/ƙàfō (*pl.* ƙàhònī),
horn (of animal), horn
for blowing

ƙai, (see ji ƙai)

ƙà̀ƙà, how ? (= yàyà)

ƙàƙƙarfā (*pl.* ƙarfàfā),
strong

ƙalau/lau, very spotlessly

ƙanè (*f.* ƙanwà ; *pl.*

ƙânnē), younger sibling
(= brother or sister)
ƙànƙanè (f. ƙànƙanùwā ;
pl. ƙanānà), small
(thing), a little
ƙanƙantà (f.), smallness
ƙanwà (f.), younger sister
(see ƙanè)
ƙārā (f), crying out, complaint to one in authority
ƙārà, v. increase, repeat
(doing something)
ƙàramī (f. ƙàramā ; pl.
ƙanānà), small (thing)
ƙārè, v. be complete, finish
ƙarfè (pl. ƙaràfā), metal ;
o'clock
— ƙarfè biyu, two o'clock
ƙarfī, strength
ƙàrƙashī, under-side
— ƙàrƙashin, under-
neath . . .
ƙàru, v. be increased, make
progress
ƙaryā (f.) (pl. ƙàryàce-
ƙàryàcē), a lie, untruth.
falseness
ƙasā (f.) (pl. ƙasàshē),
earth, soil, country,
district
nan ƙasā, here in this
country
ƙasà, on the ground, downward
— ƙasà-ƙasà, slightly
downward

ƙàshī (pl. ƙasūsuwà), bone
ƙauyè (pl. ƙauyukà), vil-
lage, rural area
ƙētàrā, v. step/cross over
ƙētàrē, v. cross (road, river,
border)
ƙi, v. refuse, dislike
ƙî, refusal, hatred
ƙirin, (see baƙī)
ƙìyayyà (f.), mutual hatred
ƙōfà (f.) (pl. ƙōfōfī), doorway
ƙòƙarī, (praiseworthy)
effort, (worthy) attempt
ƙōnà, v. burn
ƙōnè, v. burn (completely),
become burned
— yā ƙōnè ƙùrmus, it's
completely burned up
ƙōtà (f.) (pl. ƙōtōcī), handle
of, e.g. axe, hoe
ƙùrmus, (see ƙōnè)
ƙùrùnƙus, here ends the
fable/matter
ƙwai, egg(s)
ƙwarai, very much
— ƙwarai dà gàskē, very
much indeed
ƙwaryā (f.) (pl. ƙ̂ōrē),
gourd bowl
ƙyālè, v. ignore, take no
notice of
ƙyēyà (f.), back of the head

làbārì (pl. làbàrū), news,
information

— **bâ làbārì,** without warning

laɓàɓā, *v.* walk stealthily, sneak up on

laccà, (political) speech

lādā, reward, wages

Lâdì/Lādì, (see **Lahàdì**)

lāfiyà (*f.*), health, well-being, safety

làfiyayyē (*f.* **làfiyayyiyā** ; *pl.* **làfiyàyyū**), healthy, sound

Lahàdì/Lâdì (*f.*), Sunday

lâifī (*pl.* **laifōfī**), fault, crime

— **bâ lâifī,** that's all right (*lit.* there's nothing wrong)

— **lâifìn kânsà,** his own fault

lālàcē, *v.* become spoiled, deteriorate

lallē, for sure

Làràbā (*f.*), Wednesday

Lārabāwā, (see **Bàlārabè**)

lattì, lateness

lau, (see **ƙalau**)

launì (*pl.* **launōnī**), colour

Lawàl, (man's name)

lēbùrà (*pl.* **lēburōrī**), labourer

lēɓè (*pl.* **lēɓunà**), lip

lèmō/lèmū, citrus (fruit *or* tree)

likità (*pl.* **likitōcī**), doctor

linzāmì (*pl.* **linzàmai**), bit, bridle

lissāfì, act of reckoning up, arithmetic, accounting

littāfì (*pl.* **littàttàfai**), book

Littìnîn/Àttànîn (*f.*), Monday

lōkàcī (*pl.* **lòkàtai**), time

lōtò, time

— **lōtò-lōtò,** from time to time

m, well (an exclamation indicating thoughtful consideration of a matter)

mā/ma, as for . . ., on the other hand, however (an insert)

mâ, (first plural future II p-a pronoun)

ma-/wà, to/for (indirect object indicator)

ma'àikàcī (*f.* **ma'aikacìyā** ; *pl.* **ma'àikàtā**), worker

ma'àikī (*pl.* **ma'àikā**), messenger

ma'ajī (*pl.* **mà'àjìyai**), storehouse

ma'aunā (*f.*) (*pl.* **mà'àunai**), place where grain is sold

ma'aunī (*pl.* **mà'àunai**), any measure, scales

mabūdī (*pl.* **màbùɗai**), key

màcè (*f.*) (**màta-** ; *pl.* **mātā**), woman, wife

— **tamàcè/tamàtā,** female (*lit.* pertaining to woman)

macìjī (*pl.* **màcìzai**), snake

madafā/madafī (*pl.* **màdà-fai**), kitchen, cooking-place

mādàllā, splendid, fine, thank you

madarā (*f.*), (fresh) milk

madìnkī (*f.* **madìnkìyā** ; *pl.* **madìnkā**), tailor

madaurī (*pl.* **màdàurai**), thing used for tying

mafàshī (*pl.* **mafàsā**), highway robber

mafì/mafìyī (*pl.* **mafìyā**), in excess of, superior to

màganà (*f.*) (*pl.* **màgàn-gànū**), word, thing said

māgànī (*pl.* **māgungunà**), medicine

— **shā māgànī,** take medicine

magàyī, informer

magirbī (*pl.* **màgìrbai**), (type of harvesting tool shaped like a **fartanyà**)

magwajī (*pl.* **màgwàdai**), measuring rod

mahàifī (*f.* **mahaifìyā** ; *pl.* **mahàifā**), parent

mahàrbī *pl.* **mahàrbā**), hunter, one who shoots

mahàucī (*pl.* **mahàutā**), butcher, meat-seller

mahàukàcī (*f.* **mahauka-cìyā** ; *pl.* **mahàukàtā**), madman, insane person

mahautā (*pl.* **màhàutai**), place where meat is sold

mahukuntā (*pl.* **màhùkùn-tai**), law court

mahùkùrcī (*f.* **mahukur-cìyā** ; *pl.* **mahùkùrtā**), patient/long suffering person

mai (dà), (see **mayar**)

mài (*pl.* **màsu**), possessor of . . ., characterized by . . .

— **mài gidā,** head of the house, husband

— **mài tēbùr,** small market trader who (usually) displays his goods on a table

— **mài zuwà,** that which is coming (*e.g.* **satī mài zuwà** = next week)

mâi, oil, fat, grease, petrol

— **mân shānū,** cream, butter

màimakon, instead of . . .

maishē, (form of **mayar**)

majèmī (*pl.* **majèmā**), tanner

majì/majìyī (*f.* **majiyìyā** ; *pl.* **majìyā**), hearer, feeler, one who hears/feels

makà, to/for you (*m. sing.*)
(indirect object pronoun
construction)

makàɗī (*pl.* **makàɗā),**
drummer

makaɗī (*pl.* **màkàɗai),**
drum-stick

màkāhò/màkāfò (*f.*
makaunìyā ; *pl.* **màkàfī),**
blind person

màkānīkì (*pl.* **màkànìkai),**
mechanic

màkarà, *v.* be/come late,
dally

makarantā (*f.*) (*pl.*
makarantōcī), school

màkàrau, person who is
customarily late, dila-
tory person

makì/mikì, to/for you (*f.
sing.*), (indirect object
pronoun construction)

mākò, week (= **sātī)**

— **màkòn gòbe,** next week

— **màkòn jiyà,** last week

makòyī (*f.* **makòyìyā;** *pl.*
makòyā), learner,
apprentice

makù/mukù, to/for you
(*pl.*), (indirect object
pronoun construction)

makàryàcī (*f.* **makàrya-
cìyā ;** *pl.* **makàryàtā),**
liar

màkògwàrō, throat, wind-
pipe

mālàm(ī) (*f.* **mālàmā ;** *pl.*
màlàmai), teacher, Mr.

mālamancī, (playful term
coined to refer to the
mixture of Hausa and
English which people
fluent in both languages
employ in informal con-
versation)

màmā, (woman's) breast(s),
Mother

màmākì (*pl.* **màmàkai),**
being surprised, amaze-
ment

Mammàn, (man's name)

mân, (see **mâi)**

manà/mamù, to/for us (indirect object pronoun
construction)

mànà, indeed ! (an exple-
tive)

— **ī mànà,** yes indeed !

mangwàrò, mango(es),
mango tree

manì, (see **minì)**

mântā (dà), *v.* forget

màntaccē (*f.* **màntacciyā ;**
pl. **màntàttū),** forgotten
(thing), forgetful person

màntau, forgetful person

mânyā, (see **bàbba)**

— **mânya-mânyā,** impor-
tant people

maràbā, welcome !,
welcoming

màràicē, (late) evening

dà màràicē, in the (late) evening

maràs (pl. maràsā), lacking in

maràshī (f. marashìyā ; pl. maràsā), lacking in

Māris (f.), March

maròƙī (f. maròƙìyā ; pl. maròƙā), beggar, one who is requesting/ pleading

martabà (f.) (pl. marta- bōbī), high rank

Maryamù, Mary

masà/mishì, to/for him (indirect object pronoun ‘ construction)

māshì (pl. māsū), spear

masò/masòyī (f. masòyìyā; pl. masòyā), one who likes/loves

māsū, (see māshì)

masù/musù, to/for (indirect object pronoun con- struction)

màsu, (see mài)

matà, to/for her (indirect object pronoun con- struction)

mātā/màta-, (see màcè)

matsà, v. squeeze/pinch to- gether, bother

màtsu, v. be under pressure

mawàdàcī (f. mawadācìyā ; pl. mawàdàtā), wealthy person

mayar/mai (dà). v. put back, return (a thing to its place), change into, regard as

Māyù (f.), May

mazā, (see mijì, namijì)

maza, quickly

maza-maza, very quickly

mè/mēnē/mēnēnè, what (is it) ?

mètan (f.), 200

mhm̀, greetings (in reply to a greeting)

mijì (pl. mazā), husband

mikì, (see makì)

mīkìyā (f.), Ruppell's griffon (a large scaven- ger bird)

mìlyân, million

minì/manì, to/for me (in- direct object pronoun construction)

mìnistà (pl. ministōcī), government minister

minshārī, snoring

mishì, (see masà)

m'm̀, (expression of sym- pathetic concern)

mōtà (f.) (pl. mōtōcī), auto- mobile, lorry

mòtsī, movement, motion

mū, (first plural inde- pendent pronoun)

mu, (first plural p-a pronoun employed with zā, bā)

— **mu kàn,** (first plural
habitual p-a construc-
tion)

— **mu kè,** (first plural
relative continuative p-a
construction)

mu/mù, (first plural object
pronoun)

mũ, (first plural p-a pronoun employed with **bā**)

-mù, (first plural possessive
pronoun)

mūgũ (*f.* **mugunyà** ; *pl.*
miyàgū), bad/evil (person or thing)

mùgùntā (*f.*), badness,
wickedness

mukà, (first plural relative
completive p-a pronoun)

mu kàn, (see **mu**)

mu kè, (see **mu**)

mukù, (see **makù**)

mun, (first plural completive p-a pronoun)

munà, (first plural continuative p-a construc-
tion)

munāfùkī (*f.* **munāfùkā** ;
pl. **mùnàfùkai**), hypocrite

murfù/murhù (*pl.* **muràfū**),
the three stones which
form the indigenous
cooking-place, stove

muryà (*f.*) (*pl.* **muryōyī**),
voice

Mūsā, Moses

musù, (see **masù**)

mutù, *v.* die

mùtûm/mùtumì (*pl.*
mutànē), man, person

mutuncì, manliness, self-
respect

mùtùntakà (*f.*), human
nature

mwâ, (first plural future
II p-a pronoun)

mwà, (first plural p-a pronoun employed with **bā**)

na/-n (*f.* **ta/-r**), of, pertaining to (the referen-
tial)

— **na/ta biyu,** the second
one

na, (first singular relative
completive p-a pronoun)

— **na kàn** (first singular
habitual p-a construc-
tion)

— **na/ni kè,** (first singular
relative continuative p-a
construction)

nā, (first singular completive p-a pronoun)

nā-/nà- (*f.* **tā-/tà-**), belonging to (prefixed to
possessive pronouns to
form the independent
possessive pronouns)

nâ, (first singular future II
p-a pronoun)

nà, first singular p-a pronoun employed with **bā**)

-nà, be in the process of, be at (specialized verbal employed in continuative aspect constructions)

-na/-nā (*f.* **-ta/-tā**), my (first singular possessive pronoun)

na'àm, (particle of assent or interest), yes

nà'am, (reply to a call), yes ?, what ?

naɗà, *v.* wind (a turban), fold (a cloth), appoint (a person to office)

naɗèwā, folding, winding, appointing

nàɗu, *v.* be folded up, be wound, be appointed

nai, 9d

nairà, 1 naira

nākà/tākà, yours (*m. sing.*) (independent possessive pronoun)

na kàn, (see **na**)

na kè, (see **na**)

nākì/tākì, yours (*f. sing.*) (independent possessive pronoun)

nākù/tākù, yours (*pl.*) (independent possessive pronoun)

nāmà (*pl.* **nāmū**), (wild) animal, meat, flesh

namijì (*pl.* **mazā**), male, brave man

nan/nân/nàn, this/these, that/those, here/there

–– **nan dà nan,** immediately, at once

–– **nan gàrī,** in this town

–– **nan ƙasā,** in this country

nànnēmà, *v.* look all over for

nāsà/tāsà, his (independent possessive pronoun)

nāsù/tāsù, theirs (independent possessive pronoun)

nātà/tātà, hers (independent possessive pronoun)

nauyī, heaviness

–– **dà nauyī,** heavy

nawà, how much/many ?

–– **nawà-nawà,** how much each/apiece

nàwa/tàwa, mine (independent possessive pronoun)

nē/nè (*f.* **cē/cè**), is, was

nēmā, seeking, looking for

nèmā (i/ē), *v.* seek, look for

nèmammē (*f.* **nèmammiyā**; *pl.* **nèmàmmū**), sought

nènnēmà, (= **nànnēmà**)

nēmō, *v.* seek and bring here

nēsà, far away (= **nīsa**)

ngō/ungō, take hold (of what I am handing you) !

nī, (first singular independent pronoun)

ni/nì, (first singular object pronoun)

Nìjēriyà (*f.*), Nigeria

ni kè̃, (see **na kè̃** under **na**)

nīsā, distance

nīsa, afar

— **dà nīsa,** far away

nōmā (*f.*), *v.* farming

nòmā (**i/ē**), *v.* till a farm

Nūhù, Noah

nūnà, *v.* show

nŭna, *v.* become ripe

nutsè̃/nitsè̃, *v.* vanish

Nùwambà (*f.*), November

ōfìs/ōfìshī, office

òhō, what do I care !, I don't know or care

Òktōbà (*f.*), October

rabà, *v.* divide, separate

rabì, half

ràbō, one's lot, sharing out, share

ràbō/ràbuwā (*f.*), separation

ràbu (**dà**), *v.* part from, separate

rāfànī (*pl.* **ràfànai**), maternal uncle (= **kāwŭ**)

ragà, *v.* reduce

ragè̃, *v.* reduce, remain

ragì, reduction

— **bâ ragì,** there is no reduction (in price)

râi (*pl.* **rāyukà**), life

— **rânkà yà dadè̃,** may you live long ! (*lit.* may your life last a long time)

ràkē, sugarcane

rāmì (*pl.* **rāmunà**), hole (in ground, wall, earth-floor)

rân, (see **râi** or **rānā**)

rānā (*f.*), sun heat of sun, day

— **rân nan,** (on) a certain day, the other day

— **ran Tàlātà,** Tuesday

rānī, the dry season

rasà, *v.* lack, be unable to

rashì, lack

— **rashìn sanì,** ignorance, lack of knowledge

ràsît/ràsitì, receipt

ràsu, *v.* die, be in short supply

rātsè̃, *v.* swerve, stray (from road)

rawā (*f.*) (*pl.* **ràye-ràyē**), dancing, a dance

rawànī (*pl.* **rawunà**), turban

ràwayà (*f.*), yellow

— **ràwayà-ràwayà,** yellowish

rērà, *v.* sing

— **rērà wāƙà,** sing a song

rigā/rìgāyà, *v.* (have) already done, precede

rìgā (*f.*) (*pl.* **rìgunà**), gown, robe, shirt, coat

rìgàkafì, prevention

rìgāyà, v. (see rigā)

rījìyā (f.) (pl. rījiyōyī), a
well

riƙà, v. keep on doing

riƙè, v. hold

ròƙā (i/ē) v. request, beseech

ròƙō, v. a request, re-
questing

rōmō, broth

rubùtā, v. write

rùbùtū, writing, act of
writing

rufà, v. cover, close

rufè, v. cover (up/over),
close, conceal

ruwā, water, rain

--- inā ruwāna ?, what do I
care ?

--- ruwan samà, rain

--- ruwan shā, drinking
water

sā (f. sānìyā ; pl. shānū),
bull

sā, v. put, place, appoint

sā/swā, (third plural future
II p-a pronoun)

sà/swà/sù, (third plural p-a
pronoun employed with
bā)

-sà, (third singular possessive pronoun)

sā'à (f.), good luck, hour,
time

--- sā'àd dà, when . . .

-- sā'àn nan, then . . .

sàbà'in, seventy

sābō (f. sābuwā ; pl.
sàbàbbī), new (thing)

--- sābō ful, brand new

sabò dà/sabòdà, because of

sàbulù, soap

sādà, v. cause to meet

sàdu (dà), v. meet (with)

sāfē, morning

--- dà sāfē, in the morning

sāfiyā (f.), morning

sai (dà), v. (see sayar)

sai, except, then, unless,
only, until, must (etc.)

-- sai kà cê, as if (lit. you
must say)

--- sai kà ganī, you'll have
to see it (to believe it)

Sà'ìdù, (man's name)

sak, exactly (with direc-
tions—see arèwā)

sàkā (i/ē), v. release (i.e.
from prison, marriage,
etc.)

sakandàrè, secondary
school

sākè, v. change

-- sàkè fàɗā, (please) repeat (what you) said

Sakkwato, Sokoto

sàlāmù/sàlâm àlaikùn,
greetings ! (called from
outside the compound)

sallà (f.), Muslim prayers,
festival

sallàmā, v. agree to sell at price offered

samà, sky

samà, upward

— samà-samà, slightly upward

sàmā/sāmù (i/ē), v. obtain, get, come upon

Sambò, (man's name)

sàmmakō, making an early start

sāmō, v. get and bring here

sāmù, v. (see sàmā)

sàmu, v. occurred, be obtainable

sàna'à (f.) (pl. sana'ō'ī), (one's) trade, occupation, profession

sànannē (f. sànanniyā; pl. sànànnū), known

sanar (dà), v. cause to know

sanasshē, v. (form of sanar)

sàndā (pl. sandunà), stick, force

— ɗan sàndā (pl. 'yan sàndā), Government Policeman

sànē, knowledgeable

Sānī, (man's name)

sanì/san, v. know

sānìyā (f.), cow (see sà)

sànnu, greetings!, slowness, carefulness

— sànnu dà aikì, greetings in (your) work

— sànnu dà zuwà, greetings at (your) coming

— sànnu sànnu, greetings

— sànnu-sànnu, slowly

santsī, slipperiness

sanyī, damp coldness

sarkī (pl. sarākunà), chief, king

sassāfē, very early morning

— dà sassāfē, in the very early morning

sàssayà, v. keep on buying

sassayar, v. keep on selling

sassàyē, v. keep on buying until (one) has bought all of

sātà (f.), stealing

sàtā (i/ē), v. steal

sātī, week, Saturday, (= mākò), weekly wages

— sātī mài zuwà, next week

— sātī wandà ya wucè, last week

Sàtumbà (f.), September

sàu, times (used with numbers, e.g. sàu ukù = three times)

sàuka, v. descend, get down from, arrive (at)

saukar (dà), v. lift down, bring/put down

saukō, v. come down (from)

saukàƙē, = sawwàƙē

saukī, easiness

dà saukī, easily, less bothersome, (illness) be better

yanà dà saukī, it (*e.g.* illness, tiredness) is better

yā yi saukī, it got better

saurā, remainder

saura, *v.* remain. be left over

sauràyī (*pl.* **sàmàrī**), young man

saurī, quickness

dà saurī, quickly

sâwā, putting (verbal noun from **sâ**)

sawwàƙē, reduce completely, make (*e.g.* illness) better

sàyā (i/ē), *v.* buy

sayar/sai (dà), *v.* sell, cause to buy

sayârwā, selling

sayè, *v.* buy all of

sàyē, buying

sayō, *v.* buy and bring here

sàyu, *v.* be bought (completely)

sh-, (see **sh** section following this section)

sidiƙ, (see **baƙī**)

sifìrī, zero

sil, (see **baƙī**)

simintì/sumuntì, cement

sirdì (*pl.* **siràdā**), saddle, seat (of bicycle, motorcycle)

sìsì, 5 kobos

sìsìn-kwabò, ½ kobo (= **ɗàrī**)

sìsì-sìsì/sì-sìsì, 5 kobos apiece/each

sìttin, sixty

sō, *v.* want, like, love

sô, wanting, liking, loving

sōmà, *v.* begin, start

sòsai, well, correctly, exactly

sòyayyà (*f.*), mutual affection

su, (third plural p-a pronoun employed with **zâ, bâ**)

su kàn, (third plural habitual p-a construction)

su kè, (third plural relative continuative p-a construction)

sū, (third plural independent pronoun)

su/sù, (third plural object pronoun)

sù, (third plural subjunctive p-a pronoun)

sũ, (see **sà**)

-sù, (third plural possessive pronoun)

sukà, (third plural relative completive p-a pronoun)

su kàn, (see **su**)

sukàr(ī), sugar

su kè, (see **su**)

sùkùkù, despondently (an
ideophone)
- yanà zàune sùkùkù, he
was sitting despondently
sulè (*pl.* sulūluwà), shilling
Sulè, (man's name)
Sùlēmānù, (man's name)
sun, (third plural completive p-a pronoun)
sunà, (third plural continuative p-a construction)
sūnā (*pl.* sūnàyē), name,
price
- - sâ sūnā, set the price (of
an article)
sùnkwìye, bent over,
stooped
- - à sùnkwìye, bent over,
stooped
sùrukā/sùrùkuwā (*f.*),
mother-in-law
sùrukī (*f.* sùrukā ; *pl.*
sùrùkai), (father)-in-
law ; *pl.* in-laws
sùrūtù, loud (senseless)
chattering
swâ, (see sâ)
swà/sù/sà, (see sà)

shā, *v.* drink
- - shā māgànī, take medicine
— shā wàhalà, have trouble
shā (dà), (see shāyar)
shâ, drinking ; and (with
numbers 11–19 only)

shàfā (i/ē), *v.* wipe, affect a
person
shāhò (*pl.* shāhunà), hawk
shâidā, *v.* bear witness,
inform
shakkà (*f.*), doubting
— bâ shakkà, doubtless,
without doubt
shar, (see kōrè)
shārè, *v.* sweep
shàrī'à (*f.*) (*pl.* sharī'ō'ī),
administration of justice,
law, court
shāshē, (form of shāyar)
shāyar/shā (dà), *v.* water
(an animal), cause to
drink
shègàntakà (*f.*), impu-
dence, rascality
shēgè (*f.* shēgìyā ; *pl.*
shègū), bastard, illegitimate child
shēgè !, damn it !, you
bastard !
shèkarà (*f.*) (*pl.* shèkàrū),
year
shēkaràn città, five days
hence
shēkaranjiyà, day before
yesterday
shēƙà, *v.* winnow, pour out
— shēƙà dà gudù, take to
(one's) heels
shi, (third singular masculine p-a pronoun em-
ployed with zâ, bâ)

shī, (third singular masculine independent pronoun)

shī kè nan, that's that, that's the end of the matter

shi/shì, (third singular masculine object pronoun)

shidà, six

shìga, v. enter (there), go in

shìgā, entering (there)

shìgè, v. pass by (= **wucè**)

shigō, v. enter (here), come in

shin/shîn, could it be ?, I wonder . . .

shìnkāfā (f.), rice

shirū, silence

— **shiru-shiru,** quietness, taciturnity

shiryà, v. prepare ; settle quarrel

shūɗì (f. **shūɗìyā** ; pl. **shûɗɗā**), blue (thing)

shūkà, v. sow, plant seed

shūkà, planting, crops

ta, in the process of, through

ta, (third singular feminine relative completive p-a pronoun and the p-a pronoun employed with **zâ, bâ**)

— **ta kàn** (third singular feminine habitual p-a construction)

— **ta kè,** (third singular feminine relative continuative p-a construction)

ta/tà, (third singular feminine object pronoun)

tā, (third singular feminine completive p-a pronoun)

tâ, (third singular feminine future II p-a pronoun)

tà, (third singular feminine subjunctive p-a pronoun)

tà, (third singular feminine p-a pronoun employed with **bā**)

ta/-r, (see **na/-n**)

— **ta biyar,** the fifth (see also **na/-n**)

tabbàtā, v. be sure (that), confirm

tàbbàtaccē (f. **tàbbàtacciyā** ; pl. **tàbbàtàttū**), confirmed, proven (fact or person)

tabbatar (dà), v. make certain, confirm

tabɗì, (expression of utter amazement)

taɓà, v. touch ; have ever/ previously done

tàɓà kunnē, great grandchild

tāɗì, chatting

tàfasà, *v.* (water, *etc.*) boils
tàfàsasshē (*f.* tàfàsasshiyā ;
    pl. tàfàsàssū), boiled
tàfi, *v.* go (away)
— tàfi àbinkà !, scram
tàfī, palm of the hand, sole
    of the foot
tàfiyà (*f.*), travelling, going
tāgà (*f.*) (*pl.* tāgōgī), win-
    -dow (hole)
tàimakà (i/ē), *v.* help
tàimakō, help, act of
    helping
tak, (see ɗaya)
tākà, *v.* tread on, walk along
tākà, (see nākà)
tàkàlmī (*pl.* tākalmà),
    sandal, shoe, boot
ta kàn, (see ta)
takàrdā (*f.*) (*pl.* tàkàrdū),
    paper, (small) book
ta kè, (see ta)
tākì, (see nākì)
tākù, (see nākù)
takwàs, eight
talàkà (*pl.* talakāwā), com-
    mon person
Tàlātà (*f.*), Tuesday
tàlàtin, thirty
Talle, (man's name)
tamàtā, female
tàmànin, eighty
tàmbayà (i/ē), *v.* ask
tàmbayà (*f.*) (*pl.* tamba-
    yōyī), question, act of
    asking

tāmù, (see nāmù)
tanà, (third singular femi-
    nine continuative p-a
    construction)
tàntàmbayà, *v.* keep on
    asking
tarà, nine
tārà, *v.* gather, collect
tàre (dà), together (with)
tarō, 2½ kobos
tàru, *v.* be gathered to-
    gether
tāsà (*f.*) (*pl.* tāsōshī), metal
    bowl or basin ; *pl.* dishes
tāsà, (see nāsà)
tāsù, (see nāsù)
tashà/tēshà (*pl.* tashōshī),
    (railway) station
tāshì, *v.* get up, start out
    (on a journey), stand up
tātà, (see nātà)
tàttàɓà kunnē, great-great
    grandchild
tattàkē, *v.* trample under
    foot
tàtsūnìyā (*f.*) (*pl.* tātsūni-
    yōyī), fable
taurī, hardness, toughness
tàwa, (see nàwa)
tàwadà (*f.*), ink
tāyà (*f.*) (*pl.* tāyōyī), tyre
tayà, *v.* make an offer (in
    bargaining)
tēbùr(ī) (*pl.* tēburōrī), table,
    shovel
tēshà, (see tashà)

tĭcằ (*pl.* **tĭcōcī**), teacher

tīlằs, perforce, of necessity

tĭnjim, abundantly, in large numbers (an ideophone)

— **mutằnē tĭnjim**, a large number of people

tô/tŏ, well, okay

ts-, (see the **ts-** section following this section)

tufằ (*pl.* **tufāfĭ**), clothes

tùkùna, not yet, first

tukunyā (*f.*) (*pl.* **tukwằnē**), cooking-pot

tùlū (*pl.* **tūlūnằ**), pitcher

tun, since

tunằ, *v.* remember

tùnằnī, reflecting, remembering, regret, apprehensiveness

tunkìyā (*f.*) (*pl.* **tumākī**), sheep

tūrằ, *v.* push

Tūrai (*f.*), Europe

tūrè, *v.* push/knock over

tūsằ (*f.*), breaking wind

tuwō, guinea-corn or millet mush (the staple food of Northern Nigeria)

tsằdā (*f.*), expensiveness

— **yanằ dằ tsằdā = yā yi tsằdā**, it is expensive

tsāfĭ, fetish, idol

tsai (dằ), (see **tsayar**)

tsakằ/tsakiyằ (*f.*), centre, middle

— **tsakằr tsằkānī**, betwixt and between

tsằkānī, between

tsallē, jumping

— **tsàlle-tsàllē**, jumping events in track and field matches

tsằmmānī, thinking, thought

tsawō, length

tsayằ, *v.* stand (up), stop, wait

tsayar/tsai (dằ), *v.* cause to stand/stop/wait

tsàye, stopped, standing

— **à tsàye**, in a standing position, stopped

tsincè, *v.* pick up, select, find (thing)

tsìnī (*pl.* **tsīnằyē**), sharp point

tsìntā (i/ē), *v.* select, pick up

tsintsiyā (*f.*) (*pl.*) **tsintsiyōyī**), broom, type of thatching grass

tsìrārằ (*f.*), nakedness, naked

tsit, silence (an ideophone)

— **yā yi tsit**, he kept silent

tsōhō/tsōfō (*f.* **tsōhuwā** ; *pl.* **tsòfàffī**), old (person or thing)

— **tsōfon hannū**, experienced person, 'an old hand'

tsòrō, fear

tsūfa, *v.* become old

tsūfā, becoming old. ageing

tsuntsū (*f.* tsuntsuwā ; *pl.*
tsuntsàyē), bird

tsūtsà (*f.*) (*pl.* tsūtsōtsī),
worm

ùbā (*pl.* ùbànnī), father

ukù, three

Ùmarù, (man's name)

ungō, (see ngō)

ùngùlū (*f.*) (*pl.* ùngùlai),
vulture

Ùsmân, (man's name)

uwā (*f.*), mother

— uwargidā, woman of the
house, (first) wife

wâ (*f.* yâ ; *pl.* yâyyē),
elder sibling (brother or
sister) (= yàyā)

wà, (see ma-/wà)

wà/wànē/wànēnè (*pl.* su
wà), who (is it) ?

— wànē shī ?, who does he
think he is ?

waccàn, (see wancàn)

wàccē, (see wànnē)

wàcē/wàcēcè, (feminine of
wànē/wànēnè)

wàcè, (see wànè)

wadai, curse (an exclama-
tion)

— Allà wadankà, may God
curse you !

waddà, (see wandà)

wadàncân, (see wancàn)

wadàndà, (see wandà)

wadànnân, (see wannàn)

wàdànnè, (see wànè)

wàdànnē, (see wànnē)

wadansu, (see wani)

wàhalà (*f.*), trouble

wai, it is said, quote,
rumour has it that . . .

wàiwàye, turning the head
round to look

wajē, direction

— wajen, toward/to a per-
son or place, in the
presence of a person
(= wurin)

wàje, outside

wākē, bean(s)

wàkīlì (*pl.* wàkìlai), representative

wāƙà (*f.*) (*pl.* wāƙōƙī),
song, poem

wancàn (*f.* waccàn ; *pl.*
wadàncân), that. that
one

wàncan (*f.* wàccan ; *pl.*
wàdàncan), the one in
question

wandà/wândà (*f.* waddà ;
pl. wadàndà), that which,
which, who

— duk wandà, whoever

wàndō (*pl.* wandunà), pair
of trousers

Wānè (*f.* Wancè ; *pl.* Su
wānè), So-and-so

wằnē/wằnēnề, (see wằ)
wằnề (f. wằcề ; pl.
wằɗầnnề), which ?
wani (f. wata ; pl.
waɗansu), some (one), a
certain (one), a, another
wankề, v. wash (body,
clothes, pot, etc.)
wannằn (pl. waɗannân),
this, this one
wằnnē (f. wằccē ; pl.
wằɗầnnē) which one ?
wằnzāmì (pl. wằnzầmai),
barber, tatooer
wằrhakằ, at this time . . .
warkằ, v. recover from
illness
warkar (dằ), v. cure
warkề, v. recover from
illness, cure
wằsā (pl. wằsầnnī), playing,
joking, dancing
wasằlằm, (see hāzā)
wằsīƙằ (f.) (pl. wằsìƙū),
letter
wasu, (form of waɗansu)
wằshềgầrī, (= kằshềgầrī)
wata, (see wani)
watằ (pl. wằtầnnī), moon,
month
— watằ mằi zuwằ, next
month
— watằn gòbe, next month
— watằn jiyằ, last month
— watằn dằ ya wucề, last
month

wằtằkīlằ/watakīlằ/kīlằ,
probably, perhaps,
maybe (but probable)
wằtò, that is . . .
wātsề, v. become scattered
wāwā (pl. wāwằyē), fool
— wāwan barcī, heavy/
sound sleep
wayằ (f.) (pl. wayōyī),
wire, telegraph, tele-
gram, telephone
—– gidan wayằ, post office
(where telegrams may be
dispatched)
wāyề, v. become light
— gàrī yā wāyề, it dawned
wằyō, cleverness, trickiness
wâyyô, alas ! (exclamation
of despair)
— wâyyô Allằ, alas !
—– wâyyô nī, woe is me !
wejì/wajì, wedge
wòfī (pl. wōfằyē), useless
(thing or person), empty
wōhò, booing
— sun bī sù wōhò-wōhò,
they followed them
booing
wucề, v. pass by (= ficề,
shigề)
wuƙā (f.) (pl. wuƙầƙē),
knife
wunì/yinì, v. spend the day
wunì/yinì, period of day-
light
wur, (see jā)

wurgà, *v.* throw
wurgar (dà), *v.* throw
  (violently)
wurgō, *v.* throw here
wurì (*pl.* **kuɗī**), cowry shell
  (formerly used as money)
wurī (*pl.* **wuràrē**), place
— **dà wuri-wuri,** very
  early, very promptly
— **wurin,** toward/to a person or place, in the
  presence of a person
  (= **wajen**)
— **(tun) dà wuri,** promptly,
  early
wutā (*f.*), fire
wuyà (*pl.* **wuyōyī**), neck
wùyā (*f.*), difficulty

'y-, (see separate section for
  'y- following this section)
ya, (third singular masculine relative completive
  p-a pronoun)
— **ya kàn,** (third singular
  masculine habitual p-a
  construction)
— **ya kè,** (third singular
  masculine relative con-
  tinuative p-a construc-
  tion)
yā, (third singular masculine completive p-a pronoun)
yā, *v.* come
— **yā kà,** come !

yâ, (third singular masculine future II p-a pro-
  noun)
yâ, (see **wâ**)
yà, (third singular masculine subjunctive p-a pronoun)
yà, (third singular masculine p-a pronoun em-
  ployed with **bā**)
yaddà/yâddà, how, the way
  in which
yādì, yard (measurement),
  (European) cloth
ya kàn, (see **ya**)
ya kè, (see **ya**)
Yàƙubù, Jacob
yâmmā, west, (late) afternoon
— **yâmmā sak,** due west
yâmma, westward
yanà, (third singular
  masculine continuative
  p-a construction)
yankà, *v.* slaughter (animal), cut in two ; set (a
  time) ; give verdict (in a
  court case)
yankā, butchering
yankè, *v.* (= **yankà**)
— **yankè shàrī'à,** pro-
  nounce judgement (in a
  court case)
yankèwā (*f.*), cutting,
  butchering, *etc.* (from
  yankè)

yànzu, now
— har yànzu, still, up to the present
— yànzu-yànzu, right away
yar/yā (dà), v. throw away, discard
yàràntakà (f.), childishness, childhood
yàrda, v. agree, consent
yàrdā (f.), agreement, consent
yārinyà (f.), girl
yārò (pl. yârā), boy
yātsà (pl. yātsōtsī), finger
yâu, today
— yâu-yâu, this very day, today for sure
yàushè/yàushe, when ?
yâuwā/yâuwa, fine, splendid (reply to greeting)
yawà, abundance
— dà yawà, much, many
yāwò, strolling, wandering
yàyā, (see wâ)
yàyà, how ?
yayyafī, drizzle
yi, v. do, make
— yi ta yî, set about doing
yì, (see ì)
yî, doing, making
yinì, (see wunì)
yìwu, v. be possible
Yūlì, July
Yūnì, June

yunwà (f.), hunger, famine
— ji yunwà, be/go hungry
Yūsufù, Joseph

'yā (f.), daughter (= dìyā)
— 'yā màcè (pl. 'yam mātā), young woman
— 'yar cikī, type of gown
— 'yar fārì, firstborn daughter
— 'yar'ùbā, half-sister
— 'yar'uwā, sister
'yan, (see dā)
— 'yan kasā, inhabitants of a country
'yā'yā, (see da)
'Yòlà, Yola (a town near the Cameroun border)

zā, v. (specialized verbal employed as future I aspect particle), will
zâ, v. will go
zāfī, heat, pain
— yā yi zāfī, it was hot/painful
zâi, he will (third singular masculine form of future I p-a construction)
zàkarà (pl. zàkàrū), rooster, cock
zākī, sweetness
zalbè, common grey heron
zama, v. be, become, live
zamā, being, living

zāmànī (*pl.* zàmànai),
period of time
— zāmànin dâ, in olden
times
zambàr, 1000
— zambàr dubū, 1 000 000
zân, I will (first singular
form of future I p-a
construction)
zanè (*pl.* zannuwà, body-
cloth, cloth
zārè, *v.* unsheath (sword),
pull out (*e.g.* foot from
mud, stirrup, shoe, *etc.*)
zarè, *v.* snatch, grab
Zāriyà (*f.*), Zaria
zaunà, *v.* sit down, settle
(in a place)
zaunar (dà), *v.* cause to sit/
settle
zàune, seated
— à zàune, seated
zāwò, diarrhoea
zàzzàɓī, fever, malaria
Zazzagancī, the dialect of
Zaria (Zazzàu)
Zazzàu, Zaria

zīnārìyā (*f.*), gold
zìyārà (*f.*), visiting
zìyartà (i/ē), *v.* visit
zō, *v.* come
zōbè (*pl.* zôbbā), ring
zōmō (*pl.* zōmàyē), rabbit
zubà, *v.* pour
zubar/zub (dà), *v.* pour/
throw away
zubè, *v.* pour away (all of),
abort (pregnancy)
zūcìyā (*f.*) (*pl.* zūciyōyī),
heart
zùmùntā (*f.*), relationship
(by blood or marriage),
good relationship
zur, (see jā)
zūrà, *v.* start up quickly
— zūrà dà gudù, take to
(one's) heels
zùriyà/zùri'à (*f.*),
descendants
zuwà, coming ; towards
— zuwà gà . . ., to . . . (formula employed at start
of letter)

English–Hausa Vocabulary

Note : *when using the English–Hausa sections, it is recommended that the student cross-check entries with the Hausa–English section, a large dictionary and, if possible, with some occurrence of the words/constructions in context. It is very easy to be misled into wrong usage by the over-brief indications of the meanings provided in short vocabularies like this one.*

ability, **iyàwā** (*f.*)
able, be, *v.* **iyà**
according to, **ìn ji . . .,
wai . . .**
acquaintance, **idòn sanì**
adding up, **lìssāfì**
administer, *v.* **hakùntā**
adult, **bàbba** (*pl.* **mânyā**)
aeroplane, **jirgin samà**
affair, **bàtū**
affect, *v.* **shàfā (i/ē)**
affection (mutual), **sòyayyà**
(*f.*)
after, **bāyân dà**
afternoon (late), **yâmmā,
là'asàr**
ago, short while ago, **dàzu**
agree, *v.* **yàrda**
air, **iskà** (*m.* or *f.*)
alas !, **wâyyô** !
all, **dukà**
all together, **gàba daya**
allow, *v.* **barì/bar**

along, get along well, *v.*
jitu
already planned or known,
dâ mā
already, to have (done), *v.*
rigā, *v.* **rìgāyà**
all right, that's all right,
bâ lâifī
also, **kumā**
although, **kō dà, kō dà shi/
ya kè**
always, **kullum/kullun**
amazement, **màmākì**
amen, **àmin**
America, **Amirkà** (*f.*)
and, **dà, kumā**
anger, **haushī**
angry, be, **yi fushī**
animal (domestic), **dabbà**
(*f.*) (*pl.* **dabbōbī**)
— (wild), **nāmà** (*pl.* **nāmū/
nāmōmī**)
answer, *v.n.* (*f.*) **amsà**
ants, white, **gàrā** (*f.*)

ıny, **kōwànè** (*f.* **kōwàcè** ;
   pl. **kōwàɗànnè**)
anyone who, **duk wandà**
anything, **kōmē**
appoint, *v.* **naɗà**
apprentice, **makòyī**
approach, *v.* **kusa**
April, **Afrìl**
Arab, **Bàlārabè** (*f.* **Bà-**
   lārabìyā ; *pl.* **Lārabāwā**)
argument, **faɗà**
arithmetic, **lìssāfì**
arm, **hannū** (*pl.* **hannàyē**)
arrogance, **tàƙamā** (*f.*)
arrow, **kibiyà** (*f.*) (*pl.*
   kibiyōyī)
as, **kàmar**
as for, **kàm, mā/ma**
as if, **sai kà cê, kàmar**
ask, *v.* **tàmbayà** (i/ē)
at, **à**
attempt, **ƙòƙarī**
attention, pay, *v.* **kùlā**
   (dà), kasà kûnnē
audience chamber (of
   chief), **fādà** (*f.*)
August, **Àgustà**
aunt (paternal), **bābà** ;
   gwaggò/gwàggō
— (maternal), **innà/ìnnā/**
   iyà ; **gwaggò/gwàggō**
   (maternal uncle's wife)
axe, **gàtarī** (*pl.* **gāturà**)

bachelor **gwaurō/gwamrō**
   (*pl.* **gwauràyē**)

back, **bāyā**
— backwards, **bāya**
back of the head, **ƙyēyà**
   (*f.*)
bad, **mūgù** (*f.* **mugunyà** ;
   pl. **miyàgū**)
bad, go, *v.* **lālàcē**
badness, evil, **mùgùntā**
   (*f.*)
bag, **jàkā** (*f.*) (*pl.* **jakun-**
   kunà)
ball **cūrì** ; **ƙwallō**
banana(s), **àyàbà** (*f.*)
baobab tree, **kūkà** (*f.*) (*pl.*
   kūkōkī)
barber, **wànzāmì** (*pl.*
   wànzàmai)
bastard, **shēgè** (*f.* **shēgìyā** ;
   pl. **shègū**)
be, *v.* **zama, nē/cē**
bean(s), **wākē**
bear child, *v.* **haihù** (i/ē)
bear witness, *v.* **shâidā**
beard, **gēmù**
beat, *v.* **bugà**, *v.* **bùgā** (i/ē),
   v. **dòkā** (i/ē)
beat (drum), *v.* **kaɗà**,
beating, thrashing, **dūkà**
beautiful, **kyàkkyāwā** (*pl.*
   kyāwàwā)
because (of), **dòmin/don**
because of, **sabò dà/sabòdà**
become, *v.* **zama**
bed, **gadō** (*pl.* **gadàjē**)
beer, corn, **fìtō, giyà** (*f.*)
before, **kàmìn/kàfìn**

beggar, maròƙī (f. marō-ƙiyā ; pl. marôƙā)

begin, v. sōmà, v. fārà

beginning, farkō, fārì

behind, bāyan

belongings, kāyā (pl. kāyàyyakī)

bent over, sùnkwìye

Benue River, Bīnuwài (f.)

beseech, v. ròƙā

better than, fi ... kyâu

better, it would be, gāra, gwàmmà

between, tsàkānī

betwixt and between, tsakàr tsàkānī

bicycle, kèkē (pl. kēkunà)

big, bàbba (pl. mânyā)

bigness, girmā

bird, tsuntsū (f. tsuntsu-wā ; pl. tsuntsàyē)

biscuit, bìskitì (pl. biskitōcī)

bite, v. cìzā (i/ē)

black, baƙī (f. baƙā ; pl. baƙàƙē)

— blackish, baƙi baƙi

— jet-black, baƙī ƙirin/ sidiƙ/sil

blackboard, àllō (pl. allunà)

blemish, aibù̄ (pl. aibōbī)

blind person, màkāhò/ màkāfò (f. makauniyā ; pl. màkàfī)

blood, jinī

blow, v. būsà

blow on, v. hūrà

blue, shūɗì (f. shūɗiyā ; pl. shûɗɗā)

boat, jirgī (pl. jiràgē)

body, jìkī (pl. jikunà)

boil, v. tàfasà

— boiled, tàfàsasshē

bone, ƙàshī (pl. ƙasūsuwà)

book, littāfì (pl. littàttàfai)

— book cover, bangō

borrow (other than money), v. àrā (i/ē)

bottle, kwalabā/kwalbā (f.) (pl. kwalàbē/kwalabōbī)

bottom, gìndī

boundary, iyàkā (f.)

bowl, kwānò (metal) (pl. kwānōnī), kaskō (earthenware)

box, àkwàtì (pl. akwātunà)

boy, yārò (pl. yârā)

brave person, jārùmī (f. jàrùmā ; pl. jàrùmai)

bread, burōdì/brōdì

break (a stick), v. karyè

breasts, màmā

bride, amaryā (f.)

bridegroom, angò

bridge, gadà (f.)

bridle, linzāmì (pl. linzàmai)

bring, v. kāwō

broom, tsintsiyā (f.) (pl. tsintsiyōyī)

broth, rōmō

brother, ɗan'uwā (*pl.*
  'yan'uwā)
brother, half, ɗan'ùbā (*pl.*
  'yan'ùbā)
brother, younger, ƙanè (*pl.*
  ƙânnē)
bucket, gùgā (*pl.* gūgunà)
build, *v.* ginà, *v.* kafà
bull, sâ (*f.* sānìyā ; *pl.*
  shānū), bìjimī/bàjimī (*pl.*
  bìjìmai)
burn, *v.* ƙōnà, *v.* ƙōnè
bush, dājì
but, àmmā
butcher, mahàucī (*pl.*
  mahàutā)
butchering, yankā
butter, mân shānū
buttocks, gìndī
button, ànīnī (*pl.* ànìnai)
buy, *v.* sàyā (i/ē)

calabash, ƙwaryā (*f.*) (*pl.*
  ƙôrē)
call, *v.* kirā
canoe, jirgī (*pl.* jiràgē)
cap, hùlā (*f.*) (*pl.* hūlunà)
care, what do I ?, ìnā
  ruwāna ?
carefully, à hankàlī
carry, *v.* ɗaukà (i/ē)
cat, kyânwā (*f.*) (*pl.*
  kyanwōyī)
catch, *v.* kāmà
cause, dàlīlì (*pl.* dàlìlai)
cement, simintì/sumuntì

centre, tsakiyà/tsakà (*f.*)
certain, be, *v.* tabbàtā
chair, kujèrā (*f.*) (*pl.*
  kùjèrū)
chance, dāmā (*f.*)
change, *v.* sākè
change, canjì
character, halī
— good, kirkì
characterize, *v.* fayè
chase away, *v.* kòrā (i/ē)
chat, *v.* gānà
chattering, sùrūtù
chatting, tādì
cheap, it is, yā yi àràhā
cheapness, àràhā
cheat, *v.* cùtā (i/ē)
chief, sarkī (*pl.* sarākunà)
child, yārò (*f.* yārinyà ;
  pl. yârā)
childishness, yàràntakà (*f.*)
chin, haɓà (*f.*)
citrus, lèmō/lèmū
city, birnī (*pl.* birànē)
clan, zùriyà (*f.*)
clerk, àkàwū (*pl.* akāwunà)
— head clerk, bàbban
  àkàwū
cleverness, wàyō
climb, *v.* hau, *v.* hayè
close, *v.* rufè
close (to), kusa (dà)
cloth (body), zanè (*pl.*
  zannuwà)
— (imported), yādì
clothes, tufāfì (*sing.* tufà)

cloud (rain), **girgijè** (*pl.* **gizàgìzai**)

coffee, **kòfī**

coldness (dry), **d̄arī**

— coldness (damp), **sanyī**

collect, *v.* **tārà̄**

colour, **launì** (*pl.* **launōnī**)

come, *v.* **zō**

coming, **zuwà̄**

come out, *v.* **fìtō**

commoner, **talàkà̄** (*pl.* **talakāwā**)

compare, *v.* **kwatàntā**

complaint, **kūkā, k̄ārā** (*f.*)

concerning, **bàtun**

confirm, *v.* **tabbàtā**

— confirmed, **tàbbàtaccē**

continue, *v.* **cigàba**

controversy, **jà̄yayyà̄** (*f.*)

conversation, **tād̄ī, bàtū**

cook, *v.* **dafà̄**

cooked, **dà̄faffē**

— be cooked, *v.* **dàfu**

cooking-pot, **tukunyā** (*f.*) (*pl.* **tukwà̄nē**)

corn (guinea), **dāwà̄** (*f.*), **hatsī**

correct(ly), **daidai, sòsai**

country, **k̄asā** (*f.*) (*pl.* **k̄asàshē**)

courtier, **bàfādà̄/bàfādè** (*pl.* **fàdàwā**)

cow, **sānìyā** (*f.*)

co-wife, **kīshìyā** (*f.*) (*pl.* **kīshiyōyī**)

cowrie shell, **wurì** (*pl.* **kud̄ī**)

crime, **lâifī** (*pl.* **laifòfī**)

cross, *v.* **k̄ētàrē, hayè**

crow, **hànkākà̄** (*pl.* **hànkàkī**)

crowing (of cock), **cārā** (*f.*)

crying, **kūkā**

cunning, **wà̄yō**

cure, *v.* **warkar** (**dà̄**), *v.* **warkè**

custom, **àl'ādà̄** (*f.*) (*pl.* **àl'àdū**)

dance, **rawā** (*m.* or *f.*) (*pl.* **rà̄ye-rà̄yè**)

darkness, **duhù̄/dufù̄**

daughter, **'yā** (*f.*), **d̄ìyā** (*f.*)

dawn, **àsùbâ/àsùbāhì/ sùbāhì**

dawn, *v.* **gàrī yā wāyè**

day (period of daylight), **rānā** (*f.*)

— (twenty-four hours), **kwānā** (*f.*) (*pl.* **kwà̄nàkī**)

day after tomorrow, **jībi**

day before yesterday, **shēkaranjiyà̄**

deaf and dumb, **bèbàntakà̄** (*f.*)

deaf-mute, **bēbē** (*f.* **bēbìyā** ; *pl.* **bēbà̄yē**)

dear, it is, **yā yi tsà̄dā**

debt, **bāshì**

— incur a debt, *v.* **ci bāshì**

December, **D̀izambà̄** (*f.*)

depose, *v.* **fitar/fid dà̄**

descend, *v.* **sà̄uka**

descendants, zùriyà (f.)
despondent, jùrum
despondently, sùkùkù
deteriorate, v. lālàcē
diarrhoea, zāwò
die, v. mutù, v. ràsu, v.
   hàlakà
different, dàban
difficulty, wùyā (f.)
— with difficulty, dà kyar
dip out, v. kwāsà ; ɗēbō
direction, wajē
disciple, àlmājìrī (f. àlmājìrā ; pl. àlmàjìrai)
disease, cùtā (f.)
dish, tāsà (f.) (pl. tāsōshī)
dislike, v. ƙi
dispute, jàyayyà (f.)
distance, nīsā
divide, v. rabà
do, v. yi
doctor, likità (pl. likitōcī)
dog, kàrē (pl. karnukà)
donkey, jàkī (f. jàkā ; pl.
   jākunà)
door, ƙōfà (f.) (pl. ƙōfōfī)
doubt, shakkà (f.)
— doubtless, bâ shakkà
dozen, dōzìn
drink, v. shā
driver, dirēbà
drizzle, yayyafī
drummer, makàɗī (pl.
   makàɗā)
drum stick, makaɗī (pl.
   màkàɗai)

dry, v. būshè
dry season, rānī

each other, jūnā
ear, kûnnē (pl. kunnuwà)
early (very), dà wuri-wuri,
   tun dà wuri
early start (of a trip),
   sàmmakō
earth, country, ƙasā (f.)
   (pl. ƙasàshē)
easiness, saukī
east, gabàs
easy, it is, yanà dà saukī
eat, v. ci
— eat up, v. cînyē
edge, bàkī (pl. bākunà)
education, ilmì/ilìmī
effort, àniyà/niyyà (f.),
   ƙòƙarī
egg(s), ƙwai
elder brother, wâ (pl.
   yâyyē)
— elder sister, yâ (f.) (pl.
   yâyyē)
elephant, gīwā (f.) (pl.
   gīwàyē)
end, v. ƙārè
England, Ingìlà (f.)
enter (there), v. shìga
— (here), v. shigō
erect, v. kafà
error, kuskurè
establish, v. kafà
estimate, v. kwatàntā
Europe, Tūrai (f.)

European person, **Bàtūrè** (*f.* **Bàtūrìyā** ; *pl.* **Tùràwā**)

evening, late, **màràicē**

ever, to have, *v.* **taɓà**

every, **kōwànè** (*f.* **kōwàcè** ; *pl.* **kōwàɗànnè**)

everyone, **kōwā**

everything, **kōmē**

evil, **mūgù** (*f.* **mugunyà** ; *pl.* **miyàgū**), **mùgùntā** (*f.*)

exact(ly), **sòsai, daidai**

examination, **jarràbâwā** (*f.*)

— to pass an examination, **ci jarràbâwā**

— to take an examination, **yi jarràbâwā**

excel, *v.* **fi**

except, **sai**

excrement, **kāshī**

excuse me !, **gāfarà**

expel, *v.* **fitar/fid dà**

expensiveness, **tsàdā** (*f.*)

experienced person, **tsōfon hannū**

expert, **gwànī** (*f.* **gwànā** ; *pl.* **gwanàyē**)

extremely, **ƙwarai dà gàskē**

eye, **idò** (*pl.* **idànū**)

fable, **tàtsūnìyā** (*f.*) (*pl.* **tātsūniyōyī**)

face, **fuskà** (*f.*) (*pl.* **fuskōkī**)

fairness, **ādalcì**

fall short, *v.* **kāsà**

fall *v.* **fāɗì**

— fall into, *v.* **fāɗà**

— fall on, *v.* **aukà**

family, **ìyālì, zùriyà** (*f.*)

famine, **yunwà** (*f.*)

far away, **dà nīsa**

farm, **gōnā** (*f.*) (*pl.* **gònàkī**) *v.* **yi nōmā** ; *v.* **nòmā** (i/ē)

— farmer, **manòmī** (*pl.* **manòmā**)

— farming, **nōmā**

father, **bàba, ùbā** (*pl.* **ùbànnī**)

father-in-law, **sùrukī**

fault, **lâifī** (*pl.* **laifōfī**), **aibù** (*pl.* **aibōbī**)

fear, **tsòrō**

feast, **jībì**

feather(s), **gāshì**

February, **Fàbrairù**

feed, *v.* **ciyar/cī dà**

feel, *v.* **ji**

female, **tamàtā**

ferrying, **fitò**

fetish, **tsāfì**

fever, **zàzzàɓī**

few, **kàɗan**

fez, **dàrā** (*f.*)

fighting, **faɗà**

fill, *v.* **cikà**

fine !, **yâuwā/yâuwa** !

finish, *v.* **gamà, ƙārè**

find (by chance), *v.* **tsìntā** (i/ē), *v.* **tsincè**

finger, **yātsà** (*pl.* **yātsōtsī**)
finish, *v.* **ƙārè**
fire, **wutā** (*f.*), **gòbarā** (*f.*)
first, **na/ta farkō**
five kobos, **sīsì**
florin, **fàtakà, dalà** (*f.*) (*pl.*
　　dalōlī)
flour, **gàrī**
fold, *v.* **naɗà**
follow, *v.* **bi**
food, **àbinci**
fool, **wāwā** (*pl.* **wāwàyē**)
forest, **baƙin dājì**
forget, *v.* **mântā**
— forgetful person, **màntau**
formerly, **dâ**
fourth day hence, **città**
fragment, **guntū** (*pl.*
　　guntàyē)
France, **Fàransà** (*f.*)
Frenchman, **Bàfàransì** (*f.*
　　Bàfàransìyā ; *pl.*
　　Fàrànsâi)
Friday, **Jumma'à** (*f.*)
friend, **àbōkī** (*f.* **àbōkìyā** ;
　　pl. **àbòkai**)
friendship, **amincì**
frightening, **ban tsòrō**
frog, **kwàɗō** (*pl.* **kwàɗī**)
front, **gàbā**
— in front, **gàba**
— in front of, **gàban**
Fulani person, **Bàfilācè** (*f.*
　　Bàfilātà ; *pl.* **Filànī**)
full, become, *v.* **cìka**

gather, *v.* **tārà**
— be gathered, **tàru**
get, *v.* **sāmù**
get down, *v.* **sàuka**
get up, *v.* **tāshì**
girl, **yārinyà** (*f.*) (*pl.* **'yam
　　mātā**)
girl (nubile), **bùdurwā**
give, *v.* **bā/bâ**, *v.* **bāyar**
give back, *v.* **mayar/mai(dà)**
gleaning, **kālā**
go, *v.* **tàfi**, *v.* **jē**
go around, *v.* **kēwàyā**
go out, *v.* **fita**
goat, **àkwiyà** (*f.*) (*pl.*
　　awākī)
God, **Allà/Allàh**
gold, **zīnārìyā** (*f.*)
good !, **dà kyâu !**
— goodness, **kyâu**
goodness ! good heavens !
　　tabdì !
gown, **rìgā** (*f.*) (*pl.* **rìgunà**)
grab, *v.* **zarè**
grandchild, **jīkà** (*pl.* **jīkōkī**)
granddaughter, **jīkanyà**
grandfather, **kàkā** (*pl.*
　　kàkànī)
grandmother, **kàkā** (*pl.*
　　kàkànī)
grass, **cìyāwà** (*f.*) (*pl.*
　　cìyàyī)
grasshopper, **fàrā** (*pl.* **fàrī**)
gratitude, **gòdiyā** (*f.*)
grazing, **kīwò**
grease, **mâi**

great-grandchild, **tàɓà
kunnē**
— great-great-grandchild,
tàttàɓà kunnē
greed, **kwàɗàyī**
green, **kōrè** (f. **kōrìyā** ; pl.
kwârrā)
— bright green, **kōrè shar**
greet, v. **gayar/gai dà**
greetings, **gaisuwā** (f.),
barkà (f.)
ground, on the, **ƙasà**
groundnut(s), peanut(s),
gyàɗā (f.)
guava, **gwēɓà**
guest, **bàƙō** (f. **bàƙwā** ; pl.
bàƙī)

hair, **gāshì**
half, **rabì**
half-kobo, **sīsìn kwabò,
ɗàrī**
half-sister, **'yar'ùbā**
hand, **hannū** (pl. **hannàyē)**
hand, on the other, **dai, fa,
mā**
handle (hoe, axe), **ƙōtà** (f.)
(pl. **ƙōtōcī)**
handsome, **kyàkkyāwā** (pl.
kyāwàwā)
happen, v. **fàru**, v. **àuku**
— happen on, v. **yi arbà**
happiness, **farin cikì**
hardness, **taurī**
harvest, v. **gìrbā** (i/ē)
harvest season, **kàkā** (f.)

hat, **hūlā** (f.) (pl. **hūlunà)**
hatchet, **gàtarī** (pl.
gāturà)
hatred, **ƙìyayyà** (f.), **ƙī**
Hausa person, **Bàhaushè**
(f. **Bàhaushìyā** ; pl.
Hàusàwā)
hawk, **shāhò** (pl. **shāhunà)**
head, **kâi** (pl. **kawunà)**
— headache, **cīwòn kâi**
health, **lāfiyà** (f.)
— healthy, **làfiyayyē**
heap up, v. **kasà**
hear, v. **ji**
heart, **zūcìyā** (f.) (pl.
zūciyōyī)
heat, **zāfī**
heaven, **samà**
heaviness, **nauyī**
heels, take to one's, v.
shēƙà/zūrà dà gudù
help, v. **tàimakà** (i/ē)
— help, **tàimakō**
hen, **kàzā** (f.) (pl. **kàjī)**
herd (of animals), **garkè**
here, **nan/nân/nàn**
here is . . ., **gà . . .**
heron, **zalɓè**
hide, v. **ɓōyè**
hide, skin, **fātà** (f.) (pl.
fātū)
highway robber, **mafàshī**
(pl. **mafàsā)**
hoe, **fartanyà** (f.) (pl.
fartanyōyī); **gàrmā** (f.)
(pl. **garèmanī)**

hold, v. rìƙè
hole, rāmì (pl. rāmunà)
honesty, kirkì
honour, girmā
hoping, fātā, bègē
horn, ƙàhō/ƙàfō (pl.
  ƙàhònī)
horse, dōkì (pl. dawākī)
hospital, asìbitì (pl. asibitōcī)
hot season, bazarā (f.)
hour, awà (f.) (pl. awōwī)
house, gidā (pl. gidàjē)
— householder, mài gidā
how, yaddà/yâddà
how ?, ƙàƙà ?, yàyà ?
how many ?/how much ?
  nawà ?
however, dai
however, kōyàyà
however many, kōnawà
human being, ɗan Adàm
  (pl. 'yan Adàm)
human nature, mùtùntakà
  (f.)
hundred, ɗarī
hunger, yunwà (f.)
hungry, be, v. ji yunwà
hunter, mahàrbī (pl.
  mahàrbā)
husband, mijì (pl. mazā),
  mài gidā
hut, ɗākì (pl. ɗākunà)
hut, made of grass, bukkà
  (f.) (pl. bukkōkī)

hyena, kūrā (f.) (pl.
  kūràyē)
hypocrite, munāfùkī (f.
  munāfùkā ; pl.
  mùnàfùkai)

idol, tsāfì
if, ìdan/in, dà
ignorance, rashìn sanì
ignore, v. ƙyālè
illness, cīwò, cùtā (f.)
imitate, v. kwàikwayà (i/ē),
  v. kwatàntā
immediately, nan dà nan,
  yànzu-yànzu
important people, mânya-
  mânyā
impossible, be, v. fàskarà
  (i/ē)
impudence, shègàntakà (f.)
in, (à) cikin, à
increase, v. ƙārà
indeed, kàm
indication, àlāmà/hàlāmà
  (f.) (pl. àlàmai)
inexpensiveness, àrāhā
information, làbārì (pl.
  làbàrū)
informer, magàyī
inhabitants, 'yan ƙasā
inherit v. gàdā, v. gājè
injection, àllurà (f.) (pl.
  àllùrai)
injure, v. cùtā (i/ē)
ink, tàwadà (f.)
inside, cikì, (à) cikin

instead of, màimakon
intelligence, hankàlī
iron, ƙarfè

jackal, dilā
jam, v. kākàrē
joking, wàsā (pl. wàsànnī)
journey, tàfiyà (f.)
judge, àlkālī/àlƙālī (pl.
  àlkàlai/àlƙàlai)
judgement, pronounce, v.
  yankè shàrī'à
July, Yūlì
jumping, tsallē
June, Yūnì, Jun
just person, ādàlī (pl.
  àdàlai)
justice, ādalcì, shàrī'à (f.)

Kano person, Bàkanè/
  Bàkanò (f. Bàkanùwā ;
  pl. Kanāwā)
keep on (doing), v. dingà,
  v. riƙà
key, mabūdī (pl. màbùɗai)
khaki cloth, kàkī
kill, v. kashè
kind, irì
— all kinds, irì-irì
kindness, àlhērì, àlbarkàcī
king, sarkī (pl. sarākunà)
kitchen, madafā/madafī
  (pl. màdàfai)
knife, wuƙā (f.) (pl.
  wuƙàƙē)
knock over, v. tūrè

know, v. sanì/san
knowledge, ilmì/ilìmī
known, sànannē
kobo, kwabò (pl. kwàbbai)
kolanut, gōrò

labourer, lēbùrà (pl.
  lēburōrī)
lack, v. rasà, rashì
Lagos, Ìkko
lamp, fìtilà (f.) (pl. fìtilū)
language, harshè (pl.
  harsunà)
lantern, fìtilà (f.) (pl.
  fìtilū)
late, be, v. màkarà
latecomer, màkàrau
lateness, lattì
later, till, sai an jimà
laughter, dàriyā (f.)
lavatory, bāyan gidā
lawcourt, shàrī'à (f.) (pl.
  sharī'ō'ī), mahukuntā
  (f.) (pl. màhùkùntai)
lay down, v. kwantar (dà)
learner, makòyī (f. makò-
  yìyā ; pl. makòyā)
leather worker, bàdūkù (pl.
  dùkàwā)
left, hagū
— to the left, hagu
length, tsawō
lest, kadà/kâr
let, allow, v. barì/bar
letter, wàsīƙà/wàsīkà (f.)
  (pl. wàsìƙū)

liar. maƙàryàcī (f. maƙaryacìyā ; pl. maƙàryàtā)

lie, ƙaryā (f.) (pl. ƙàryàce-ƙàryàcē)

lie down, v. kwântā

life, râi (pl. rāyukà)

lift, v. ɗagà

light (fire), v. hūrà

like, v. sō

like, kàmar

limit, iyàkā (f.)

lip, lēɓè (pl. lēɓunà)

little, ƙàramī (f. ƙàramā ; pl. ƙanānà), ƙànƙanè (f. ƙànƙanùwā ; pl. ƙanānà)

— a little, kàɗan

live, v. zama

lizard, ƙàdangarè (pl. ƙàdàngàrū)

load, kāyā (pl. kāyàyyakī)

loan (money), bāshì

— (not money), arō

lock. v. kullè

locust, fàrā (f.) (pl. fàrī)

loincloth, bàntē

long, dōgō (f. dōguwā ; pl. dōgàyē)

look (at), v. dūbà

— look everywhere, v. duddùbā

look for, v. nèmā (i/ē)

looking at, kallō

lot, ràbō

love, v. sō

luck, sā'à (f.)

lunatic, mahàukàcī (f. mahaukacìyā ; pl. mahàukàtā)

machine, kèkē (pl. kēkunà)

madman, mahàukàcī (f. mahaukacìyā ; pl. mahàukàtā)

madness, hàukā

make, v. yi

malaria, zàzzàɓī

male, namijì (pl. mazā)

man, mùtûm (pl. mutànē)

mango(es), mangwàrò

many, dà yawà

March, Māris (f.)

mare, gōɗìyā (f.)

market, kàsuwā (f.) (pl. kāsuwōyī)

marriage, aurē

marriage feast, angwancì

marry, v. àurā (i/ē)

marsh, fàdamà (f.) (pl. fadamōmī)

matchet, àddā (f.) (pl. addunà)

matter, bàtū

matter, it doesn't, bâ kōmē

May, Māyù (f.)

meal, jībì

measure, v. gwadà, v. aunà

measuring stick, magwajī (pl. màgwàdai)

meat, nāmà

mechanic, **màkānīkì** (*pl.*
màkànìkai)

meddlesomeness, **kàràm-
bằnī**

medicine, **māgànī** (*pl.*
māgungunà)

meet, *v.* **hàɗu,** *v.* **sàdu**

— (with), *v.* **gàmu (dà)**

memory, **tùnànī**

merchant, **àttājìrī** (*pl.*
àttàjìrai)

mercy, **jîn ƙai**

— have, *v.* **ji ƙai**

merely, **kawài**

metal, **ƙarfè** (*pl.* **ƙaràfā**)

middle, **tsakiyà/tsakà** (*f.*)

milk, **madarā** (*f.*)

millet, **gērō**

million, **zambàr dubū,
mìlyân**

minister, **mìnistà** (*pl.*
ministōcī)

misfortune, **hàsārà** (*f.*)

mistake, **kuskurè**

Monday, **Lìttìnîn** (*f.*)

money, **kudī**

monkey, **birì** (*pl.* **birai**)

month, **watà** (*pl.* **wàtànnī**)

— last month, **watàn jiyà,
watàn dà ya wucè**

— next month, **watàn gòbe,
watà mài zuwà**

moon, **watà** (*pl.* **wàtànnī**)

morning, **sāfē, sāfìyā** (*f.*)

mother, **màmā** (*f.*), **uwā**
(*f.*)

mother-in-law, **sùrukā** (*f.*)

motor, **mōtà** (*f.*) (*pl.*
motōcī)

— motor boy, **kàren mōtà**

mount, *v.* **hau,** *v.* **hayè**

mountain, **dūtsè** (*pl.*
duwàtsū)

mouse, **ɓērā** (*pl.* **(ɓēràyē**)

mouth, **bàkī** (*pl.* **bākunà**)

Mr., **mālàm** (*f.* **mālàmā** ;
pl. **màlàmai**)

much, **dà yawà**

multitude, **tulì**

must, **dōlè, tīlàs**

nakedness, **tsìrārà** (*f.*)

name, **sūnā** (*pl.* **sūnàyē**)

namely, **wàtò**

nape of the neck, **ƙyēyà** (*f.*)

Native Administration,
en'è (*pl.* **en'è-en'è**)

near (to), **kusa (dà)**

necessity, of, **tīlàs**

neck, **wuyà** (*pl.* **wuyōyī**)

need, **bùkātà** (*f.*) (*pl.*
bùkàtū)

needle, **àllurà** (*f.*) (*pl.*
àllùrai)

new, **sābō** (*f.* **sābuwā** ; *pl.*
sàbàbbī)

— brand new, **sābō ful**

news, **làbārì** (*pl.* **làbàrū**)

— I have good news,
àlbishìrī

nevertheless, **duk dà hakà**

next, **mài zuwà**

next day, **kàshḕgàrī**
Niger River, **Kwârà** (*f.*)
night, **darē**
— at night, **dà (dàd) darē**
night, spend the, *v.* **kwāna**
ninepence, **nai**
no, **ā'à**
nonsense !, **habà**
north, **arḕwā**
— due north, **arḕwā sak**
— north-east, **arḕwā masò
gabàs**
— northward, **arḕwa**
— north-west, **arḕwā masò
yâmma**
not, **bà ... ba, bà ... ba**
notice, take notice of, *v.*
kùlā (dà)
November, **Nùwambà** (*f.*)
now, **yànzu**
nuisance, **kàràmbànī**

obtain, *v.* **sāmù/sàmā (i/ē)**
occupation, **sàna'à** (*f.*) (*pl.*
sana'ō'ī)
October, **Òktobà** (*f.*)
of, **na/ta, -n/-r**
of course !, **mànà** !
offer (bargaining), *v.* **tayà**
office, **ōfìs** (*pl.* **ōfisōshī)**
oil, **mâi**
old, **tsōfō/tsōhō** (*f.* **tsōfuwā** ; *pl.* **tsòfàffī)**
— become old, *v.* **tsūfa**
one, **ɗaya, gùdā**
— one only, **ɗaya tak**

once, at, **nan dà nan**
only, **kaɗai, kawài, kurùm**
open, *v.* **būɗè**
opportunity, **dāmā** (*f.*)
or, **kō**
order, **dòkā** (*f.*) (*pl.*
dōkōkī)
order, in order to, **dòmin/
don**
outside, **wàje**
padlock, **kwàɗō** (*pl.* **kwàɗī)**
pain, **cīwò, zāfī**
palm tree (deleb), **giginyà**
(*f.*)
palm (of hand), **tàfī**
paper, **takàrdā** (*f.*) (*pl.*
tàkàrdū)
parent, **mahàifī** (*f.* **mahai-
fīyā** ; *pl.* **mahàifā)**
parents, **iyàyē**
parents-in-law, **sùrùkai**
part from, *v.* **ràbu dà**
pass (by), *v.* **wucè**, *v.* **shigè**
— exam, *v.* **ci**
passenger, **fasànjà** (*pl.*
fasanjōjī)
path, **hanyà** (*f.*) (*pl.*
hanyōyī)
patience, **hàƙurī**
patient, be, *v.*, **hàƙurà**
pay, *v.* **biyā**
peasant, **talàkà** (*pl.*
talakāwā)
pen, **àlkalàmī** (*pl.* **alkalumà)**
pencil, **fensìr** (*pl.* **fensirōrī)**

perforce, dōlè, tīlàs

perhaps, wàtàkīlà/wata-
kīlà/kīlà

perish, v. hàlakà

person, mùtûm (pl. mutànē)

perspiration, gùmī

petrol, mâi

pick up, v. ɗaukà (i/ē)

pig, àladè (pl. àlàdai)

pile, v. kasà

pilgrimage, hajì

pinch, v. matsà

pitcher, tùlū (pl. tūlūnà)

place, wurī (pl. wuràrē)

place, v. ajìyē, v. sâ

plan, dàbārà (f.) (pl.
dàbàrū)

plant, v. shūkà

plate, tāsà (f.) (pl. tāsōshī)

play, playing, wàsā (pl.
wàsànnī)

please, don Allà

pleasantness, dādī

plenty, yawà

plough, gàrmā (f.) (pl.
garèmanī)

pocket, àljīfū/àljīhū (pl.
aljīfunà)

poem, wāƙà (f.) (pl.
wāƙōƙī)

policeman (Government),
ɗan sàndā (pl. 'yan
sàndā)

— (N.A.), ɗan dòkā (pl.
'yan dòkā)

polish, v. gōgà

porridge, tuwō

possible, be, v. yìwu

post office, gidan wāyà, fâs
ōfìs

pot (cooking), tukunyā (f.)
(pl. tukwànē), kaskō

potato(es), dànkalì

pound, ₦2, fâm (f.)

pour, v. zubà

— pour away, v. zubar/zub
(dà)

praise God !, àlhamdùlillāhì

prayers (Muslim), sallà

prefer, v. fi sô

pregnancy, cikì

prepare, v. shiryà

prevent, v. hanà

prevention, rìgàkafì

previously, dâ

primary school, firamàrè

probably, wàtàkīlà

profession, sàna'à (f.) (pl.
sana'ō'ī)

prosperity, arzìkī/azzìkī

prosperous, become, v.
arzùtā

pull, v. jā, v. jāwō

pull out, v. cirè, v. zārè

pumpkin, kàbēwà (f.) (pl.
kàbèyī)

punishment, hòrō

pupil, àlmājìrī (f. àlmā-
jìrā ; pl. àlmàjirai)

push, v. tūrà

— over, v. tūrè

put, v. ajìyē, v. sâ

put down, v. **saukar (dà)**
put on (clothes), v. **jità**

quarrel, **faɗà**
quarter, **kwatà** (f.)
question, **tàmbayà** (f.) (pl.
  tambayōyī)
quickly, **maza, dà saurī**

rabbit, **zōmō** (pl. **zōmàyē**)
rain, **ruwan samà**
rainy season, **dàmunā** (f.)
raise, v. **ɗagà**
rank, high, **martabà** (f.)
ransom, v. **fànsā (i/ē)**
rat, **ɓērā** (pl. **ɓēràyē**)
raw, **ɗanyē** (f. **ɗanyā** ; pl.
  ɗanyū)
read, v. **karàntā**
reading, **kàràtū**
really ?, **àshē ?**
reap, v. **gìrbā (i/ē)**
reason, **dàlīlì** (pl. **dàlìlai**)
receipt, **ràsitì, ràsît**
receive, v. **kàrɓā (i/ē)**
recently, **ɗàzu**
recover (illness), v. **warkà,**
  v. **warkè**
red, **jā** (pl. **jājàyē**)
— reddish, **ja-ja**
— bright red, **jà wur/jir/zur**
redeem, v. **fànsā (i/ē)**
reduce, v. **ragè,** v. **sawwàƙē,**
  v. **sauƙàƙē**
reduction, **ragì**
refuse, v. **ƙi**
regarding, **bàtun**

relationship, **zùmùntā** (f.)
relatives, **dangì**
reliability, **amincì**
remain, v. **saura**
— remainder, **saurā**
remedy, **māgànī**
remember, v. **tunà**
— remembering, **tùnànī**
remove, v. **kau/kawad dà** ;
  ɗēbè, v. **kwāshè,** v. **fitar/**
  fid dà
repair, v. **gyārà,** v. **gyârtā**
repeat (word), **sàkè fàɗā**
replace, v. **mayar/mai (dà)**
representative, **wàkīlì** (pl.
  wàkìlai)
request, v. **ròƙā** ; (n.) **ròƙō**
rest, **hūtū,** v. **hūtà**
— resting, **hūtàwā** (f.)
restore, v. **kōmar dà**
return (here), v. **dāwō**
— (there), v. **kōmà**
reward, **lādā**
rice, **shìnkāfā** (f.)
riding, **hawā**
right, to the, **dāma** (f.)
righteous person, **ādàlī** (pl.
  àdàlai)
ring, **zōbè** (pl. **zôbbā**)
ripen, v. **nùna**
river, **kògī** (pl. **kōgunà**)
road, **hanyà** (f.) (pl.
  hanyōyī)
rock, **dūtsè** (pl. **duwàtsū**)
roofing pan (material),
  kwānò (pl. **kwānōnī**)

room, ɗākì (pl. ɗākunǎ)
rope, igiyǎ (f.)
rub, v. gōgǎ
rule, dòkā (f.) (pl. dōkōkī)
rumour has it that ..., wai
run, v. gudù
— running, gudǔ

saddle, sirdì (pl. sirǎdā)
sadness, baƙin cikì
safety, lāfiyǎ (f)
said, it is said that ..., wai
sale, no !, àlbarkà
salt, gishirī
same, all the, duk ɗaya
sandal, tàkàlmī (pl.
    tākalmà)
Saturday, Àsabàr (f.), Sātī
say, v. cê, v. fàɗā (i/ē)
saying, cêwā
scales, ma'aunī
scheme, dàbārà (f.) (pl.
    dàbàrū)
school, makarantā (f.) (pl.
    màkàràntū, makaran-
    tōcī)
— school-slate, àllō (pl.
    allunà)
seated, à zàune
secondary school,
    sakandàrè
secret, in; à ɓòye
see, v. ganī/gan/ga
see from afar, v. hàngā (i/ē)
seed, irì
seek, v. nèmā (i/ē)

seize, v. kāmà
self, kâi
self-respect, mutuncì
sell, v. sayar/sai dà
send, v. àikā (i/ē)
sense, hankàlī
separate, v. rabà
separation, ràbō/ràbuwā
    (f.)
September, Sàtumbà (f.)
set aside, v. ajìyē
settle (in place), v. zaunà
sew, v. ɗinkà
— sewing, ɗinkì
sewing machine, kèken
    ɗinkì
shade, inuwà (f.)
share, ràbō
sharp point, tsìnī (pl.
    tsìnàyē)
sheep, tunkìyā (f.) (pl.
    tumākī)
ship, jirgī (pl. jiràgē)
shoe, tàkàlmī (pl. tākalmà)
shoot, v. hàrbā (i/ē)
— shooting, harbì
short, gàjērē (f. gàjērìyā ;
    pl. gàjèrū)
— shortness, gajertà (f.)
shop, kàntī (pl. kantunà)
shovel, shēbùr, tēbùr (pl.
    shēburōrī, tēburōrī)
show, v. nūnà
shut, v. rufè
sign, àlāmà/hàlāmà (f.) (pl.
    àlàmai)

silence, **shirū**

similarity, **kàmā**

sing a song, v. **rērà wāƙà**

singly, **ɗai-ɗai**

sister, **'yar'uwā**

— older, **yàyā**

— younger, **ƙanwà**

sit down, v. **zaunà**

skill, **gwànintà** (f.)

skin, **fātà** (f.) (pl. **fātū**)

sky, **samà**

slaughter, v. **yankà**, v. **yankè**

slave, **bāwà** (f. **bâiwā** ; pl. **bāyī**)

— slavery, **bàutā**

sleep, **barcī**

— (sound), **wāwan barcī**

slightly, **kàɗan**

slipperiness, **santsī**

smallness, **ƙanƙantà** (f.)

smoke, **hayāƙī**

snake, **macìjī** (pl. **màcìzai**)

snap, v. **karyè**

snatch, v. **zarè**

sneak up on, v. **laɓàbā**

snoring, **minshārī**

soap, **sàbulù**

so-so, **dāma-dāma**

so-and-so, **wānè** (f. **wancè** ; pl. **su wānè**)

sole (foot), **tàfī**

son, **ɗā** (pl. **'yā'yā**)

song, **wāƙà** (f.) (pl. **wāƙōƙī**)

soon, **an jimà**

sort, **irì**

— all sorts, **irì-irì**

south, **kudù**

sow, v. **shūkà**

space, **fīlī** (pl. **fīlàyē**)

spear, **māshì** (pl. **māsū**)

speech (political), **laccà** (f.)

speech, **màganà** (f.) (pl. **màgàngànū**)

spend a long time, v. **daɗè**

spend a time, v. **jimà**

spend one day, v. **wunì/yinì**

splendid !, **yâuwā/yâuwa** !

spoil, v. **ɓātà**

spoon, **cōkàlī** (pl. **cōkulà**)

squeeze, v. **matsà**

stamp (postage), **kân sarkī**

stand up, v. **tāshì**, v. **tsayà**

stark naked, **ɓutuk**

start, v. **sōmà**, v. **fārà**

start out, v. **tāshì**

station, **tashà/tēshà** (pl. **tashōshī**)

steal, v. **sàtā** (i/ē)

stench, **ɗòyī**

stick, **sàndā** (pl. **sandunà**)

still, **har yànzu**

stomach, **cikì**

— stomach ache, **cīwòn cikì**

stone, **dūtsè** (pl. **duwàtsū**)

stool, **kujèrā** (f.) (pl. **kùjèrū**)

storehouse, **ma'ajī** (pl. **mà'àjìyai**)

stop, v. **tsayà**

storm, **hadarì/hadirì**

story, làbārì (pl. làbàrū)
stove (stone), murfù/
   murhù (pl. muràfū)
stranger, bàƙō (f. bàƙwā ;
   pl. bàƙī)
stray, v. rātsè
strength, ƙarfī
strolling, yāwò
strong, ƙàƙƙarfā (pl.
   ƙarfàfā)
student, ɗālìbī (pl. ɗàlìbai),
   àlmājìrī (f. àlmājìrā ;
   pl. àlmàjìrai)
study, v. karàntā
— studying, kàràtū
subdue, v. dannè
sufficient, be, v. ìsa
— sufficient, ìsasshē
sugar, sukàr
sugarcane, ràkē
sun, rānā (f.)
Sunday, Lahàdì/Làdì (f.)
sunset, màgàribà
superior to, ɱafì/mafìyī
   (pl. mafìyā)
sure, be, v. tabbàtā
sure, for, lallē
surpass, v. fi
surprise, màmākì (pl.
   màmàkai)
swamp, fàdamà (f.) (pl.
   fadamōmī)
sweep, v. shārè
sweetness, zāƙī
swerve, v. rātsè
swimming, iyò

table, tēbùr (pl. tēburōrī)
tailor, maɗìnkī (pl.
   maɗìnkā)
tall, dōgō (f. dōguwā ; pl.
   dōgàyē)
tanner, majèmī (pl.
   majèmā)
tattoo marks, jàrfā (f.)
tax, hàrājì
teacher, mālàm (f.
   mālàmā ; pl. màlàmai),
   tìcà (pl. tìcōcī)
tear, v. tsāgà
telegram, wayà (f.) (pl.
   wayōyī)
telephone, wayà (f.) (pl.
   wayōyī)
tell, v. gayà
ten kobos, sulè (pl.
   sulūlukà)
tenth, of a penny, ànīnī
   (pl. ànìnai)
termites, gàrā (f.)
test, examination, jarrà-
   bâwā (f.)
test, v. gwadà
thank, v. gōdè
— thanks, gòdiyā (f.)
— thank you, nā gōdè
that, can/cân/càn
that, wancàn (f. waccàn ;
   pl. waɗàncân)
theft, sātà (f.)
then, sā'àn nan
there, can/cân/càn
there is/are, v. àkwai, v. dà

there is no/not, v. bābù/bâ
thief, ɓàrāwò (pl. ɓàràyī)
thing, àbù (pl. abūbuwà)
thinking, tsàmmānì, câ
third, sulùsī
this, these, nan/nân/nàn
thought, tsàmmānì
thousand, alìf, dubū,
  zambàr
thrash, v. bùgā (i/ē)
thrashing, bugù
three days hence, gātà
throat, màƙōgwàrō
through, ta
throw, v. jēfà, v. wurgà
throw at, v. jèfā (i/ē)
throw away, v. yar/yā dà
throwing at, jīfà
Thursday, Àlhàmîs (f.)
thus, hakà
tie, v. ɗaurè
till a farm, v. nòmā (i/ē)
time, lōkàcī (pl. lòkàtai),
  lotò, sā'à (f.)
— from time to time, lōtò-
  lōtò
times, sàu
times, in olden, zāmànin dâ
tin, gwangwan (pl.
  gwangwàyē)
tired, be, v. gàji
tiredness, gàjiyà (f.)
today, yâu
— today week, ì ta yâu
together (with), tàre dà
toilet, bāyan gidā

tomorrow, gòbe (f.)
tongue, harshè (pl.
  harsunà)
tools, kāyan aikì
tooth, haƙōrī (pl. haƙòrā)
top, kâi
top, on top of, à kân
tortoise, kùnkurū (pl.
  kunkurà)
touch, v. taɓà
toughness, taurī
toward, wajen, zuwà
town, gàrī (pl. garūruwà)
trade, sàna'à (f.) (pl.
  sana'ō'ī)
trader (itinerant), farkē/
  falkē (pl. fatàkē)
tradition, àl'ādà (f.) (pl.
  àl'àdū)
train, jirgin ƙasā
trample, v. tattàkē
travel, tàfiyà (f.)
tread on, v. tākà
tree, itàcē (pl. itātuwà)
trouble, wàhalà (f.)
— have trouble, shā
  wàhalà
trousers, wàndō (pl.
  wandunà)
truth, gàskiyā (f.)
Tuesday, Tàlātà (f.)
turban, rawànī (pl.
  rawunà)
turn, v. jūyà
tyre, tāyà (f.) (pl. tāyōyī)

uncle (maternal), **kāwù/ kàwū** (*pl.* **kàwùnai), rāfànī** (*pl.* **ràfànai)**

— (paternal), **bappà/bàba**

uncooked, **ɗanyē** (*f.* **ɗanyā;** *pl.* **ɗanyū)**

underneath, **ƙàrƙashin**

understand, *v.* **fàhimtà (i/ē),** *v.* **gānè,** *v.* **ji**

unit, **gùdā**

unless, **sai**

unsheath, *v.* **zārè**

until, **har, sai**

upward, **samà**

urine, **fìtsārī**

usefulness, **àmfànī**

useless (thing), **wòfī** (*pl.* **wōfàyē)**

vanish, *v.* **nutsè/nitsè**

very much, **ƙwarai, ƙwarai dà gàskē, ainù(n)**

village, **ƙauyè** (*pl.* **ƙauyukà)**

visit, *v.* **zìyartà (i/ē)**

voice, **muryà** (*f.*) (*pl.* **muryōyī)**

voyage, **tàfiyà** (*f.*)

vulture, **ùngùlū** (*f.*) (*pl.* **ùngùlai)**

waist, **iyā gìndī**

wait for, *v.* **jirā,** *v.* **dākàtā**

wall, **bangō**

wandering, **yāwò**

want, *v.* **sō**

wash, *v.* **wankè**

watch, **àgōgō** (*pl.* **agōgunà)**

water, **ruwā**

— drinking water, **ruwan shâ**

water-pot, **tùlū** (*pl.* **tūlūnà)**

way, **hanyà** (*f.*) (*pl.* **hanyōyī)**

way, by way of, **ta**

wealth, **arzìkī/azzìkī**

wealthy person, **mawàdàcī** (*f.* **mawadācìyā ;** *pl.* **mawàdàtā)**

wear, *v.* **jità**

wedge, **wejì/wajì**

Wednesday, **Làràbā** (*f.*)

week, **mākò, sātī**

weeping, **kūkā**

weigh, *v.* **aunà**

welcome !, **maràbā !**

well, **rījìyā** (*f.*) (*pl.* **rījiyōyī)**

well !, **àshē !**

well . . ., **tô/tò . . .**

well-being, **lāfiyà** (*f.*)

west, **yâmmā**

— westward, **yâmma**

wet-mix, *v.* **dāmà**

what about ?, **fà ?**

whatever, **kōmē**

when, **lōkàcîn dà, sā'àd dà**

when ?, **yàushè ?/yàushe**

whenever, **kōyàushè/ kōyàushe**

where ?, **ìnā ?**

— where, **îndà**

wherever, **kō'ìnā/kōìnā**

whether, **kō**

which, **wandà** (*f.* **waddà** ;
 pl. **waɗàndà**)

which ?, **wànè** ? (*f.* **wàcè** ;
 pl. **wàɗànnè**)

while, after a, **an jimà, jìm
 kàɗan**

white, **farī** (*f.* **farā** ; *pl.*
 faràrē)

— snow-white, **farī fat**

who, whom, **wandà** (*f.*
 waddà ; *pl.* **waɗàndà**)

who ?, **wà/wànēnè** ? (*pl.* **su
 wà** ?)

whoever, **duk wandà**

whoever, **kōwànēnè** (*f.*
 kōwàcēcè)

why ?, **dom mè** ?

why !, **ai** !

wife, **màcè** (*pl.* **mātā**), **uwar
 gidā**

— father's wife (not one's
 mother), **gwaggò/
 gwàggō**

win, *v.* **ci**

wind, **iskà** (*m.* or *f.*)

wind, *v.* **naɗà**

wind, breaking, **tūsà** (*f.*)

window, **tāgà** (*f.*) (*pl.*
 tāgōgī)

wing, **fiffikè** (*pl.* **fikàfikai**)

winnow, *v.* **shēƙà**

wipe, *v.* **shàfā** (**i/ē**)

with, **dà**

woe is me !, **wâyyô nī** !

woman, **màcè/màta-** (*f.*)
 (*pl.* **mātā**)

I wonder . . . ?, **shin/
 shīn** . . . ?

wood, **itàcē** (*pl.* **itàtuwà**)

word, **màganà** (*f.*) (*pl.*
 màgàngànū)

work, **aikì** (*pl.* **ayyukà**)

worker, **ma'àikàcī** (*f.*
 ma'aikacìyā ; *pl.*
 ma'àikàtā)

worm, **tsūtsà** (*f.*) (*pl.*
 tsūtsōtsī)

worry, **dāmù**, *v.* **dàmā**

worthlessness, **banzā**

wound, **cùtā** (*f.*)

write, *v.* **rubùtā**

writing, **rùbùtū**

yam(s), **dōyà** (*f.*)

yard, **yādì**

year, **shèkarà** (*f.*) (*pl.*
 shèkàrū)

— last year, **bàra** (*f.*)

— next year, **bàɗi** (*f.*)

— this year, **bana** (*f.*)

yellow, **ràwayà** (*f.*)

yes, **ī, na'àm, nà'am** ?

yesterday, **jiyà** (*f.*)

yet (not yet), **tùkùna**

youngest (of children), **àutā**

youth, **sauràyī** (*pl.* **sàmàrī**)

zero, **sifìrī**

SWAHILI

D. V. PERROTT

Swahili is a relatively easy language to learn. There are no real difficulties of pronunciation and none of spelling, and it is quite possible for the student working alone to master the language.

This book covers the whole of the Swahili language without being in any sense a formal grammar. It begins by explaining the construction of a Swahili sentence, using about a dozen of the commonest words, and then goes on to show the changes caused by different classes of nouns and the various verb tenses. At the end of each graded lesson there is a list of new words and an exercise.

TEACH YOURSELF BOOKS

SWAHILI DICTIONARY

D. V. PERROTT

This concise working dictionary contains all the Swahili words the student is likely to hear or read, and forms a companion book to *Teach Yourself Swahili*.

The Swahili-English and English-Swahili sections of the dictionary each contain an extensive vocabulary, and care has been taken to include words appropriate to the circumstances of life in East Africa. The compiler has also included a concise Swahili grammar at the beginning of the dictionary, along with practical notes on pronunciation.

TEACH YOURSELF BOOKS

YORUBA

E. C. ROWLANDS

This book provides a complete introductory course in Yoruba, the mother tongue of more than 10 million people living in Western Nigeria, in parts of Northern Nigeria and in Benin.

The book is concerned with the generally accepted 'standard' Yoruba which is widely understood even where regional dialects exist. The course assumes no previous knowledge of the language and every stage is illustrated with examples and exercises. Pronunciation, grammar and syntax are comprehensively covered and the book will equip you with a basic, everyday vocabulary.

TEACH YOURSELF BOOKS